D0946723

Auld Reekie

An Edinburgh Anthology

Auld Reekie

An Edinburgh Anthology

Selected and edited by
RALPH LOWNIE

With a Preface by
ALEXANDER M^cCALL SMITH

TIMEWELL
PRESS

First published in Great Britain in 2004 by
Timewell Press Limited
10 Porchester Terrace, London W2 3TL

Selection copyright © Ralph Lownie 2004
All rights reserved

No part of this publication may be reproduced,
stored in a retrieval system or transmitted, in any form
or by any means, electronic, mechanical, photocopying,
recording or otherwise, without the prior
permission of the publisher.
A catalogue record for this title is available
from the British Library.

ISBN 1 85725 204 7

Typeset by Antony Gray
Printed and bound in Great Britain by
Biddles Ltd, King's Lynn

For C. M. L

Contents

Edinburgh is truly a city of names and by-names. Even her own hasn't escaped variation. Dunedin! Edina!! The Athens of the North!!! All these are more than a bit bookish. But the country folk called her 'Auld Reekie'; and though this name is based on the same characteristic that gets London dubbed 'The Smoke', you can't help thinking it's more affectionate.

James T. R. Ritchie, *The Singing Street* (1964)

Preface

Edinburgh is a city which has many lovers. Those who visit or those who live here often have a feeling for the city that is close to a passion, and, like all lovers, they are keen to share this with others. So a collection of writings about Edinburgh will always be welcome to those who wish to convey to others, or savour for themselves, those things that make the Scottish capital such an entrancing place.

And what a wonderful collection it is that Mr Lownie has compiled for us! There are historical snippets, garnered from a very wide range of sources, well-known and not-so-well-known facts, statistics, and vignettes of the characters and incidents that have made the city so interesting and appealing. And these have been chosen with care, humour, and – most important of all – with love. Mr Lownie is a distinguished citizen of this town who has given his heart to his city. Now he makes that gift one that we can all share – and we are grateful to him indeed.

Alexander McCall Smith

Introduction

Her Attraction

The combination of historic association with a matchless beauty which no change can efface gives Edinburgh her supreme attraction. By universal judgment, Edinburgh has a place, possibly the highest place, in the small group of the great towns of Europe conspicuous for romance and physical charm.

Sir Henry Campbell-Bannerman, *Speeches* (1908)

Nomenclature

Edinburgh perhaps emerges from prehistory in the first half of the second century, inasmuch as it may have been the British *Alauna*, rockplace, which Ptolemy lists among the 'towns' of the *Votadini*, a British tribe who inhabited southeast Scotland and northeast England in Roman times; but it is clearly identified in the late sixth century, when the heroic poems of the *Gododdin* (the Votadini name in its later Welsh form, to be pronounced roughly as *gau-'dauth-een* with *th* as in 'the') named the place both as *Eidyn* and as *Din Eidyn* or 'Fort Eidyn', and also described it as *Eidyn ysgor* or *Eidyn gaer*, the stronghold or fortified town of Eidyn. All these forms use 'Eidyn' (pronounced *'aid-in*) as a proper name, and the same is true of the later versions made for the invading groups of Anglians and Gaelic-speaking Scots, typified in the note *'Dunedene*, which is in English *Edineburg'* given in the ninth-century *Life of St Monenna*: for while British *din* could be translated (no doubt, as usually happens in such circumstances, by conquered Britons for the benefit of new

overlords) as equivalent to Anglian *burh* or Gaelic *dun*, it
is evident that *Eidyn* had to be left untranslated.

The fanciful form 'Edwinesburgh' is a palpable fake
that appears in the time of David I and was probably an
attempt to manufacture a link with Edwin, first Christian
king of Northumbia.

Stuart Harris,
The Place Names of Edinburgh (1996)

Her Standing

The first thing which must strike any stranger is that
Edinburgh is both by natural ordinance and man's con-
trivance a Capital. It was made to rule; it did rule; and
it was robbed of its command. Its kingdom was absorbed.
It became the head-place of a province . . .

You can see at a glance that Edinburgh was meant to
put its stamp on Scotland, not to take its orders from
London. In appearance it is sovereign to the heart of its
stones . . . It is the natural capital of a divided country.

Ivor Brown, *Summer in Scotland* (1952)

Her Place

It is a thousand years since the first houses began to
huddle beneath the protection of Edinburgh Castle Rock
and to form themselves into a conscious unit. It is not
much less than a thousand years since that unit, under the
name of Edinburgh, began to be the most important
Scottish town; and it is over six hundred years since it

14

became the official and recognized Capital, the seat of the Court and the Government. Since then Edinburgh's growth has been the scene of violent intrigue in high places and much bloody action amongst kings and nobles; she has had her periods of prosperity and international fame, alternating with those of neglect and decay, but she has as a city throughout the centuries grown on the whole easily and with confidence. She has grown by slow design and by deliberate effort, striking her roots deeper with every expansion. She has never swollen to an unmanageable size and has always remained a conscious unit.

Moray McLaren, *The Scots* (1951)

Her Proud Position

The ancient and famous metropolis of the North sits overlooking a windy estuary from the slope and summit of three hills. No situation could be more commanding for the head city of a kingdom; none better chosen for noble prospects. From her tall precipice and terraced gardens she looks far and wide on the sea and broad champaigns. To the east you may catch at sunset the spark of the May lighthouse, where the Firth expands into the German Ocean; and away to the west, over all the carse of Stirling, you can see the first snows upon Ben Ledi.

But Edinburgh pays cruelly for her high seat in one of the vilest climates under the heaven. She is liable to be beaten upon by all the winds that blow, to be drenched with rain, to be buried in cold sea fogs out of the east, and powdered with the snow as it comes flying southwards from the Highland hills. The weather is raw and boisterous in winter, shifty and ungenial in summer, and downright meteorological purgatory in the spring. The delicate die early, and I, as a survivor, among bleak winds and plumping rain, have been sometimes tempted to envy them their fate. For all who love shelter and the blessings of the sun, who hate dark weather and perpetual tilting against squalls, there could scarcely be found a more unhomely and harassing place of residence. Many such aspire angrily after that Somewhere-else of the imagination, where all troubles are supposed to end. They lean over the great bridge which joins the New Town with the Old – and watch the trains smoking out from under them and vanishing into the tunnel on a voyage to brighter skies. Happy the passengers who shake off the dust of Edinburgh, and have heard for the last time the cry of the east wind among her chimney-tops! And yet the place establishes an interest in people's hearts; go where they will, they find no city of the same distinction; go where they will, they take a pride in their old home.

Robert Louis Stevenson,
Edinburgh: Picturesque Notes (1879)

Her Chief Assets

Edinburgh's chief assets are her natural beauties. Where is there another city with green mountains and great cliffs rising from its midst, and a view of the sea, with ships and islands, to be seen from its crowded thoroughfares? Other great cities have magnificent buildings, great parks and gardens – man has made them beautiful cities by his work; but Edinburgh possesses gifts straight from the hand of God, and some of them have not yet been spoilt.

Dear to the heart of the resident is the view seen as one

comes down the Mound on a winter's afternoon at sunset, when the Castle stands dark against the glorious red of the western sky, and, across the belt of gardens, Princes Street, with its illuminated shop windows, its rows of lamps, its moving lines of cars with coloured lights, looks like a necklace of flashing jewels.

Famous is the 'Marmion view' from the south – the view that Scott loved and Turner painted – but with denser massing now of suburb than they saw, reaching right up the furzy knoll where Marmion stood. Here is the Castle in all its majesty, the Grassmarket and Cowgate huddled picturesquely under its precipices, and the descending spine of the High Street, St Giles's open crown over the roofs, and then the maze and glitter of domes and pinnacles and steeples, with the North Sea beyond.

But of all views of Edinburgh the most mystically beautiful is that seen from the Calton Hill by night. The city is close about you, but in the darkness there is isolation. Across a gulf of impenetrable gloom there is spread a panorama of heights and depths, beaded by a myriad of lights, the depths seeming reflected from the heights, like the starry sky seen in a deep pool. As you encircle the hill, you find always some new phantasy of light and gloom, until on the side towards the Firth there seems a stretch of flat country garlanded with lights that dip and rise with every undulation of the land down to the lip of the sea, and all round the coast every point and headland is studded and coloured with sea lights, while far out in the mid-Firth flashes the great Eye of the revolving light of Inchkeith.

Rosaline Masson, *Edinburgh* (1904)

17

The Planners

War and Peace alike were its enemies. Edinburgh was twice the subject of vengeance: corpulent King Harry VIII instructed his armies to leave not a stick standing nor a soul alive in 1544; and in 1596 Jamie Saxt's advisers recommended the city's obliteration and replacement by a monument as an awful warning to others against accommodating religious riots. As war receded, the capital nearly fell victim to reason and baroque town planning. Only national poverty (if the Earl of Mar is to be believed) prevented the Old Town's removal, and substitution by the construction of a splendid new town on the flat plains of Leith. It remains fortunate to survive where it does.

In the face of the zeal of reformers, the ambitions of monarch and court, and the designs of improvers and planners, Edinburgh proved deeply unshakeable. Indeed, it seemed to have a life of its own.

Charles McKean, *Edinburgh: Portrait of a City* (1991)

A Plea

Lord Cockburn, Letter to Lord Provost: I wish I could impress upon them, and indeed upon the whole community, the fact, and its consequences, that, for its public importance, Edinburgh, except its beauty, has really very little to depend upon.

It has little trade; which, in some views, may be a misfortune. Mercifully it has almost no manufactures, – that is, tall brick chimneys, – black smoke; – a population precariously fed, – pauperism, disease, and crime, all in excess. Some strange efforts have occasionally been made to coax these things to us; but a thanks-deserving Providence has hitherto been always pleased to defeat them. For, though manufactures be indispensable, they need not be everywhere. Blight should be confined to as few parts of the field as possible. There should be Cities of Refuge. Hence the envy which is said that Perth sometimes has of Dundee, is nearly inconceivable. One would have thought that there was no Perth man (out of the asylum) who would not have rejoiced in his unstained tranquillity, in the delightful heights that enclose him, – in his silvery Tay, – in the quiet beauty of his green and level Inches. Yet it is said that some of them actually long for steam engines on Kinnoul Hill, and docks, and factories, and the sweets of the Scouring burn. But I do not believe this. It is incredible. Long may both they and we be spared. We have better things to give us an interest. – Chiefly some traces, the more interesting that they are faded, of the Ancient Royalty and national independence of Scotland, and of a once resident nobility; – the seat of the Supreme Courts of Justice; – a College of still maintained celebrity; and our having supplied a greater number of eminent men to literature, to science, and to the arts, than any one town in the empire, with the single exception of London.

But none of these things, nor all of them, make it Edinburgh. Other places have some of them, or greater attractions. But no other place excites the same peculiar interest. Deducting foreign students, there is probably not one stranger out of each hundred of the many who visit us, who is attracted by anything but the beauty of the city and its vicinity.

It is not our lectures, nor our law, nor our intellectual reputation, that gives us our particular fame. It is our curious, and matchless, position, – our strange irregularity of surface, – its picturesque results, – our internal features and scenery, – our distant prospects, – our varied, and ever-beautiful neighbourhood, – and the endless aspects of the city, as looked down upon from adjoining heights, or as it presents itself to the plains below. Extinguish these, and the rest would leave it a very inferior place. Very respectable; but not what it is.

George Bruce, *Some Practical Good* (1975)

An Appropriate Motto

This weird sense of the city as a sort of starry ladder has so often come upon me when climbing the Edinburgh ways in cloudy weather, that I have been tempted to wonder whether any of the old men of the town were thinking of the experience when they chose the strange and splendid motto of the Scotch capital. Never, certainly, did a great city have a heraldic motto which was so atmospherically accurate. It might have been invented by a poet . . .

The motto of Edinburgh, as you might still see it, I think, carved over the old castle gate, is '*Sic Itur ad Astra*' – 'This way to the stars.'

G. K. Chesterton, *Daily News*, 5 December 1905

First Impressions

~

Auld Reekie

'This, then, is Edinburgh?' said the youth, as the fellow-travellers arrived at one of the heights to the southward, which commanded a view of the great northern capital – 'this is that Edinburgh of which we have heard so much?'

'Even so,' said the falconer; 'yonder stands Auld Reekie; you may see the smoke hover over her at twenty miles' distance, as the goss-hawk hangs over a plump of young wild ducks; ay, yonder is the heart of Scotland, and each throb that she gives is felt from the edge of Solway to Duncansbay Head. See, yonder is the old Castle; and see to the right, on yon rising ground, that is the Castle of Craigmillar, which I have known a merry place in my time.'

'Was it not there,' said the page in a low voice, 'that the Queen held her court?'

'Ay, Ay,' replied the falconer – 'Queen she was then, though you must not call her so now . . . '

Sir Walter Scott, *The Abbot* (1820)

Auld Reekie Again

Poor old Edinburgh, it lies there on its hill-face between its castle and Holyrood, extremely dim to us at this two-centuries' distance; and yet the indisputable fact of it burns for us with a strange illuminativeness; small but unquenchable as the light of stars. Indisputably enough, Old Edinburgh is there; poor old Scotland wholly, my old respected Mother! Smoke-cloud hangs over old

Edinburgh, – for, ever since Aeneas Sylvius's time and earlier, the people have had the art, very strange to Aeneas, of burning a certain sort of black stones, and Edinburgh with its chimneys is called 'Auld Reekie' by the country people. Smoke-cloud very visible to the imagination: who knows what they are doing under it! Dry as dust with his thousand Tomes is dumb as the Bass Rock, nay dumber, his Tomes are as the cackle of the thousand flocks of geese that inhabit there, and with deafening noise tell us nothing. The mirror of the Firth with its Inchkeiths, Inchcolms and silent isles, gleams beautiful on us; Old Edinburgh rises yonder climbing aloft to its Castle precipice; from the rocks of Pettycur where the Third Alexander broke his neck, from all the Fife heights, from far and wide on every hand, you can see the sky windows of it glitter in the sun, a city set on a hill. But what are they doing there; what are they thinking, saying, meaning there? O Dryasdust! – The gallows stands on the Borough Muir; visible, one sign of civilisation . . .

Thomas Carlyle, *Historical Sketches* (1898)

Dun-Edin

. . . and who, indeed that has once seen Edinburgh, with its couchant crag-lion, but must see it again in dreams, waking or sleeping? My dear Sir, do not think I blaspheme when I tell you that your great London as compared to Dun-Edin, 'mine own romantic town', is as prose compared to poetry, or as a great rumbling, rambling, heavy epic compared to a lyric, bright, brief, clear, and vital as a flash of lighting. You have nothing like Scott's monument, or, if you had that, and all the glories of architecture assembled together, you have nothing like Arthur's Seat, and above all you have not the Scotch national character; and it is that grand character after all which gives the land its true charm, its true greatness.

Charlotte Brontë, letter, 30 July 1850

Touch of Royalty

Edinburgh is obviously regal. She is plainly a capital. She has the superiority complex of a capital, which is openly reviled, and secretly admired, by all provinces. Her exclusiveness is the exclusiveness of the aristocrat who has tried out most things and knows exactly what she does not wish to do. Such snobberies as she may possess – and what city does not posses them? – have little to do with money. It would be, I feel, more difficult for a man of no quality to buy himself into Edinburgh than into any other city, with possibly the exception of Dublin.

I have used the wrong pronoun to Edinburgh. This city is 'he', not 'she'. Edinburgh is as masculine as London. The three great feminine capitals are Paris, Vienna and Dublin; the first two have all the lure of woman, and the last has all her charm and all her spite. But Edinburgh, London, Berlin, and Rome are as masculine as a herd of steers. I am told that New York is feminine; but I cannot say.

The air of Edinburgh seems to demand a viceroy. You feel that there should be a throne somewhere. The shuttered windows of Holyrood affect me rather as the drawn blinds of Buckingham Palace when no standard

flies from the mast and the guard is changed in St
James's. No matter how unpalatial Holyrood may be it is
still tremendously a palace. You feel that in the throne-
room, to round off Edinburgh's appearance of coronation,
should be a Prince of Scotland.

H. V. Morton, *In Search of Scotland* (1929)

Contrasts

A city of contradictions, where the statue of Charles II
tramples the grave of John Knox in Parliament Square,
where poverty dwells in panelled rooms with elaborately
heraldic ceilings, and the darkest close may hold traces of
Scotland's proudest families. The King's palace stands in
a slum, and the sons of citizens are educated amid the
magnificence of George Heriot's College, a building
where stone has been treated like some precious metal, fit
monument for a prince among goldsmiths . . .

But across the valley where the Nor' Loch used to be,
where now in summer rosy hydrangeas and tall lilies
grace Princes Street Gardens, how different is the town
that we discover! Spacious, dignified, self-conscious, laid
out in crescents, terraces, and parallelograms, with every
here and there a vista as lovely as it is unexpected. The
land falls away in a mist of treetops and smoke towards
Leith and the Firth of Forth, with glimpses of the hills of
Fife so clear you think you could touch them, or else so
dim and uncertain you can hardly tell where sky stops and
hills begin. And all is framed in the grey pseudo-Greek
architecture of nineteenth-century Edinburgh with pillars,
porticoes, and pediments complete. Severer, less ornate,

and better proportioned than the sham-Renaissance style beloved to-day, it cannot compare with the earlier Scottish domestic architecture; but it has character and interest as a symbol of the society that erected it, a society at once haughty, cultured, and well-bred, combining real hospitality with elaborate manners and the age-old Scottish passion for display. The novelist, Henry Mackenzie, said of the houses of the new town that they were 'calculated for show, not convenience' – and indeed all this part of Edinburgh looks like that.

Flora Grierson, *Haunting Edinburgh* (1929)

A City for all Seasons

Edinburgh is, of course, a city for all seasons, not of Autumn only. There are days when the grey skies and rough winds of winter seem prepared at last to yield to something better and the first timid unofficial blossoms appear in unexpected places – bow-headed snowdrops on fragile stems in soil-filled crevices in the rock faces of the Calton Hill; crocuses in Queen Street Gardens and Greyfriars kirkyard. Perhaps they have been visible for days but gone unnoticed: television in winter is for many more magnetic than urban nature rambles. For a day, maybe two, the air is warmer, less abrasive, commensurate with the lengthening hours of daylight. On such days the stones of the city shed their almost-permanent charcoal-grey and become embarrassed in the unexpected sunshine. There is not yet much warmth from the sun; and Edinburghers, whose bent figures resemble remarkably those first snowdrops, turn corners still in anticipation of the traditional onslaught of a snell and boisterous wind. But it is unmet, and they relax slightly within the high-collared comfort of their tweeds; they straighten their backs and release the digital security of their hats – and suspect the pattern of the weather.

Ken Jones, *With Gold and Honey Blest* (1979)

A Recent Impression

The first obvious impression that Edinburgh produces is of a rocky splendour and pride. It is a city built upon rock and guarded by rock. The old town is perched on the ridge which runs up from Holyrood to the Castle, and on the other side, to the east, rise the two shapes of the Salisbury Crag and Arthur's Seat. Princes Street with its spacious gardens and its single line of buildings has this magnificent panorama as its missing side.

Behind Princes Street, on the gradual slope running down to the Water of Leith, lies the New Town. This is the town of Hume. Everything in it breathes spaciousness, order and good sense; the houses present a dignified front to the world; they suggest comfortable privacy and are big enough for large parties, and seem admirably planned to withstand the distractions and allow the amenities of a rational city life. The New Town was due to the foresight and enterprise of an Edinburgh provost more than a hundred years ago and to the taste of the architects he employed, and it is probably one of the finest pieces of town-planning extant. It shows that a little over a hundred years ago Edinburgh possessed a boldness of foresight and a standard of achievement which at that time were remarkable.

Taken together the Old Town and the New produce an effect of spacious design. The design of the Old Town is a result of the rocky formation which is its base, the design of the New purely architectural. The Old Town is by now mostly slums, and parts of the New are falling into the same state. Beyond this nucleus of the city lie Victorian, Edwardian and Neo-Georgian suburbs, most of them, and the last more particularly, shapeless and graceless. In these the great majority of the population live.

Edwin Muir, *Scottish Journey* (1935)

Vista

Beautiful city of Edinburgh!
Where the tourist can drown his sorrow
By viewing your monuments and statues fine
During the lovely summer-time
I'm sure it will his spirits cheer
As Sir Walter Scott's monument draws near,
That stands in East Princes Street
Amongst flowery gardens, fine and neat.
And Edinburgh castle is magnificent to be seen
With its beautiful walks and trees so green,
Which seems like a fairy dell;
And near by its rocky basement is St Margaret's well,
Where the tourist can drink at when he feels dry,
And view the castle from beneath so very high,
Which seems almost towering to the sky.
Then as for Nelson's monument that stands on the
                                        Calton hill,
As the tourist gazes thereon, with wonder his heart
                                        does fill

As he thinks on Admiral Nelson who did the
Frenchmen kill.
Then, as for Salisbury crags, they are most beautiful
to be seen,
Especially in the month of June, when the grass
is green,
There numerous molehills can be seen,
And the busy little creatures howking away,
Searching for worms amongst the clay;
And as the tourist's eye does wander to and fro
From the south side of Salisbury crags below,
His bosom with admiration feels all aglow
As he views the beautiful scenery in the valley below;
And if, with an observant eye, the little loch beneath
he scans,
He can see the wild ducks swimming about and
beautiful white swans.
Then, as from Arthur's seat, I'm sure it is a treat
Most worthy to be seen, with its rugged rocks and
pastures green
And the sheep browsing on its sides
To and fro, with slow-paced strides,
And the little lambkins at play
During the livelong summer-day.
Beautiful city of Edinburgh! the truth to express,
Your beauties are matchless I must confess,
And which no one dare gainsay,
But that you are the grandest city in Scotland at
the present day!

William McGonagall, Edinburgh (1887)

A Painter's View

Why is Edinburgh not at least as well known as Paris? Why has Edinburgh not produced her Utrillo, her Pizarro, her Monet, her Buffet? Is Edinburgh any less dramatically inspiring than Paris?

I choose to paint Edinburgh because I want everyone to share my joy in her. I want her citizens to see how extraordinary their ordinary everyday surroundings are.

I want the visitor to miss nothing, to see more than the obvious, more than the Castle and Princes Street. I want them to see the humour in the shape of Edinburgh chimney-pots and roofs and crow-stepped gables, the drama of plunging townscapes glimpsed through the mouth of a close.

There is an essential joy about living in Edinburgh that no other city can provide for me: not San Francisco or Rio, despite their superb balance of man-made beauty and nature; not Paris, for Paris is too large; not brand-new Brazilia, because it is brand-new: not even Florence or Munich or Copenhagen, because ultimately I am committed to the British way of life. It is the joy of her suddenness, her accessibility, her profound beauty that one can rediscover over and over again, on foot, from medieval huddle through Georgian elegance to wild sweeping hills, all within the one city boundary . . .

In her composition, Edinburgh is a compound of miracles, an enchantment which no town-planner in his senses would ever have dared to dream.

Richard Demarco, *A Life in Pictures* (1995)

31

Bookman's Paradise

Edinburgh is a city of libraries – a bookman's paradise. It shelters more noble collections than probably any other city of its size within the British dominions. And this is as it should be, for is not Edinburgh the capital of an intelligent and cultivated people, the heart of a national literature?

W. Forbes Gray,
A Literary Centre of a Literary Capital (1946)

Nostalgia

Its quaint, grey, castled city, where the bells clash of a Sunday, and the wind squalls, and the salt showers fly and beat. I do not even know that I desire to live there; but let me hear, in some far land, a kindred voice sing out, 'O why left I my hame?' and it seems at once as if no beauty under the kind heavens, no society of the wise and good, can repay me for my absence from my country. And though I think I would rather die elsewhere, yet in my heart of hearts I long to be buried among good Scots clods. I will say it fairly, it grows on me with every year: there are no stars so lovely as Edinburgh street-lamps. When I forget thee, Auld Reekie, may my right hand forget its cunning!

Robert Louis Stevenson,
The Silverado Squatters (1883)

Abroad

I leave the busy, crowded street
    To step within your silent aisles,
Where the dead hearts of centuries beat,
    Beneath your storied roof, St Giles'!
Where choir and chapel void and vast
Are filled with spirits of the Past!

In golden shafts and rainbow spears
    The light falls soft on oak and stone,
So filters through nine hundred years
    The glory that is Scotland's own;
For these your sombre walls include
Our country's pride of nation-hood!

The feet of heroes tread your pave
    While echo to their fame replies;
The voice of Knox still fills your nave;
    Dead Stewart in your South Aisle lies!
Your roof and steeple once again
Are rampart for Queen Mary's men!

The sound of trampling feet intrude
    A slow procession winds in state
Out of the grey-towered Holyrood
    And up the mourning Canongate.
'Tis great Montrose they carry home
To his long rest beneath your dome!

Around me stand, Time's trusted fanes,
    The tributes to our later dead;
The triumph fadeth, there remains
    But grief – the tears that Scotland shed;
And dark upon your splendid walls
The stained old colours droop like palls!

Deep falls the early winter eve,
　　And deeper grows the winding spell
That old Romance will always weave
　　Around the shrine we love so well!
Oh! House of Heroes, proud, apart,
How much you hold of Scotland's heart!

Will Ogilvie,
The Land We Love (1832)

The City

I thought that Bristol, taking in its heights and Clifton and its rocks and its river, was the finest city in the world; but Edinburgh with its castle, its hills, its pretty seaport, conveniently detached from it, its vale of rich land lying all around, its lofty hills in the back ground, its views across the Firth: I think little of its streets and its rows of fine houses, though all built of stone, and though everything in London and Bath is beggary to these; I think nothing of *Holyrood House*; but I think a great deal of the fine and well-ordered streets of shops; of the regularity which you perceive everywhere in the management of business; and I think still more of the absence of all that foppishness, and that affectation of carelessness, and that insolent assumption of superiority, that you see in almost all the young men that you meet with in the fashionable parts of the great towns in England. I was not disappointed; for I expected to find Edinburgh the finest city in the kingdom. Conversations at Newcastle, and with many Scotch gentlemen for years past, had prepared me for this; but still the reality has greatly surpassed every idea that I had formed about it. The *people*, however, still exceed the place; here all is civility; you do not meet with rudeness, or even with the want of a disposition to oblige, even in persons in the lowest state of life.

William Cobbett,
Tour in Scotland (1833)

Charm

Auld Reikie! wale o' ilka town
That Scotland kens beneath the moon;
Whare couthy chiels at e'ening meet
Their bizzing craigs and mou's to weet:
And blythly gar auld Care gae bye
Wi' blinkit and wi' bleering eye . . .
Then, Reikie, welcome! Thou canst charm.

Robert Fergusson,
from *Auld Reekie, A Poem* (1773)

Peculiar Characteristics

The Scottish capital is one of the few cities of the empire that possesses natural features, and which, were the buildings away, would, while it ceased to be *town*, become very picturesque *country*. And hence one of the peculiar characteristics of Edinburgh. The natural features so overtop the artificial ones, – its hollow valleys are so much more strongly marked than its streets, and its hills and precipices than its buildings, – Arthur's Seat and the Crags look so proudly down on its towers and spires, –

and so huge is the mass, and so bold the outline of its Castle rock and its Calton, compared with those of the buildings which over-top them, – that intelligent visitors, with an eye for the prominent and distinctive in scenery, are led to conceive of it rather as a great country place than as a great town. It is a scene of harmonious contrasts. Not only does it present us with a picturesque city of the grey, time-faded past, drawn out side by side, as if for purposes of comparison, with a gay, freshly-tinted city of the present, rich in all the elegancies and amenities; but it exhibits also, in the same well-occupied area, town and country; as if they, too, had been brought together for purposes of comparison, and as if, instead of remaining in uncompromising opposition, as elsewhere, they had resolved on showing how congruously, and how much to their mutual advantage, they could unite and agree.

Hugh Miller,
Edinburgh and its Neighbourhood (1864)

Midnight

Glasgow is null,
Its suburbs shadows
And the Clyde a cloud.

Dundee is dust
And Aberdeen a shell.

But Edinburgh is a mad god's dream,
Fitful and dark,
Unseizable in Leith
And wildered by the Forth,
But irresistibly at last
Cleaving to sombre heights
Of passionate imagining
Till stonily,
From soaring battlements,
Earth eyes Eternity.

Hugh MacDiarmid,
The Complete Poems (1978)

Athens of the North

Travellers have generally agreed that Edinburgh has a strong resemblance to Athens, and the inhabitants have apparently been willing to humour them by planting happy adaptations and variations of Athenian buildings on prominent places and cutting down tall trees. Thus some see the Royal High School on Calton Hill as the Temple of Theseus; Dugald Stewart the philosopher and Robert Burns the poet are both commemorated by adaptations of the choragic monument to Lysicrates; the observatory on Calton Hill is the Temple of the Winds. Most pointed of all the resemblances, there stands on the top of Calton Hill the Parthenon itself, reduced presumably by the onslaught of the Scots weather to a peristyle. But Nature's reproductions are even more convincing. From the spur of the Pentlands immediately above Colinton the resemblance of the view to that from the bottom of Mount Anchesmus is said to be undeniable. Bulessus is the Hill of Braid; the Castle Hill is the Acropolis; Lycabettus joined to Areopagus form the Calton Hill; and the Firth of Forth is the Aegean Sea. Inchkeith is, of course, Aegina, and the hills of the Peloponnesus rise in Fife.

James Bone,
The Perambulator in Edinburgh (1911)

Classical Praise

Install'd on hills, her head near starry bowers,
Shines Edinburgh, proud of protecting powers.
Justice defends her heart; Religion east
With temples; Mars with towers doth guard the west;
Fresh Nymphs and Ceres serving, wait upon her,
And Thetis, tributary, doth her honour.
The sea doth Venice shake, Rome Tiber beats,
While she but scorns her vassal water's threats.
For sceptres nowhere stands a town more fit,
Nor place where town, world's queen, may fairer sit;
But this my praise is, above all most brave,
No man did e'er defame thee but a slave.

William Drummond of Hawthornden,
Edinburgh (1616)

Sour Grapes

If Edinburgh has not given the creative spirit due place, the creative spirit has not been deluded as to Edinburgh's false position. It is a significant fact that with all the romance attached to it it has never been made the subject of any good, let alone any great, poem. It could not have failed to inspire the poets if there had not all along been something wrong with its pretensions – some essential falsity the instincts of their genius could never be deluded by. Even in prose – except for guidebook stuff and gossipy historical matter – it makes a poor showing; an anthology of excerpts with the slightest pretensions to rank as literature would be an exceedingly slim volume indeed, and its principal contributors would almost all be foreigners.

Lewis Grassic Gibbon and
Hugh Mac Diarmid,
*Scottish Scene: or The Intelligent
Man's Guide to Albyn* (1934)

A View

. . . From the top of the Calton Hill you look down upon hundreds of blue smoke-wreaths curling upward from the chimneys of the resting and restful town, and in every direction the prospect is one of opulence and peace. A thousand years of history are here crystallized within the circuit of a single glance, and while you gaze upon one of the grandest emblems that the world contains of a storied and romantic past, you behold likewise a living and resplendent pageant of the beauty of to-day. Nowhere else are the Past and the Present so lovingly blended.

William Winter,
Gray Days and Gold (1890)

A Magic City

Princes Street is all they say it is. On one side the excellent shops. Then the trim gardens, the Scott Memorial (did ever any other man of letters have such a monument, and, if so, where?), the pleasant low front of the National Gallery of Scotland, and other buildings.

Then the mysterious steaming chasm of the railway. And then – oh, magnificent! – the grey windowed and turreted cliff – for that is the only way to describe it – of the Old Town, with the Castle dominating. What a place!

Two things make Edinburgh so unbelievably grand, so incredible to modern eyes. The first is the way in which it goes up and up, window above window, building piled on building, and breaks everywhere into the most fantastic skylines . . . The second characteristic. All Edinburgh appears to have been built of the same grey sandstone, so that, unlike all other big towns, it wears a face of one colour throughout.

J. B. Priestley,
Sunday Despatch, 19 May 1929

Edinburgh Architecture

I think Edinburgh is the most beautiful city in Europe. I have not seen all the cities in Europe but I have seen a good many and have no fear whatsoever in making that statement . . . One noticed with relief in Edinburgh, after England, how attractive details, such as the granite stones in the streets, had been preserved. What a pity it would be if Edinburgh copied England and covered the place with tarmacadam! What a relief to see iron lamp-posts which are in scale with the streets!

John Betjeman, *The Scotsman*, 25 October 1957

The Strong Tie

From an early age I have felt a strong interest in Edinburgh, though attached to Edinburgh by no other ties than those which are common to me with multitudes; that tie which attaches every man of Scottish blood to the ancient and renowned capital of our race; that tie which attaches every student of history to the spot ennobled by so many great and memorable events; that tie which attaches every traveller of taste to the most beautiful of British cities; and that tie which attaches every lover of literature to a place which, since it has ceased to be the seat of empire, has derived from poetry, philosophy, and eloquence a far higher distinction than empire can bestow.

Lord Macaulay, speech delivered
at Edinburgh election on 29 May 1839

Places

OLD TOWN

Her Potential

It seemed as if the rock and castle assumed a new aspect every time I looked at them; and Arthur's Seat was perfect witchcraft. I don't wonder that anyone residing in Edinburgh should write poetically.

Washington Irving, *Correspondence* (1907)

The Castle

In every point of view, however, the main centre of attraction is the Castle of Edinburgh. From whatever side you approach the city – whether by water or by land – whether your foreground consists of height or of plain, of heath, of trees, or of the buildings of the city itself – this gigantic rock lifts itself high above all that surrounds it, and breaks upon the sky with the same commanding blackness of mingled crags, cliffs, buttresses and battlements. These, indeed, shift and vary their outlines at every step, but everywhere there is the same unmoved effect of general expression – the same lofty and imposing image.

J. G. Lockhart,
Peter's Letters to His Kinsfolk (1819)

Castle Rock

To scale the rock was merely child's play for the Edinbro' callants. It was my own favourite diversion. I soon found that the rock contained all manner of strange crypts, crannies, and recesses, where owls nestled, and the weasel brought forth her young; here and there were small natural platforms, overgrown with long grass and various kinds of plants, where the climber, if so disposed, could stretch himself, and either give his eyes to sleep or his mind to thought; for capital places were these same platforms either for repose or meditation. The boldest features of the rock are descried on the southern side, where, after shelving down gently from the wall for some distance, it terminates abruptly in a precipice, black and horrible, of some three hundred feet at least, as if the axe of nature had been here employed cutting sheer down, and leaving behind neither excrescence nor spur – a dizzy precipice it is, assimilating much to those so frequent in the flinty hills of Northern Africa, and exhibiting some distant resemblance to that of Gibraltar, towering in its horridness above the neutral ground . . .

George Burrow, *Lavengro* (1851)

The One o'clock Gun

It is now one in the afternoon; and at the same instant of time, a ball rises to the summit of Nelson's flagstaff close at hand, and, far away, a puff of smoke followed by a report bursts from the half-moon battery at the Castle.

This is the time-gun by which people set their watches, as far as the sea coast or in hill farms upon the Pentlands.

Robert Louis Stevenson,
Picturesque Notes (1879)

> Each Day the great Gun booms at one,
> That instant Calton Ball falls down
> That minute every watch comes out
> Of every pocket in the Town.
> The Gun on Sabbath makes no sound;
> Are we not rapt in thoughts profound!

Evelyn Beale and Winifred Christie,
An Edinburgh Alphabet (1908)

The Drummer Boy

One of Edinburgh's most famous underground legends revolves around the discovery of a tunnel in the dungeons of Edinburgh Castle in the early nineteenth century. The City Council was curious to find out where this newly unearthed passage went, but the entrance wasn't large enough to allow exploration – unless the explorer happened to be a particularly small one.

Since there were no midgets in the vicinity, the Council decided to send a ten-year-old boy into the tiny aperture to see where the tunnel went to. This may sound like a heartless thing to do, but in those days, thousands of orphans were employed to climb inside chimneys and sweep them – so many Edinburgh children were used to crawling through small, dark spaces. To be fair to the councilmen,

47

they did give the lad a tiny drum – and told him to beat it as he went. That way they could monitor his progress.

The child wriggled into the cold, black passage and wormed his way out of sight, frantically beating the drum. As the faint rat-tat-tat sound travelled under the High Street, councilmen followed safely along on top, listening to the poor lad's progress. At a spot just short of the Tron Church the drumming stopped. It did not start up again.

Edinburgh Council had a dilemma. Though life was cheap among the city's slum children they couldn't keep sending ten-year-old after ten-year-old into the tunnel – there was no telling how many they might get through. Instead, the Council quietly sealed the entrance back up. It was never reopened.

Local residents will tell you that on some nights, if there is no traffic around, a faint but frantic drumming can be heard below the streets around the Tron Kirk. In 1994, a woman on a private tour of underground vaults collapsed after hearing the drummer-boy story. When she came to, she told her astonished companions the reason for her fainting fit. She had heard a drumming behind her just before the story was told.

Jan-Andrew Henderson,
The Town below the Ground (1999)

The Royal Mile

The largest, longest and finest street for Buildings and Number of Inhabitants, not in Britain only, but in the World.

Daniel Defoe,
*A Tour Through the Whole
Island of Great Britain* (1769)

You have seen the famous street at Lisle, la Rue Royale, leading to the Port of Tournay, which is said to be the finest in Europe; but which I can assure you is not to be compared either in length or breadth to the High Street at Edinburgh . . . The style of building here is much like the French: the houses, however, in general are higher, as some rise to twelve, or one in particular to thirteen stories in height. But to the front of the street nine or ten stories is the common run; it is the back part of the edifice which, by being built on the slope of an hill, sinks to that amazing depth, so as to form the above number. This mode of dwelling, tho' very proper for the turbulent times to which it was adapted, has now lost its convenience: as they no longer stand in need of the defence from the Castle, they no more find the benefit of being crowded together so near it. The common staircase which leads to the apartments of the different inhabitants, must always be dirty, and is in general very dark and narrow. It has this advantage, however, that as they are all of stone, they have little to apprehend from fire, which in the opinion of some, would more than compensate for every other disadvantage. In general, however, the highest and lowest tenements are possessed by the artificers, while the gentry and better sort of people dwell in fifth and sixth stories.

Edward Topham, *Letters from Edinburgh* (1776)

Some of these old buildings contained up to twenty apartments, some small, some grand. Ours was one of the latter; I think at one stage two had been knocked into one. There was a large drawing room, a library, a dining room, six bedrooms and a bathroom. A large kitchen with a pantry, a scullery, and a sleeping closet constituted the servant's quarters. There had been buildings on this site since the fifteenth century. From time to time they had fallen or burnt down and new dwellings had been constructed on the ruins. The architecture of the High Street had the character of an antiquated, stone shanty town. Houses had grown piecemeal, by accretion and alteration. Windows were all sizes – actually a pleasing diversity – and installing water closets and modern plumbing required real ingenuity.

William Boyd, *The New Confessions* (1987)

The Slums

The slums from which they were rescued were fearsome places. The old 'lands' in the High Street and Canongate and in the closes and wynds, courtyards and alleyways leading off them, were simply groups of dwellings or tenements under one roof and having a common entry. For long they had housed both rich and poor together, the social level going down as you went up – sometimes for fourteen floors, reckoned the highest housing in Europe. But with the development of the New Town in what had been open countryside to the north of the original city, the richer folk moved out to the more salubrious environment, leaving the old lands to degenerate drastically.

In McLevy's day two of the most notorious were known respectively as the Holy Land and the Happy Land. Another, the Cock and Trumpet, so called from the carved stone crest of the Acheson family over the door, was a brothel from his time until shortly before the Second World War, when it was bought, saved from demolition and restored by the fifth Marquess of Bute. Hill and Adamson, the pioneer photographers, have a photograph taken in McLevy's heyday of

50

one of the girls standing in the doorway under the cock and trumpet emblem. Acheson House now respectably houses the office and showroom of the Scottish Craft Centre, but few others of Edinburgh's fine mediaeval houses survived their declension into slumdom. Today even parts of the New Town are disappearing: the splendid tenements of St James's Square have been replaced by probably the ugliest building Edinburgh has ever seen, a shopping centre described by one American as a bad imitation of a bad American original, a disgrace to the City and to the architectural profession, balefully visible over a wide area.

G. Scott Moncrieff,
*James McLevy: The Casebook of
a Victorian Detective* (1975)

The Lands

Here I was in this old, black city, which was for all the world like a rabbit-warren, not only by the number of its in-dwellers, but the complication of its passages and holes. It was indeed a place where no stranger had a chance to find a friend, let be another stranger. Suppose him even to hit on the right close, people dwelt so thronged in these tall houses, he might very well seek a day before he chanced on the right door. The ordinary course was to hire a lad called a *caddie*, who was like a guide or pilot, led you where you had occasion, and (your errands being done) brought you again where you were lodging . . . We took shelter under a pend at the head of a close or alley. Being strange to what I saw, I stepped a little further in. The narrow paved way descended swiftly. Prodigious tall houses sprang up on each side and bulged out, one story beyond another, as they rose. At the top only a ribbon of sky showed in. By what I could spy in the windows, and by the respectable persons that passed out and in, I saw the houses to be very well occupied; and the whole appearance of the place interested me like a tale.

Robert Louis Stevenson, *Catriona* (1893)

St Giles

In its general exterior, this church presents by no means a fine specimen of the Gothic architecture, although there are several individual parts about the structure which display great beauty – the tower above all which rises out of the centre of the pile, and is capped with a very rich and splendid canopy in the shape of a Crown Imperial. This beautiful tower and canopy form a fine point in almost every view of the city of Edinburgh; but the effect of the whole building, when one hears and thinks of it as a Cathedral, is a thing of no great significance.

J. G. Lockhart,
Peter's Letters to His Kinsfolk (1819)

And from long banishment recal Saint Giles,
To watch again with tutelary love
O'er stately Edinburgh throned on crags.
A blessed restoration, to behold
The Patron, on the shoulders of his priests
Once more parading through her crowded streets
Now simply guarded by the sober powers
Of science, and philosophy, and sense!

William Wordsworth, *Excursion* (1814)

Visitors to Edinburgh express surprise that the metropolitan church of the capital, the great city of Scottish Presbyterianism, bears the name not of Scotland's patron, St Andrew, nor of her Celtic missioner, Columba, but of an obscure French Benedictine monk.

The cult of St Giles (Egidius or Aegidius in Latin) was brought to Britain during the period of the Crusades . . . For almost two centuries there were constant contingents of Scots travelling through France to embark at the Mediterranean ports. Their route was down the Rhone valley to Arles near which the abbey town of St Gilles, on a bend in the river, was rapidly becoming the main port of embarkation . . .

Probably many crusaders prayed in the great church of St Gilles for safety on their journey. On their return to Scotland they would remember him and request further favours from him . . . In Edinburgh, during the reign of Alexander I, a new church was erected for the citizens and it was probably then that the patronage of the French saint began.

The official title of the church everybody calls St Giles' cathedral is the High Kirk of Edinburgh . . . It was only a cathedral, in the sense of being the seat of a bishop, for a few years when Charles I created Edinburgh an episcopal see. Under Presbyterianism the term 'cathedral' is no more than honorary.

Edwin Sprott Towill, *The Saints of Scotland* (1978)

High Street

In the centre of the High Street, in front of the Black Turnpike, the ancient citadel of the town-guard cumbered the thoroughfare till near the close of last century, protected by its ungainly utility from the destruction that befell many a building of rare historical interest. During Cromwell's impartial rule in Edinburgh it formed the scene of many of his acts of 'guid discipline, causing drunkardis ryd the trie meir, with stoppis and muskettis tyed to thair leggis and feit, a paper on thair breist, and a drinking cap in thair handis.' This obsolete instrument of punishment, the wooden mare, still remained when Kay, the caricaturist, made his drawing of the old guardhouse, immediately before its destruction; and it is shown in the woodcut, along with the Black Turnpike and the adjacent tenement where, in 1566, Queen Mary and Darnley were entertained by Lord Home. The chronicles of the old place of petty durance, could they now be recovered, would furnish many an amusing scrap of antiquated scandal, interspersed at rare intervals with the graver deeds of such disciplinarians as the Protector, or the famous sack by the Porteous mob. There such fair offenders as the witty and eccentric Miss Mackenzie, daughter of Lord Royston, found at times a night's lodging, when she and her maid sallied out disguised as *preux chevaliers* in search of adventures. Occasionally even a grave judge or learned lawyer, surprised out of his official decorum by the temptations of a jovial club, was astonished on awaking to find himself within its impartial walls, among such strange bedfellows as the chances of the night had offered to its vigilant guardians. The demolition of the Cross, however, rendered the existence of its unsightly neighbour the more offensive to civic reformers. Fergusson, in his *Mutual Complaint of the Plainstanes and Causey*, humorously represents it as one of the most intolerable grievances of the latter, enough to 'fret the hardest stane'; and at length in 1785 its doom was pronounced, and its ancient garrison removed to the New Assembly Close, then recently deserted by the directors of fashion. There, however, they were pursued by the enmity of their detractors. The proprietors of that fashionable district of the city were scandalised at the idea of such near neighbours as the *Town-Rats*; and by means of Protests, Bills of Suspension, and the like weapons of modern civic warfare, speedily compelled the persecuted veterans to beat a retreat. They took refuge in premises provided for them in the Tolbooth, but the destruction of their ancient stronghold may be said to have sealed their fate. They lingered on for a few years, maintaining an unequal and hopeless struggle against the restless spirit of innovation that had beset the Scottish capital, until at length, in the year 1817, their final refuge was demolished, the last of them were put on the town's pension list, and the truncheon of the constable replaced the venerable firelock and Lochaber-axe.

Sir Daniel Wilson,
Memorials of Edinburgh in the Olden Time (1848)

Tolbooth

It was a foul and unwholesome den: many of the guiltless inmates were so wasted that they were rather like frightful effigies of death than living men. Their skins were sinews in a manner very awful to see. Their eyes were vivid with a strange distemperature, and there was a charnel-house anatomy in the melancholy with which they welcomed a new brother in affliction, that made me feel, when I entered among them, as if I had come into the dark abode of spectres, and manes, and dismal shadows.

John Galt, *Ringan Gilhaize* (1823)

Parliament Square

All the people of business at Edinburgh, and even the genteel company, may be seen standing in crowds every day, from one to two in the afternoon, in the open street, at a place where formerly stood a market-cross, which (by the bye) was a curious piece of Gothic architecture.

Tobias Smollett,
The Expedition of Humphrey Clinker (1771)

Fire at the Tron – 1824

An alarm was given that the Tron Church was on fire. We ran out from the Courts, gowned and wigged and saw that it was the steeple, an old Dutch thing composed of wood, iron and lead and edged all the way up with bits of ornament. Some of the sparks of the proceeding night had nestled in it, and had at last blown its dry bones into flames. There could not be a more beautiful fireworks . . .

Lord Cockburn, *Memorials of His Time* (1856)

A countryman, who had left town when the old spire of the Tron Chuch was blazing like a torch, and the large group of buildings nearly opposite the Cross still enveloped in flame from ground-floor to roof–tree, passed our work–shed, a little after two o'clock, and, telling us what he had seen, remarked that, if the conflagration went on as it was doing, we would have, as our next season's employment, the Old Town of Edinburgh to rebuild. And as the evening closed over our labours, we went in to town in a body to see the fires that promised to do so much for us. The spire had burnt out, and we could but catch between us and the darkened sky the square abrupt outline of the masonry a-top that had supported the wooden broach, whence, only a few hours before, Fergusson's bell had descended in a molten shower. The flames, too, in the upper group of buildings, were restricted to the lower stories and flared fitfully on the tall forms and bright swords of the dragoons, drawn from the neighbouring barracks, as they rode up and down the middle space, or gleamed athwart the street on groups of wretched–looking women and ruffian men, who seemed scanning with greedy eyes the still unremoved heaps of household goods rescued from the burning tenements.

Hugh Miller, *My Schools and Schoolmasters* (1854)

The Luckenbooths

For some inconceivable reason, our ancestors had jammed into the middle of the principal street of the town, leaving for passage a narrow street on the north, and on the south, into which the prison opens, a narrow crooked lane, winding between the high and sombre walls of the Tolbooth and of the adjacent houses on one side, and the buttresses and projections of the Old Church upon the other. To give some gaiety to this sombre passage (well known by the name of the Krames), a number of little booths or shops, after the fashion of cobblers' stalls, are plastered as it were against the Gothic projectments and abutments, so that it seemed as if the traders had occupied with nests bearing the same proportion to the building, every buttress and coign of vantage, as the martlet did in Macbeth's Castle. Of later years these booths have degenerated into mere toy shops . . . but at the time of which we write, hosiers, glovers, hatters, mercers, milliners, and all who dealt in the miscellaneous wares now termed 'haberdashers' goods', were to be found in the narrow alley.

Sir Walter Scott, The Heart of Midlothian (1818)

> The ancient Krames whaur weanies tottit
> Whaur a' wee wairdless callants trottit
> Though scantlt fed, and scrimply coatit
> To spend their a'
> On dirlin' drums or ba's that stottit
> Against the wa'.

James Ballantine,
Lament for Ancient Edinburgh (1856)

Grassmarket

The Grassmarket has retained its character almost un-spoilt. Many of the old lands have been pulled down: the cross of the Knights Templar, who owned much property here and in the West Bow, has gone from the housetops, and new buildings have appeared. Yet the Grassmarket remains one of the loveliest things in Edinburgh, with the mellow quiet aspect of a district that has seen much and endured much. Its quiet has often been broken, by the cries of martyred covenanters, by the shouts of the mob that Porteous fired on, by the clattering of knights in armour and noble ladies to the tourneys that James IV loved to hold hard by, in full view of his court, assembled on the Castle. Squealings and gruntings have rent its air on the cattle–market days; much innocent blood of pigs and kine had stained its causeway long before the reformers died here for their faith. For as early as 1477 James III forebade 'all quyck bestis, ky, oxen', to be brought within the city walls.

But nothing can lastingly dispel the quiet that hangs over the Grassmarket, like a legacy from the days when James I built here a convent for Cornelius of Zurich, who came over, at the King's invitation, to found the order of the Franciscans and promote education in Scotland . . . From the time that the Flodden Wall was built in 1513 the Grassmarket had its West Port, second in importance only to the West Bow, and always plentifully supplied with the heads of traitors . . . It was through the West Port that Claverhouse rode, to waste his life in the cause of a worth-less King. But the Grassmarket knew its most magnificent days when Edinburgh received a new-crowned king or his bride, coming from foreign ports. Under the West Port have passed Mary of Gueldres from Holland, Mary Tudor from England, Madeleine of France, first love of James V, who died so young, said righteous Scotland, because she loved dancing and so offended the jealous and severe God of the reformers. And barely a year after her death came the lovely Mary of Guise, to be welcomed by Edinburgh in the Grassmarket. And here her daughter

Mary, Queen of Scotland, has been greeted with praise in the days of her glory, with insults and abuse in the time of her fall. James VI was welcomed here, in 1590, by 'Solomon and the twa wemen', and here his Queen, Anna of Denmark, received the keys of the city from an angel descending from the battlements.

Flora Grierson, *Haunting Edinburgh* (1929)

Cowgate

You stand on the South Bridge and, looking down, instead of a stream you see the Cowgate the dirtiest, narrowest, most densely peopled of Edinburgh streets. Admired once by a French ambassador at the court of one of the Jameses, and yet with certain traces of departed splendour, the Cowgate has fallen into the sere and yellow leaf of furniture brokers, second-hand jewellers and vendors of deleterious alcohol. These second-hand jewellers' shops, the trinkets seen by bleared gaslight, are the most melancholy sights I know. Watches hang there that once ticked comfortable on the fobs of prosperous men, rings that were once placed by happy bridegrooms on the fingers of happy brides, jewels in which lives the sacredness of deathbeds. What tragedies, what disruptions of households, what fell pressure of poverty brought them here! Looking in through the foul windows, the trinkets remind me of shipwrecked gold embedded in the ooze of ocean – gold that speaks of unknown, yet certain, storm and disaster, of the yielding of planks, of the cry of drowning men. Who has the heart to buy them, I wonder? The Cowgate is the Irish portion of the city. Edinburgh leaps over it with bridges; its inhabitants are morally and geographically the lower orders. They keep to their own quarters, and seldom come up to the light of day. Many an Edinburgh man has never set foot in the street; the condition of the inhabitants is as little known to respectable Edinburgh as are the habits of moles, earthworms, and the mining population.

Alexander Smith, A Summer in Skye (1865)

The Nor' Loch

He who now sees the wide hollow space between the Old and New Towns, occupied by beautiful gardens, having their continuity only somewhat curiously broken up by a transverse earthen mound and a line of railway, must be at a loss to realise the idea of the same space presenting in former times a lake, which was regarded as a portion of the physical defences of the city. Yet many, in common with myself, must remember the by no means distant time when the remains of this sheet of water, consisting of a few pools, served as excellent sliding and skating ground in winter, while their neglected grass–green precincts too frequently formed an arena whereon the high and mighty quarrels of Old and New Town *cowlies* were brought to a lapidarian arbitration.

The lake, it after all appears, was artificial, being fed by springs under the Castle Rock, and retained by a dam at the foot of Halkerston's Wynd [where the North Bridge now stands]; which dam was a passable way from the city to the fields on the north. Bower, the continuator of Fordun, speaks of a tournament held on the ground, *ubi nunc est lacus*, in 1396, by order of the queen [of Robert III], at which her eldest son, Prince David, then in his twentieth year, presided. At the beginning of the sixteenth century a ford upon the North Loch is mentioned. Archbishop Beatoun escaped across that ford in 1517, when flying from the unlucky street-skirmish called *Cleanse the Causeway*.

The North Loch was the place in which our pious ancestors used to dip and drown offenders against morality, especially of the female sex. The Reformers, therefore, conceived that they had not only done a very proper, but also a very witty thing, when they threw into this lake, in 1558, the statue of St Giles, which formerly adorned their High Church, and which they had contrived to abstract.

Robert Chambers, Traditions of Edinburgh (1825)

The Bridges to the New Town

Edinburgh in the mid–eighteenth century had barely expanded since its earliest days. The centre of Edinburgh consists of the Royal Mile and the Grassmarket, with a few outlying villages such as Broughton and Canonmills. The social classes lived together in the same streets, crowded on top of one another. There were no street names to be seen and people relied on the ever-present caddies to show them to their desired destination. Coal burned in open fires, simple creuze lamps lit many homes and water was supplied through the city water wells. But the eighteenth century was an era in which Edinburgh went through its biggest changes and developments. It was a time when David Hume and Adam Smith expounded their theories of philosophy and economics and when Scottish architects led the world in civic design. This ferment of cultural and intellectual endeavour is known as the Age of Enlightenment.

The years 1750–1800 witnessed the rise of Scotland's

capital to world class status. The largest and most ambitious of the city's projects was undoubtedly that of the New Town to be located north of the medieval city. Based on a design by the young and largely unknown architect, James Craig, the gridiron structure of Princes Street, George Street and Queen Street gradually took shape in the 1760s and 1770s, and the higher echelons of society made their homes within its classical porticoes.

It was [also] clear to the city developers that access to these new areas would be difficult, with the Old Town built along a steep ridge of rock sloping sharply away on each side. To drive carriages down these narrow passageways and up the other side would have been impossible. It was proposed that two bridges be built to span the valleys on either side of the Royal Mile. The North Bridge would cross the marshy trough left by the Nor' Loch and the South Bridge would span the Cowgate.

These ambitious plans for the city of Edinburgh began to take shape in 1765 with the partial draining of the stinking Nor' Loch and the building of the North Bridge towards what would become the New Tow. A serious set back came in 1769 when the North Bridge collapsed taking five lives. It was rebuilt on firmer foundations and reopened in 1772. The next stage of the development was a corresponding bridge to the south of the Royal Mile, first mooted in 1775. After the appointment of Trustees in 1785, the architect Robert Kay drew up a series of plans and the foundation stone was laid on 1 August of that year. The nineteen great stone arches, the three storey buildings and the wide road running along the top were finished in less than three years, described by an observer as *an operation of astonishing celerity.*

Alan J. Wilson and Des Brogan,
Hidden and Haunted Underground Edinburgh (1999)

The Markets

One of the first places which came to my recollection, was the market for fruit and vegetables. It was held underneath the North Bridge and the adjoining space towards the Waverley Bridge. This market was handed over to the Corporation in 1869. For many years, the Market was held in the open air, but in the early 'seventies the Corporation decided to provide a covered market. Owing to the soft nature of the ground, the foundation had to be made on thick wooden piles. After the pillars were erected on the top of these piles, the Market was roofed over, and it was called the Waverley Market, which was opened in 1877, where fruit, flowers, etc. are sold to the present time.

In those days, there were comparatively few greengrocers', butchers' or fishmongers' shops, but all commodities were obtainable in the Markets in different parts of the town. The largest and central market was situated near the top of Cockburn Street. It was entered by a short flight of steps, a few yards higher up the street than the present long flights of stairs known as Fleshmarket Close, at the back of the Scotsman Buildings. There was also another entrance through a pend in the North Bridge, where a short flight of steps led down to the top market. The Market was arranged in terraces. The top one was for Veal, Poultry and Rabbits, the Flesh Market was on the second terrace, and the open air Fish Market was entered from the Flesh Market by a flight of wide stairs. It was surrounded by covered stalls, which were occupied by retailers of various kinds of fish. The fishwives from Newhaven and Fisherrow, with their baskets and creels formed two rows in the centre of the Market.

The Fish Market was on the level of the present railway,

as was also the Vegetable Market mentioned above. Besides these markets there was a peculiar institution called 'the Plout', which was an open air market near the top of Cockburn Street, held on Saturday nights. There, dogs, cats, and pigeons and other birds were sold and exchanged. It was a common sight to see a man or boy with a pigeon or two sticking out of his coat pockets.

D. A. Small,
Through Memory's Window
(unpublished memoirs 1860–1927)

The Canongate

The palace of Holyrood house stands on the left, as you enter the Canongate – This is a street continued from hence to the gate called Nether Bow, which is now taken away; so that there is no interruption for a long mile, from the bottom to the top of the hill on which the Castle stands in a most imperial situation – Considering its fine pavement, its width, and the lofty houses on each side, this would be undoubtedly one of the noblest streets in Europe, if an ugly mass of mean buildings, called the Lucken-Booths, had not thrust itself, by what accident I know not, into the middle of the way, like Middle-Row in Holborn.

Tobias Smollett,
The Expedition of Humphry Clinker
(1771)

Canongate Kirk

The church came to the Canongate before the houses. But that is an old story, a story that takes us back to 1128, when King David I decided to have the Abbey Kirk of the Holy Rood or Cross, erected as a thanksgiving to God for being rescued from what had looked like almost certain death from the antlers of a fierce stag while hunting. The vision of a cross appearing between the antlers made him consider his survival as truly an act of God, and as his thanksgiving for deliverance the Abbey of Holyrood (as we now call it) was built.

The parish kirk of the Canongate is not the same as that built by David I. The foundations of the Abbey Church stand now in ruins beside the Palace of Holyroodhouse. The present building is, for our part of the world, fairly new, for it was built in 1688 by order of James VII and II.

Ronald Selby Wright,
The Kirk in the Canongate (1956)

A View of the Canongate

Often in boyhood, when walking along the Bridges, was I tempted to halt for a few moments to look down at a brawl in the Cowgate, far below. That part of Auld Reekie, curiously enough, always seemed a place by itself, a quarter into which, unarmed or unguarded, only the most intrepid ventured. Like the Cowcaddens of Glasgow, the Cowgate of Auld Reekie had acquired a reputation for lawlessness far in excess of what it deserved. Its denizens seldom sallied forth to the fairer parts of the city: seldom did we penetrate into theirs, except when accompanying some antiquarian excursion where numbers guaranteed safety. In those days, we unwarrantably regarded the Cowgate's inhabitants as the sort of folk with whom we should never allow ourselves to come into contact, and whom we should embrace in our vision only when at a respectable distance – folk that most of us, when obliged to pass along the Bridges, we were thankful to be able to avoid by means of the quite modest viaduct giving to the South Bridge its name. This bridging of the gap between the two halves of Allan's drapery ensured that, so far as *we* were concerned, the Cowgate and its dusty dwellers would be kept in their proper place! Yet, we had been told that artists were in the habit of finding their way into this nether region, pitching their camp-stools on its doorsteps to capture on canvas this vista or that, this ancient turret, that historic close. And what seemed even more remarkable to us children, brought up in the notion that this was the abode of ghosts and bogles and bad, bad men, was that the artists invariably managed to escape by nightfall, unhurt and unmolested.

The Cowgate for generations had an unenviable reputation; and one can hardly say that the conduct of its habitués at 'chuckin'-oot time' on a Saturday night entitled it to our better esteem. Its men-folk, collarless and tie-less, its womenfolk, usually happed about in frayed tartan shawls, were a sorry representation of the human kind, scrambling into, or oozing out of, public-houses, lodging-houses, or missions, sinning and sorrowing through most of their earthly sojourn.

Alasdair Alpin MacGregor, *Auld Reekie* (1943)

Greyfriars Kirk

One of our famous Edinburgh points of view: and strangers
are led thither to see, by yet another instance, how
strangely the city lies upon her hills. The enclosure is of an
irregular shape; the double church of Old and New
Greyfriars stands on the level at the top; a few thorns are
dotted here and there, and the ground falls by terrace and
steep slope towards the north. The open shows many slabs
and table tombstones; and all around the margin the place
is girt by an array of aristocratic mausoleums appallingly
adorned.

Robert Louis Stevenson, *Picturesque Notes* (1879)

The Flodden Wall

The Flodden Wall is important in the history of Edinburgh,
for long defining the City bounds. Nor, for some 250 years,
did the people risk building themselves houses outside it,
but instead, as the population increased, piled storey upon
storey to a height that made Edinburgh unique amongst
the cities of Europe: the skyscraper community of its day.
They reached eventually nine or ten storeys, and some of
the 'lands' may have had up to fourteen from the lower level
of the back-lanes from which their walls towered up to 130
feet in height. It should be added that some archivists
dispute those figures with considerable warmth: but they
certainly have some contemporary support.

The Flodden Wall ran south from the south-east corner
of the Castle rock across the end of the Grassmarket to
which it struck a parallel line below Heriot's Hospital,

bulging out to enclose the Greyfriars' Church, ran above the head of Candlemaker Row, by the Kirk o' Field (the site of the University), and turned north again just short of the Pleasance. It followed the march between Edinburgh and Canongate and turned west near the site of the Waverley Station to where its place was taken by the waters of the Nor' Loch which served to protect the City from the north. It was an elaborate structure of considerable height, with towers, crenellations, loop-holes, and embrasures. Its gateways were heavily defended. They were the West Port at the end of the Grassmarket: the Bristo Port: the Cowgate Port: and the Netherbow Port at the Canongate. Below the Netherbow Port the wall was formed of the houses on the west side of Leith Wynd, whose inhabitants, in time of danger, were bound to block doors and windows opening on the wynd. There was a slight extension of the wall north in 1560, to enclose Trinity College, whose lovely little church had been founded by Mary of Gueldres in 1462, and whose site is now a mesh of L.N.E.R. railway lines: and a second small extension south up the Vennel to include the High Riggs, in 1622. A portion of this extension remains alongside Heriot's, which was erected shortly afterwards on the burgh's new territory here. Otherwise the Flodden Wall remained unchanged as the boundary of the City until the expansion into the New Town in the eighteenth century.

George Scott-Moncrieff, *Edinburgh* (1947)

Calton Hill

On Calton Hill
The Twelve pillars
Of this failed Parthenon
Made more Greek by the Cargo boat
Sailing between them
On the cobwebby water of the Firth
Should marry nicely with the Observatory
In the way complements do
Each observing the heavens
In its different way.

Norman MacCaig, 'Inward Bound' from
The White Bird (1973)

Arthur's Seat

The city's ancient volcano could be seen for miles around. From such a distance it appeared as a misty, blue hill with a few dim, central hollows. Close up it was a fierce, dark-cliffed mountain with precipitous streams of red and black rocks below which were piled long screes of rusty gravel covered with patches of grass and wind-bent thorn bushes. Arthur's Seat was only one of many outbursts of vulcanism in Scotland. Its dim hollows could now be seen as dark basins where millions of years ago fires had spurted, where thundering ash and molten lava had filled the cavities, and poured out over miles of the surrounding countryside. It stood high above the city – a dramatic landscape and a lonely one. Black and red sharp-edged cliffs rose above the path circling the hill, and beneath it, far below the steep scree slopes, one looked down upon formal white crescents, over criss-crossing roads between old houses, over spires and domes, and across to the stubborn knob of the Castle Rock – that great plug of hard black basalt which had outlived a whole series of huge, primeval eruptions. Even the moving ice-sheets had not levelled it.

Elspeth Davie, *Coming to Light* (1989)

Overlooking a pastoral hollow as wild and solitary as any in the heart of the Highland mountains: there, instead of the roaring of the torrents, we listened to the noises of the city, which were blended in one loud indistinct buzz – a regular sound in the air, which in certain moods of feeling, and at certain times, might have a more tranquillizing effect upon the mind than those which we are accustomed to hear in such places. The castle rock looked exceedingly large through the misty air: a cloud of black smoke over-hung the city, which combined with the rain and mist to conceal the shapes of the houses – an obscurity which added much to the grandeur of the sound that proceeded from it. It was impossible to think of anything that was little or mean, the goings-on of trade, the strife of men, or everyday city business – the impression was one, and it was visionary; like the conceptions of our childhood of Bagdad or Balsora when we have been reading The Arabian Nights' Entertainments.

Dorothy Wordsworth,
Recollections of a Tour in Scotland (1803)

The Meadows in Autumn

A haar hings over the Meadows like snow,
it gets at the leaves on the trees,
they fall, flutter yellow. And silent to the ground
every leaf will drop.

I walk ahint the birlin leaves as
well-trained Council man follows
me. He has new-fangled machine
And containing bag. Some escape
to soar into the unkent.

Duncan Glen,
Journey into Scotland (1991)

Nelson's Printing Works

At Hope Park End, now Buccleuch Street, stood Nelson's
Printing Works, which were burned down in 1878. The
loss was stated to be £200,000. I remember going to see
the fire, and the fire engines working. They were called
manual fire engines because the pumps were worked by
man power; a very feeble instrument with which to attack
a big fire. The engines were drawn by long ropes by the
firemen and anyone who liked to join in, when horses
were not available. The volunteers were paid at the rate
of one shilling an hour and liquid refreshment over and
above. The handsome pillars at the east end of the
Melville Drive were erected by Meesrs. Nelson as a mark
of their gratitude to the city, for having allowed them to
use part of the East Meadows for a time. The pillars at

the other end of the Drive, were erected as a memorial of the 1886 Exhibition held in the West Meadows, where 'Old Edinburgh' was reproduced. The Exhibition was a huge success. There was a surplus said to be £3,000.

D. A. Small,
Through Memory's Window
(unpublished memoirs 1860–1927)

Salisbury Crags

If I were to choose a spot from which the rising or setting sun could be seen to the geatest possible advantage, it would be that wild path winding around the foot of the high belt of semicircular rocks, called Salisbury Crags, and marking the verge of the steep descent which slopes down into the glen on the south-eastern side of Edinburgh. The prospect, in its general outline, commands a close-built, high-piled city, stretching itself out beneath in a form, which, to a romantic imagination, may be supposed to represent that of a dragon; now, a noble arm of the sea, with its rock, isles, distant shores, and boundary of mountains; and now, a fair and fertile campaign country, varied with hill, dale and rock, and skirted by the picturesque ridge of the Pentland mountains. But as the path gently circles around the base of the cliffs, the prospect, composed as it is of these enchanting and sublime objects, changes at every step, and presents them blended with, or divided from, each other, in every possible variety which can gratify the eye and the imagination. When a piece of scenery, so beautiful yet so varied – so exciting by its intricacy, and yet so sublime – is lighted up by the tints of morning or of evening, and displays all that variety of shadowy depth, exchanged with partial brilliancy, which gives character even to the tamest of landscapes, the effect approaches near to enchantment.

Sir Walter Scott,
The Heart of Midlothian (1818)

Holyrood Park

Snow and solo, Holyrood Park at night;
Flakes so brittle footsteps can press no print;
Sky reflects the earthly pallor,
Shadows of evening are blanched of darkness.

Star nor moon, no break in the haze of white.
Outline none to sharpen the lion crag;
Wide terrain of hill and parkland
Empty of creature beside my walking.

Round the frozen loch sleep the ruffled swans
Geese and lesser fowl in their sheltering;
Dogs and humans huddle safely,
Lights of the city for hibernation.

Days are dark in winter, and nights are pale.
Blankly folded into each other's sphere;
Tessa Ransford: is are muffled, humbled;
Silent I, alone, travel forward.

Far ahead I see, by the gate, the trees,
Hardened branches blurred by the pallid light;
Nearly home I find beneath them
Circles of softness where earth is warmer.

Friends grow distant, lost in their own distress;
Each of us alone bears what winter brings;
Stiffened, frosted, leafless, upright,
Yet, unawares, we make fonder patches.

Tessa Ransford, *Shadows from the Greater Hill* (1987)

Holyrood House

After monarchy was restored, Charles II showed a liberal attention to the condition of his ancient metropolis. A new Palace, built upon the site of the former, and connected with its venerable relics, was erected, after the plans of Sir William Bruce of Kinross, by Robert Milne, the King's mason. The work, though in the French taste of Louis XIV's reign, does honour both to the architect and the builder. It is a quadrangle, built around a central court, surrounded with piazzas. The front is very handsome. It is two stories high, and flat in the roof, closing the inner court as with a screen, and giving access to it under a handsome cupola, surmounted by an imperial crown, executed in stone work. At each angle of the front the building projects and rises above the line, being decorated with turrets at the angles. The other three sides of the palace are three stories high, but plain and unornamented.

The attention of Charles was also turned to the abbey-church, which he fitted up anew as a chapel-royal, to be set apart in future for the use of the royal family – the installation of the Knights of the Thistle – and other occasions of regal solemnity. A throne was erected for the sovereign, and stalls for twelve knights of the order; an organ was again introduced, and the whole interior of the chapel was, at considerable expense, put into complete repair. But it was again destined to feel the violating rage of civil discord.

Though James II or VII of Scotland contributed something to the splendour of the palace of his ancestors, he was finally the cause of its being raised through the same obstinate bigotry by which he forfeited three kingdoms. When he ascended the throne, amongst injudicious measures in favour of Popery, he thought proper not only to have mass celebrated in the chapel-royal at Holyrood House, but also to establish a Roman Catholic printing press and Popish schools there. These acts of bigotry drew down the displeasure of the people at once upon the government and the very building itself, which was doubly odious as the residence of Perth the chancellor, the Popish minister of a Popish monarch.

At length, 10th December 1688, the insurrection assumed an organized and formidable aspect. A great number of the youths of the city assembling with arms in their hands, such they could procure in haste, marched towards the abbey in something like military array. The assailants forced their way into the palace and chapel, where, unfortunately, not contented with wreaking their displeasure upon the Popish vestments and images which fell into their hands, they laid the chapel utterly waste, tearing down the seats, stalls and carved ornaments, breaking even into the recesses of the dead, to tear from the coffins the remains of kings and nobles who lay buried in the choir, and leaving the whole a scene of devastation and ruin.

Want of skill and stupidity completed the desolation of this ancient chapel. The Barons of Exchequer, with well-meant attention to its repair, had directed a new roof to be imposed on the ancient walls. But this roof was of freestone, and unhappily, its weight proved too great for the frailty of walls, already nearly six hundred years old. It fell within two years after it had been put up, breaking down and ruining the groundwork, and the shafts of the columns, and encumbering the whole interior. In this state it still remains.

Sir Walter Scott,
Provincial Antiquities (1826)

I took one more walk through Holyroodhouse, the mansion of ancient kings: but how melancholy an appearance does it make now! The stately rooms are dirty as stables: the colours of the tapestry are quite faded; several of the pictures are cut and defaced. The roof of the royal chapel is fallen in; and the bones of James the Fifth, and the once beautiful Lord Darnley, are scattered about like those of sheep or oxen. Such is human greatness!

John Wesley, *Journal* (1827)

The Palace of Holyrood has been left aside in the growth of Edinburgh and stands grey and silent in a workman's quarter among breweries and gas works. It is a house of many memories. Great people of yore, kings and queens, buffoons and grave ambassadors, played their stately farce for centuries in Holyrood. Wars have been plotted, dancing has lasted deep into the night, murder has been done in its chambers. There Prince Charlie held his phantom levees, and in a very gallant manner.

Robert Louis Stevenson,
Picturesque Notes (1879)

Queen Mary's Bath-House

Time that has dinged down Castels and his toures,
And cast great crowns like tinsel in the fire,
That halds his hand for palace nor for byre,
Stands sweir at this, the oe of Venus' boures.
Not time himself can dwell withouten flowers,
Though aiks main fa' the rose sall bide entire;
So sall this diamant of a queen's desire
Outflourish all the staines that Time devours.
Many a strength his turrey-heid sall tine
Ere this sall fa' whare a queen lay in wine,
Whose lamp was her ain lily flesh and star,
The walls of luve the mair triumphant are
Gif luve were waesome habiting that place;
Luve has maist years that has a murming face.

Lewis Spence,
The Queen's Bath-House, Holyrood (1953)

The Transition

It took the Old Town barely 50 years to die. David Hume
left Riddle's Court in the Lawnmarket for St David's Street
in 1769, and Robert Chambers claimed that the last person
of quality to live in the High Street – Governor Fergusson
of Pitfour – departed in 1817. For the remainder of the
nineteenth century, those who lived in the Old Town were
those who had no choice. Lower professionals, tradesmen,
and craftsmen followed the middle classes out to the suburbs
in repeated waves, and skilled workers constructed themselves five separate colonies of houses on marginal

suburban land. When the scandal of the Burke and Hare murders erupted in the West Port, however, Walter Scott returned – in a carriage – to the streets he had walked as a student, filled with horror and remorse that, had people like him remained in the Old Town, perhaps it might not have sunk so low.

Michael Lynch [Ed.],
The Oxford Companion to Scottish History (2001)

THE NEW TOWN

'New Town': everywhere else in Scotland, it meant the likes of Glenrothes and Livingston, places built from nothing in the fifties and sixties. But in Edinburgh, the New Town dated back to the eighteenth century. That was about as new as the city liked things.

Ian Rankin, *Dead Souls* (1999)

I think myself peculiarly happy in being permitted to address the citizens of Edinburgh on the subject of architecture, for it is one which, they cannot but feel, interests them nearly. Of all the cities in the British Islands, Edinburgh is the one which presents most advantages for the display of a noble building; and which, on the other hand, sustains most injury in the erection of a commonplace or unworthy one. . . . As far as I am acquainted with modern architecture, I am aware of no streets which, in simplicity and manliness of style, or general breadth and brightness of effect, equal those of the New Town of Edinburgh.

John Ruskin,
Lectures on Architecture and Painting (1854)

A Thought for Ruskin

An important but lonely challenge had come earlier with *Rowand Anderson's* Venetian-French Gothic National

Portrait Gallery (1885). Paid for by the owner of *The Scotsman* with the encouragement of Lord Bute, this was a belated acknowledgement of the force of Ruskin's diatribe against the city's confirmed classicism (*Edinburgh Lectures*, 1856) The cardboard scenic-Gothic of Playfair's Free Church College on the Mound (1846, now New College) also excited Ruskin's rage. Whatever would he have said of the brute classicism of the United Free Church office (1909, now Church of Scotland) in George Street?

John Gifford et al,
Edinburgh (Pevsner) (1984)

❦

Craig's Plan

The prospect of the extension of the Royalty [i.e. lands received as a gift from the Crown] and the start on the construction of the North Bridge in 1765 had prompted the magistrates to consider what regulations should be made about 'building in the fields to the north'. They realised, doubtless, that without some encouragement by them their new property might for long remain un-developed. They probably also reckoned that unless they guided developments in a suitable way, the vision of 1758 would not be realised – the vision, that is, of a town distinguished by 'the neatness and accommodation of its private houses, the beauty and conveniency of its numerous streets and open spaces, of its buildings and bridges, its large parks and extensive walks . . . '

On 21 May 1766 it was noted in the Town Council Minutes that six plans had been received, and on 2 August that Plan No. 4 by Mr James Craig had been adjudged the best.

Craig's plan has been fervently eulogised and contemptuously derided. The New Town owes its superiority, says Arnot, partly to 'the whole being built conform to a regular and beautiful plan'. But in the Dictionary of National Biography the same plan is dammed as 'utterly destitute of any inventive ingenuity or any regard for the natural features of the ground'. The truth is that the plan is entirely sensible, and almost painfully orthodox.

A. J. Youngson,
The Making of Classical Edinburgh (1966)

The Neo Classic Kirks

The two earliest of the New Town churches, St Andrew's and St George's were intended by James Craig to stand in the squares terminating the George Street ridge, the main axis of his planning scheme, but the former, having its site usurped for other purposes, had to be built in a less distinguished place on the north side of George Street. In a competition held by the Town Council, the design chosen for this church was that of Major Andrew Frazer of the Engineers. The church as built consists of an oval auditorium with gallery, fronted by an entrance vestibule and a well-proportioned portico with Corinthian columns and pediment. The graceful spire which combines so happily with the rest of the building was designed by William Sibbald and superseded Frazer's design which was of stumper proportions. It was completed in 1789, four years after the remainder of the church.

The sister church of St George's was built in 1814 from the design of Robert Reid, which superseded a rather better one by Robert Adam, who was responsible for the fine treatment of Charlotte Square in which it stands. Its façade with large plain Ionic columns is rather course and out of scale with the rest of the square. Strangely enough, too, the dome surmounts, not the church proper which is of shallow Greek cross plan, but a large vestibule. The interior, though good is less well proportioned than that of St Andrew's.

George Hay,
*The Architecture of Scottish
Post-Reformation Churches* (1957)

By comparison with contemporary Nancy, therefore, Craig's New Town is a poor affair – merely two squares joined by a straight central street flanked by two others. This is basically simple, rectilinear or grid-iron planning, and is exceedingly old. The exact elements and essential relations of Craig's plan, indeed, are to be seen in the town of Richelieu, near Tours, built to the order of Cardinal Richelieu in 1633. Here are two squares, joined centrally by a straight street, with a flanking street on each side. Richelieu is, of course, far smaller than the New Town of Edinburgh, and the proportions are different; the squares are not far separated from one another, the streets are narrow, the houses relatively high. But the general form is precisely the same. No one familiar with Edinburgh can walk through the streets of Richelieu without being struck by the similarity. Whether Craig knew anything about Richelieu we cannot tell. The rectilinear approach which is common to both these plans is, of course, much older than Richelieu.

What makes Craig's New Town so pleasing, then, even to-day? It cannot be the originality of its design. Craig was not only not original, but he even failed to make use of several new ideas available to him – the circus, for example, or the effect made by two symmetrical buildings, taller than the rest, at the entrance to a square. The principal reason for Craig's success – in so far as a reason is to be found in Craig's share of the work – is the excellent use of the site. The two outer streets – Princes Street and Queen Street – have houses on one side only, and these look outwards across the street, in one case over the low ground towards the Castle and High Street, in the other down the slope towards the Firth of Forth and the distant hills of Fife. This feeling of spaciousness combined with order is no doubt enhanced by the good proportions of the streets and buildings.

A. J. Youngson,
The Making of Classical Edinburgh (1966)

Regents Road

It is more astonishing than an Eastern dream. A city rises up before you painted by fire on night. High in air a bridge of lights leap the chasm; a few emerald lamps, like glow-worms, are moving silently about in the railway station below; a solitary crimson one is at rest. That ridged and chimneyed bulk of blackness, with splendour bursting out of every pore, is the wonderful Old Town, where Scottish history mainly transacted itself; while, opposite the modern Princes Street is blazing throughout its length.

Alexander Smith,
A Summer in Skye (1865)

Princes Street

Princes Street by night is yet another matter; Princes Street by night is a poem. Come to it after dark from the Calton Hill, and see the long ribbon lying in the blue of a northern evening against the black shadow of the old town, the misty hollow of the gardens, the high line of shops; all asleep and quiet except when now and again the shriek and rattle of a train brings pity for the traveller who is leaving Edinburgh. And all is spangled with little lights – golden windows high up in the lands of the Lawnmarket; the cool white lights on standards that teach good citizens how 'M.O.H. says – spitting spreads disease'; the moving coloured stars, red and green, violet and blue, to tell the initiate whither each tram will take him; or great pools of light from a cinema or some shop that has lift its windows gleaming long after its doors are locked. Faint behind it all, the melancholy bulk of the Castle is just discernible; I do not remember ever seeing a light up there, and sober Scots do not indulge in the red jelly *Schloss-beleuchtung* that periodically sets Heidelberg Castle ablaze. Overhead, like a great full-blown moon, the clock face of the North British Hotel looms on its monstrosity of a tower, which the kindliness of evening makes almost imposing. Everything is lovely and unreal, beautiful with a kind of accidental beauty more natural to Scotland than the intended beauty of artistic nations.

Flora Grierson, *Haunting Edinburgh* (1929)

Princes Street Again

Nor has Edinburgh, or its 'New Town', much reason to
complain if the impression of its beauty be drawn from the
aspect and situation of the street which is at once the
favourite promenade and the centre of its business life.

'Her face is her fortune,' some one had said of the
Scottish capital; and if the High Street be the deep heart,
Princes Street is the fair face of Edinburgh. 'The most
magnificent esplanade in Europe,' the citizens are fond of
thinking it; and many widely-travelled strangers have
promptly granted the claim . . . But the glory of Princes
Street, which gives it charm and distinction above other
thoroughfares, is its prospect towards the south, its outlook over the valley which once held the Nor' Loch to the
Old Town and the Castle. It was happy in being saved
from the fate, destined for it by the vandals of a century
ago, of being 'built on both sides' . . . By doubling its front
Princes Street would not merely have spoiled, it would
have completely destroyed its character. As it is, the
guests at its hotel windows and the passengers on its
crowded foot pavements and on the broad stream of its
cars and carriages look across, as from a platform built to
yield them the prospect, to the huge and shadowy bulk of
the Rock, the long verdant sweep of the Castle Braes, and
the sky-climbing broken masses of the High Street houses,
crowned by spire and dome and pinnacle, and separated
from them only by a quarter of a mile of air and a light
screen of foliage.

John Geddie, *Romantic Edinburgh* (1900)

Life in Edinburgh for the incomer who is there for only a short visit will seem to centre in and around Princes Street. It is only as you stay on or come again and again and get to know the general life of the citizens that you realise that Princes Street for the Edinburgh man and woman is a mere, if lovely, thoroughfare. Life for them really goes on in those other streets, crescents, circuses and squares beyond 'The Street'. Some of those quarters are very beautiful, the Edinburgh that arose at the end of the eighteenth century and the beginning of the nineteenth. Others are no better than any other city of the kind. But always you will be coming across corners and vistas to which you will say 'Oh!' and 'Ah!' That is Edinburgh.

George Rowntree Harvey, *A Book of Scotland* (1949)

The wind hurried him along Princes Street. It blew with a bellow and a buffet on his stern and half-lifted his feet from the pavement. It beat his ears with a fistful of snow, and clasped his ribs with icy fingers. It tore the clouds from the sky, and laid bare, as if beyond the darkness, the cold grey envelope of outer space. Heads bent and shoulders thrusting like Rugby forwards in a scrum, east-bound pedestrians struggled against it, and westward travellers flew before it with prodigious strides. To the left, towering blackly, like iron upon the indomitable rock, was the Castle. To it also the storm seemed to have given movement, for as the clouds fled behind its walls the bulk of its ancient towers and battlements appeared to ride slowly in the wind's eye, as though meditating a journey down the cavernous channel of the High Street to Holyroodhouse, its deserted sister.

Eric Linklater, *Magnus Merriman* (1934)

The zephyr of the Waverley
Is full of fun and play
If on the station steps they meet,
He whisks folk off their very feet,
And drops them down in Princes Street.
The stout policeman stationed there
Will pick them up with tender care,
And as they breathless, gasp and wheeze,
Will say 'Oh aye, that's just a breeze!'

Evelyn Beale and Winifred Christie,
An Edinburgh Alphabet (1908)

The Mound

The bottom of the Mound, the National Gallery of Scotland with its Ionic columns and the gallery of the Royal Scottish Academy with its Doric columns, and on either side of them the valley with trees in cold-burnt leaf and flower-beds in cinderglow, and along the opposite brink of the valley the mile-straight stretch of Princes Street, concealing behind its architectural confusion the eighteenth-century classical grace of the New Town. He saw it all with disturbing clarity, the familiar revealed as unfamiliar. He saw it all and was excited by it and felt obliged to explain his excitement. There was no magic in the unfamiliarity, nothing that had dropped out of God's sleeve. It was caused by the slant of the sun and by the unusual stillness and dryness of the air: this October light, making a long thrust from the south-east, had a cold-tempered point that whittled every outline against the sky, laid bare every sunward surface, sliced off clean shadows and cut out a deep perspective; this northern air had its own power of refraction, and, indeed, its own power of heady stimulation.

James Allan Ford, *A Statue for a Public Place* (1965)

Princes Street Gardens

Down by the baundstaund, by the ice-cream barrie,
There is a sait that says, Wilma is Fab.
Sit doun aside me and gieze your gab,
Just you and me, a doun, and a weecock-sparrie.

Robert Garioch, 'In Princes Street Gardens'
from *Collected Poems* (1977)

The Royal Bank of Scotland

One of the provisions of the Treaty of Union concerned the establishment of an equivalent company, empowered to ingather the assets of the Darien Company and to reimburse those people in Scotland who had lost money in one way or another because of the Union. This company found itself in possession of surplus funds from time to time and lent these monies at interest. This proved to be so profitable that an application was made to the Crown for permission to carry on the business of banking and the Royal Bank of Scotland was granted its Royal Charter in 1727.

In Edinburgh, perhaps the most important Georgian building now owned by the bank is the former head office at 36 St Andrew Square. Built of Ravelston stone between 1772–75 as the town house of Sir Laurence Dundas of

Kerse, then M.P. for the city, it was designed by Sir William Chambers of Ripon and was bought by the bank in 1825 on its removal from the 'Crosbie' house, to the north (now occupied by the Norwich Union Insurance Society). The bank later made interior alterations, notable amongst which is the domed banking hall added in 1858 to the design of the Edinburgh architects Peddie and Kinnear. The banking hall in its grand simplicity, though not in its playful Greek detail, is nearer to Sir John Soane's great Bank of England interiors (now demolished), than to the other, more opulent Victorian banking halls of Edinburgh and other cities in Britain – or to the Roman Pantheon with which it is sometimes compared; though the latter's dedication to the planetary deities is recalled by the star pierced bank dome.

Edinburgh Tatler, March 1971

George Street

From George Street, which crowns the ridge, the eye is led down sweeping streets of stately architecture to the villas and woods that fill the lower ground, and fringe the shore; to the bright azure belt of the Forth with its smoking steamer or its creeping sail, and beyond, to the shores of Fife, soft blue, and flecked with fleeting shadows in the keen clean light of spring, dark purple in the summer heat, tarnished gold in the autumn haze; and farther away still, just distinguishable on the paler sky, the crest of some distant peak, carrying the imagination into the illimitable world.

Alexander Smith, *A Summer in Skye* (1865)

On the third day of my visit to Edinburgh I went round the shops in George Street, pottering in the old bookshops and looking also for some fishing tackle for a friend in Oxford. George Street is one of the finest streets I have ever seen. Its broad straight length is lined on both sides with splendid buildings and at either end there is a beautiful square, one is called Charlotte Square and the other St Andrew Square. It has a stately atmosphere. Most visitors to Edinburgh will remember Princes Street first; but after walking there many times, I feel that its north side is a little too commercial and unstable for the name. It would have been a common street had it not been linked to the grandeur of the Castle. George Street, on the other hand, will always be magnificent on its own account.

Chiang Yee,
The Silent Traveller in Edinburgh (1948)

The Poets

And that smoother toun that cares
(though New they caa it yet!)
for its offices and auld Adam squares.
And Rose Street; a gallus gett
whaur e'en livin Scottish poets are met.

A lang bouky hash-a-pie. Aye
the loud and cheerie blethersket
kennin aabody and aye sinkin lang
dram for dram wi skeerie haunds.

Pubs aawhaur! Abbotsford there
and Milne's wi its photos o MacDiarmid,

91

MacCaig, S. G. Smith – and mair;
and still there's Paddy's, and them hid
frae tourists and aa the unco guid.

A hauchlin theeveless gommerill
aye at hame in the Abbotsford
or the Goth, slaverin in a gless
and greedy for her hingin owre.

Duncan Glen,
The Autobiography of a Poet (1986)

Rose Street – Milne's Bar

Cigarette smoke floated
in an Eastern way
a yard above the slopped tables.

The solid man thought
nothing could hurt him
as long as he didn't show it.

A stoicism of a kind. I
was inclined to agree with him,
having had a classical education.

To prove it, he went on telling
of terrible things that had
happened to him –

Norman MacCaig, *Collected Poems* (1988)

Among the distinguished visitors to Milne's Bar were Stevie
Smith, Dylan Thomas and W. H. Auden. So famous did the
gatherings there become that 'the Rose Street poets' were

forced to decamp a few yards east to the much more elegant establishment, the Abbotsford. With its ornate plasterwork, island bar and wooden panelling the Abbotsford remains much as it was when it was patronised in the 1960s.

Andrew Lownie,
The Literary Companion to Edinburgh (2000)

A Little Sin in Rose Street

Cease, ye prudes, your envious railing!
Lovely Burns has charms: confess!
True it is she has ae failing:
Had ae woman ever less?

Robert Burns, *Poems* (1773)

Editor's Note: A poem to his namesake – the well-known Miss Burns of Rose Street who graced Kay's Portraits.

Charlotte Square

March is here and the snell winds whustle and blaw,
Eddyin aff the elegant Adam stanes,
Nippin the nebs o' the passers by. They a'
Coorie into their claes, chill-cauld to their banes.

Nakit trees in the gairden chitter and shak
But at their ruits a ferly confronts oor e'en:
Crocuses, gowden, purple and snaw-white, brak
Oot o' their sheaths, defiant o' winds that keen.

Heralds o' Spring, your tabards are bricht wi' faith.
Noo in an ugsome warld I'll no' despair,
Mindin the blithesome flouers that feared nae skaith,
Crocuses a' in a lowe in Charlotte Square.

Douglas Fraser, Rhymes o' Auld Reekie (1973)

Another Prospect

Facing due east is the symmetrical façade
of St George's Church, Adam design
discarded yet harmonious, its coffered
dome imposing on Edinburgh's skyline.

It stands aloof from the traffic
encircling the Square, the din and fumes
where bedecked fillies once clopped. I jump back
as a souped-up motorcycle zooms.

too close for comfort. In the garden
are thousands of blue and yellow crocuses,
where Lord Cockburn stood to listen
to the corncrakes in the dewy grass.

Stewart Conn, Stolen Light: Selected Poems (1998)

Thistle Court

When the first stone came to be laid in the First New
Town, the site chosen was Rose Court, now known as
Thistle Court, on the northern side of the line of George
Street. In the subsequent street design the Court became
an adjunct of Thistle Street which, together with Rose

Street to the south of George Street, was built as a mews lane (each had a subsidiary lane for stabling behind it) for 'shopkeepers and others'.

The initial house in Thistle Court was built in 1767 by a wright called John Young, who described it as a tenement, though with the characteristics of a country villa. This was a early instance of entrepreneurial risk-taking, in effect a testing of the water, Young having accepted a financial inducement to proceed, and public interest would no doubt be measured by the large crowd which assembled to witness the commencement of building operations. That steps to create the First New Town were taken immediately afterwards can be seen as confirmation that the temperature of the water was considered to be acceptable.

It was James Craig himself who laid the foundation stone of Rose (Thistle) Court on 26th October 1767. Two rubble-built semi-detached houses stand at either end facing a narrow garden, those on the west side being the plainer and more unpretentious and now serving the purposes of an electricity sub-station. The warm pink stonework of the eastern houses is enhanced by a pediment over the two centrally-positioned doors, and a lamp on a projecting iron bracket above them is an additional feature of distinction which has been preserved. Each house has two storeys and an attic, the latter lit by two dormer windows.

Thistle Court constitutes the earliest surviving example of New Town architecture.

Joyce M. Wallace,
Historic Houses of Edinburgh (1987)

Queen Street Gardens

There were no prettily laid out gardens then between Heriot Row and Queen Street, only a long strip of unsightly grass, a green, fenced by an untidy wall and abandoned to the use of the washer-women. It was an ugly prospect, and we were daily indulged with it, the cleanliness of the inhabitants being so excessive that, except on Sundays and 'Saturdays at e'en', squares of bleaching linens and lines of drying ditto were ever before our eyes.

Elizabeth Grant of Rothiemurchus,
Memories of a Highland Lady (1898)

The town was bathed in that luminous silver and pale gold glow which the northern autumn alone can produce. There are always one or two days of this exquisitely peaceful benevolence even after the great storms break and before the purgatory of an Edinburgh winter begins. The trees in the Heriot Row gardens that had of late been bending beneath the wind stood motionless and delicate as filigree. Their discarded leaves lay heaped in brown, yellow, and here and there crimson on the grass of the gardens and in the streets. The sky was of the palest most flawless blue. Even the grey Georgian houses facing uphill and to the south had lost their severity and had, in the deep, silver interstices of their stones, caught something of the sunlight in which they had been bathed all day long.

Moray McLaren, *The Pursuit* (1959)

On the Dean Bridge in June

White lamps the chestnut-tree adorn,
The lilacs and the golden-rain,
The snowy and the rosy thorn
Are rife with blossom once again.

Though on this pleasance June bestows
His gifts with such a lavish hand,
Not like a beggar hence he goes;
His largess reaches all the land.

But from the Bridge I lean and look,
Going and coming, late and soon,
And thank God for this flowery nook,
The paradise of peerless June.

Henry Johnstone,
Two Edinburgh Poems –
A Volunteer Haversack (1902)

A Darker Dean Bridge

Where many a man
Alas has ran
There in an evil hour
And cast away
His life that day
Beyond all human pow'r.

Robert McCandless (1887)

97

INNER SUBURBS

The Botanical Gardens

The Botanic Garden is well situated and very easy to reach from the centre of the city. The rain stopped as I went out and took a tramcar to Hanover Street and then another to the Garden. Remembering my favourite haunts, I first went to the Rock Garden, where masses of different heathers were about to open their tiny buds. I had seen this glorious purple carpet a year before and had been amazed at the variety of species, a number of which come from America. As Scotsmen always take great pride in their heathers, it is fitting that there should be a good show of them in the Botanic Garden. What they regard as the true heather is called Ling and has cross-leaves up the stalk and a cluster of big bell-like flowers at the top. I do not remember anything particular about the heathers in my own country. We have a herbal plant the name of which, phonetically, is Ling, though it is not a heather. It is curious that two countries as far apart as China and Scotland have the same word for a native plant although Chinese is a monosyllabic language and English a poly-syllabic. Ling sounds to me more like a Chinese word than an English one, and I wondered how it came to be used for a species of heather. Perhaps botanists can explain it, or maybe there is a local legend about it.

Presently I came to another favourite haunt, the small lake or pool. I stood on the brink looking towards a group of pine trees slightly to my right, whose strong blackish trunks and twisted branches with their masses of deep blue needles commanded the scene. In front of the pines many trees of varying heights and shades of green formed a sort of slope, their long, slender branches, some adorned with small flowers, hanging right down into the water. A small punt floated near by. Close to where I stood was a large cluster of water-lily leaves and buds; otherwise the smooth surface of the water was only broken by a few reeds sticking up here and there. As there was no wind, I could detect one or two blue dragonflies clinging to the top of the reeds. On my left was a low rhododendron bush in full bloom, covered with clusters of five or six brilliant vermilion flowers. Many fine species of rhododendrons have come from my country, and they are linked in my mind with China just as heather is with Scotland.

Chiang Yee,
The Silent Traveller in Edinburgh (1948)

South of the Rhododendron Walk, from a small eminence in the Garden, there is a good broad view of the city, reaching from the unfinished Acropolis on the Calton Hill to the distant slopes of the Pentlands. The Castle on the Rock rises in the midst of the view, and far to the left of it Edinburgh's private and domestic mountain, Arthur's Seat, is elevated above the Salisbury Crags that loom, from here, as if they impended upon the rough North Sea. Spires and pinnacles advertise the innumerable churches of the city: the two St Georges, the solid burden of Playfair's, St Stephen's in front of the towering steeple of the High Church, St Andrew's and the Tron and the Crown of St Giles. There is woodland in the foreground, such charming woodland, with pine-needles on its little paths and blue Tibetan poppies, or yellow primulas, to enliven the shadow of the conifers; and always a new prospect of trees and flowers as the visitor more deeply invades the climbing pattern of the wood.

Eric Linklater,
Edinburgh (1960)

Fettes

I was born in this city of grey stone and bitter wind,
Of tenements sooted up with lying history:
This place where dry mounds grow crusts of hate, as rocks
Grow lichens. I went to school over the high bridge
Fringed with spikes which curiously, repel the suicides;
And I slept opposite the rock garden where the survivors,
Who had left Irving and Mallory under the sheet of snow,
Planted the incarvillea and saxifrages of the Himalayas.

Ruthven Todd,
'In Edinburgh' (1940)

Leith

The port of Leith was from very early times one of the chief ports at which timber was imported. It is indeed rather curious that timber should have been brought into Scotland at all, for the forests of the country were large enough to have supplied all the wood that was necessary. Whatever the reason may be, the fact is that timber has long formed one of the staples of Leith. In this matter, again, the city of Edinburgh took up a very strong position. It not only claimed a right to make merchandise of all the timber coming into Leith and Newhaven as against the unfortunate inhabitants of these places, or any other 'strangeris', but even as against the King himself, or rather his representatives. The King, however, seems to have had a rather sturdy comptroller of customs at the port about 1517, and he was not so easily overruled by the citizens of Edinburgh on the occasion of a Dutch ship arriving there. His resolute conduct led to a scene on the shore of Leith. Robert Bertoun (the comptroller) and the 'men of Leith' took possession of its cargo, and held it against the Edinburgh people. This led to an action in the Court of Session, in which the Edinburgh litigants got rather the worst of it.

James Campbell Irons,
Leith and its Antiquities (1898)

The Corporations of Leith

In early times the working life of Leithers was carried out under the aegis of four incorporations, the mariners, the brewers and maltmen, traders (such as coopers, cordiners, bakers and others), and the merchants and shopkeepers, their original charter having been granted by the Logans of Restalrig in the sixteenth century. The members of these incorporations, who could not of course be burgesses, could only protect their interests by erecting monopolies that were as jealously guarded as those of the craft guilds of Edinburgh. This state of affairs was not remedied until 1734 when, by a declaration of their independence from the Town, the Leith traders were no longer referred to as unfree. Each incorporation had originally established an altar to its patron saint in the parish church, and contributions were made by the members towards defraying the costs involved as well as to a much-needed fund for relieving the poor and the infirm.

The Incorporation of Coopers of Leith made common cause with the Fleshers and Masons in upholding the altar of St John in the New Kirk of Our Lady, and it was this church which, after many vicissitudes, became at last the Parish Church of South Leith.

Joyce M. Wallace,
Traditions of Trinity and Leith (1985)

Newhaven

Newhaven is a small fishing village, situated about a mile further up the Forth than Leith. It possesses a stone and a chain pier, but neither the one nor the other has sufficient depth of water to admit of the approach of seamers of large size. The London boats, accordingly, now land and take on board their passengers at Granton, a little farther up the Firth, where a low-water pier has recently been constructed by the Duke of Buccleuch. The inhabitants of Newhaven are a laborious and hardy race. They form a distinct community, rarely intermarrying with any other class. The male inhabitants are almost all fishermen, and the females are constantly occupied in vending the produce of their husbands' industry in the markets or streets of Edinburgh. When provoked, the *fishwives* display resources of abuse quite equal to their Billingsgate contemporaries . . . Although a very hard-working people, they rarely indulge in an excessive use of ardent spirits. The quantity they consume is, indeed, very considerable, but the prodigious loads with which they are burdened, may be allowed to form some apology for the occasional use of such a stimulus, and their constant exercise in the open air appears to prevent any injurious effects from following the indulgence.

Black's *Circle Through Edinburgh* (1851)

Wha'll buy my caller herrin'?
They're bonnie fish and halesome farin'
Buy my caller herrin' drawn frae the Forth.

Lady Nairn, 'Caller Herrin'

O' a' the waters that can hobble
A fishing yole or sa'mon coble,
An' can reward the fisher's trouble,
Or south or north,
There's nane sae spacious and sae noble
As Frith o' Forth.

In her the skate an' codlin sail,
The eel fu' souple wags her tail,
Wi' herrin, fleuk, and mackarel,
An' whitins dainty:
Their spindle-shanks the labsters trail,
Wi' partans plenty.

Robert Fergusson,
'Caller Oysters' (1773)

The Chain Pier

Opposite the Georgian porticos of Trinity Crescent, feued about 1824 when sea bathing was becoming popular in Trinity and before the sands of Portobello superseded it, the Chain Pier had been built out into the water. It was designed by a man called Parrot and cost £4000. The pier was constructed in 1821 and, when King George IV paid his famous visit to Scotland the following year, it was considered as a possible disembarkation point, instead of The Shore at Leith, for 'the sacred foot of Majesty'. But Trinity had to forego that honour; the claims of Leith to be the royal port of entry for the nation were too well founded to be set aside. It did, however, receive the feet of a very different and this time departing king, the exiled and abdicated Charles X of France. Pursued by his creditors, he had been welcomed to Holyrood Palace under its ancient rights of sanctuary from debt, but in 1832, with old-style, pre-Revolution monarchy anathema in France and the newly passed Reform Act decreasing his popularity in Edinburgh, he and his household stepped from the Chain Pier on to a steam packet bound for Hamburg on the 18th of September. He had become an anachronism in his own lifetime and died five years afterwards, aged 79.

The Chain Pier was used by steamdriven boats plying up and down the River Forth but, not being suitable for large vessels, was soon abandoned for the advantages of Granton Harbour . . . It eventually fell into decay and was finally swept away in a storm around the end of last century.

Joyce M. Wallace, *Traditions of Trinity and Leith* (1985)

Granton

Beyond the Dean Bridge the country began. Even after Fettes and the masters' houses were built, Davidson's Mains was a country village, and a little further on a steep wooded bank overhung a strip of yellow sand – quite a broad strip at low tide – with little islands dotting the stretch of water between it and the coast of Fife.

It must have been one of the most beautiful inland beaches in the world till they built a breakwater at Granton, which altered the set of the tides. The sands were drowned, and the containing wall at the foot of the bank was breached; and when I last saw it, in 1904 or so, the trees were dying in a salt-water swamp. . . . I am sure the Granton breakwater was planned to be of use to the community, and I hope that it has proved its worth, but one cannot help regretting the loss of a really beautiful place.

Mrs L. K. Haldane, *The Scotsman*,
18 May 1954

A favourite Sunday walk was to the Breakwater. Down Granton Road we went, perhaps visiting the farm in Rosebank Road on the way, till at the top of Granton Steps we looked down at the Forth, the Breakwater and harbour and East and West Piers and beyond to the Kingdom of Fife. The Paddle steamer *William Muir* sailed from the East Pier to Burntisland. A line of railway ran to a platform on the berth for from 1859 until 1890, when the Forth Bridge was opened, the world's first train ferry crossed from here to Fife.

We went down the steps to the Granton Hotel, crossed

the road and a few yards to the west passed through an archway made by the railway line. We went along, either on the giddy-making smooth outside stones with the steep slope of unhewn stones below to the sea, or skipped and jumped on the rough blocks in the middle. Halfway out were steps from which men, and in those days only men, could bathe. They left their clothes in heaps and to my admiration swam about out of their depths. Some had quick dips even in January.

Our parents, their minds no doubt on domestic matters like dinner or the maid's day out, often turned before the end. It was best when we had time to go right to the harbour light on the wooden platform where men fished or sat and smoked, their lines fastened to the rails looking after themselves. Crossing the slatted footbridge gave a feeling of adventure for you could look down and see the tide running below.

Elaine Mary Wilson,
Tak' Tent o' Time (1992)

Merchiston Tower

This fortalice is situated upon the ascent, and nearly about the summit, of the eminence called the Borough-moor-head, within a mile and a half of the city walls. In form, it is a square tower of the fourteenth or fifteenth century, with a projection on one side. The top is battlemented, and within the battlement, by a fashion more common in Scotland than in England, arises a small building, with a steep roof, like a little stone cottage, erected on the top of the tower. This sort of upper-story, rising above the battlements, being frequently of varied form, and adorned with notched gables and with turrets, renders a Scottish tower a much more interesting object than those common in Northumberland, which generally terminate in a flat battlemented roof, without any variety of outline . . .

Being so near Edinburgh, Merchiston did not escape being garrisoned during the bloody period of Queen Mary's reign, or rather her son's. Each baron's house in Mid-Lothian was in those melancholy days attacked and defended, and the gibbet was the fate of the prisoners on both sides . . .

It is not from the petty incidents of a cruel civil war that Merchiston derives its renown, but as having been the residence of genius and science. The celebrated John Napier of Merchiston was born in this weather-beaten tower, according to the best accounts, about the year 1550; and a small room in the summit of the building is pointed out as the study in which he secluded himself while engaged in the mathematical researches which led to his great discovery.

To the inventor of the logarithms, (called from him, 'Napier's bones') by which process the power of calculation is so much increased, David Hume, no grantor of propositions, declares the title of a great man is more justly due, than to any other whom his country ever produced . . .

The battlements of Merchiston Tower command an extensive view, of great interest and beauty.

Sir Walter Scott, *Miscellaneous Prose* (1827)

Merchiston

Perhaps the strangest house ever built in Edinburgh was Rockville or, as it was variously known, The Pagoda, The Chinese House, Tottering Towers and Crazy Manor. Rockville, described as 'a building to delight every child who enjoys a fairy tale', stood at the corner of Napier Road and Spylaw Road in Merchiston and was built by Sir James Gowans in 1858 as his own home. Gowans was an architect, a railway engineer, a quarry owner, Edinburgh's Lord Dean of Guild and was knighted by Queen Victoria in 1886 for organising the International Exhibition in Edinburgh.

Rockville consisted of a three-storey house with a five storey, 64-foot tower of Oriental influence. Its projecting stone dormers, decorative iron balusters, massive chimneys and ornate gables gave it an eerie Gothic appearance. The interior was spacious with hot water and gas in all the rooms and a kitchen with the motto 'Waste Not Want Not' carved in stone over the cooking range. The acre of sunken garden included various statues, a bas-relief of Gowans as a master-mason, a stone table carved with gowans (Scots for wild daisies) and a gate lodge like a diminutive Hansel and Gretel house. The external walls of Rockville were built in a chequerboard pattern with a mosaic infill of coloured stones in a sandstone framework. The stones were selected from every quarry in Scotland, with samples from the Continent and China, and gave the building a rich effect of lightness and sparkle. The coloured granites produced a mainly reddish tint with highlights of green crystals of iron pyrites, an amethyst-like purple stone, silver mica and glittering quartz.

Proposals to demolish Rockville in the mid-1960s caused

a public outcry. Details of Rockville were even sent to the publicity manager of Disneyland suggesting that he might consider buying 'Edinburgh's Wonderhouse'. Rockville was finally demolished in 1966.

J. K. Gillon, *Eccentric Edinburgh* (1990)

Morningside

In the district where the Urquhart-Innes lived, all the houses resembled little castles and were enclosed by high garden walls topped with broken glass, so that anyone walking through the streets felt himself an outcast from society and hastened back to the pubs and narrow pavements at the east end of the city . . . Not all these stately residences had been able to continue to play their pristine roles. One had a large brass plate to tell that behind these love-discouraging walls lurked St Devenick's School for Girls, another shamefacedly admitted to being the 'Brasenose Hotel, Open to non-residents', a third was Miss Newbattle's Nursing Home and a fourth the regional headquarters of the gas council.

Robert Kemp, *The Maestro* (1956)

Colinton

The neighbourhood of Colinton, situated under the shadow of the hills and set upon the banks of the Water of Leith, abounds in old castles and mansion houses – Colinton, Spylaw, Woodhall, Hailes, Dreghorn, Redhall; and, as we pass on our way to Colinton by Craiglockhart Hill and its ruined tower, we recall the history of the strong Castle of Redhall that gallantly withstood a week's siege at the hands of Oliver Cromwell and his army in 1650.

Redhall was owned in 1672 by the notorious John Chiesley, the Laird of Kersewell near Carnwath, and of Dalry House, Edinburgh, who shot Sir George Lockhart of Carnwath, then President of the Court of Session, in the Old Bank Close, in 1689, in revenge for a Court decision in a family litigation.

In many of these old residences we read to-day the story of our transition age. The seventeenth-century Castle of Dreghorn belongs to the War Department. Colinton House and Policies, with cedar-trees and holly hedges dating from 1680, has been purchased by Merchiston Castle School. Woodhall House, of the ancient family of Foulis, that once housed the famous 'Bannatyne Collection' of Scottish poetry, presented to the Advocates' Library in 1770, is a private residence.

Much of the history of Colinton is epitomised in the words 'Romans', 'Cromwell, 1650', 'Covenanters, 1666', 'Charles, 1745', inscribed on the capital of the tall monument erected by the late R. A. Macfie of Dreghorn, close to the roadside above the castellated lodge at Dreghorn Bridge.

Will Grant,
The Call of the Pentlands (1927)

Duddingston

In summer a shield of blue, with swans sailing from the reeds; in winter, a field of ringing ice. The village church sits above it on a green promontory; and the village smoke rises from among goodly trees. At the church gates, is the historical joungs, a place of penance for the neck of detected sinners, and the historical luping-on stane, from which Dutch-built lairds and farmers climbed into the saddle. Here Prince Charlie slept before the Battle of Prestonpans; and here Deacon Brodie, or one of his gang, stole a plough coulter before the burglary in Chessels Court.

The surface is thick with people moving easily and swiftly and leaning over at a thousand graceful inclinations; the crowd opens and closes, and keeps moving through itself like water; and the ice rings to half a mile away, with the flying steel. As night draws on, the single figures melt into the dusk until only an obscure stir, and coming and going of black clusters, is visible upon the loch. A little longer, and the first torch is kindled and begins to flit rapidly across the ice in a ring of yellow reflection, and this is followed by another and another, until the whole field is full of skimming lights.

Robert Louis Stevenson,
Picturesque Notes (1879)

The Zoo

I first visited the Edinburgh Zoo on a September morning in 1943. Immediately I entered it I could see that it lay on the slope of a hill, and was thus better situated than the

London Zoo and rather like a small-scale Whipsnade. The first creatures I saw were two polar bears, one lying in the water and the other rolling his head continuously from side to side as if to say 'Oh! So hot, Oh! So hot!' I stood watching him for a while, wondering whether he had adapted himself to the Edinburgh climate or not, and whether he might not now find the Arctic regions a little too cold for him. Near the polar bear enclosure was a group of penguins, the common kind with a black half-circle on the chest like a necklace. They were all standing close together. There was no formal pool to enable them to show off their swift underwater movements as there is in the London Zoo. Nor did I see any king penguins among them. To me the king penguin always suggests a dignified elderly peer in evening dress. Perhaps there are no king penguins in the Edinburgh Zoo because there is no House of Lords in Edinburgh to provide material for comparison!

Chiang Yee,
The Silent Traveller in Edinburgh (1948)

OUTER SUBURBS

Lothian burn

Up here, scarcely
birdsong even: only

the labials and gutterals
of this burn as it gurgles

downhill, locality of accent
in vowel and consonant,

each circumlocution
through heather and sandstone

traced by inflection
and sharp interjection

until, in a mossy outcrop,
it comes to a glottal stop.

Stewart Conn,
Stolen Light (1998)

Pentland Hills

The tropics vanish, and meseems that I,
From Halkerside, from topmost Allermuir,
Or steep Caerketton, dreaming gaze again.
Far set in fields and woods, the own I see
Spring gallant from the shallows of her smoke,

Cragged, spired and turreted, her virgin fort
Beflagged. About, on seaward-drooping hills,
New folds of city glitter. Last the Forth
Wheels ample waters set with scared isles,
And populous Fife smokes with a score of towns.

Robert Louis Stevenson,
Hills of Home (1913)

The Pentland Bounds

Skirting the lower end of Clubbiedean, the line of frontier makes straight up into the hills, through whins and heather, and tussocky grass, behind the Malleny rifle-ranges and the Kirk Road to Currie, to the watershed at a height of 1300 feet; then it plunges down the other side for a mile or so into the valley of the Logan Burn, bounded by the greater heights of the Pentlands – the Kips, Scald Law, Carnethy, and Turnhouse. It embraces, at a height of 1124 feet above sea-level, the Bonaly reservoir, and, crossing the well-footed right-of-way path, it passes near, on the hillside to the left, the ruins of the Capelaw shepherd's house, but does not descend so far as to Glencorse Loch, under the wood-enclosed waters of which are sunk the chapel and graveyard of St Catherine's-of-the-Hopes, or to the 'King's Seat', from whence the Bruce is said to have watched the encounter with the White Hart which won for the Sinclairs of Roslin the Forest of Pentland.

The town's boundary harks back again to the summit of the pass at the head of the Howden Burn – the 'Tap o' Howden'; then climbs to the crown of Allermuir, 1615 feet above sea-level, and holds the watershed, by the 'Windy Door Nick' and the crest of Caerketton, until, with a bold leap or two, it comes back, past the side of Lothianburn golf-course and the new Public Park of Hillend, to beaten paths again at the junction of the Penicuik and Biggar high roads. It encloses the highest and widest range of hill-country – the feeding-ground of sheep, the home of the grouse, the curlew, and the white hare – that is anywhere to be found within municipal jurisdiction.

This mountain-fringe of Edinburgh is a home of romance and of literary memories, as well as of nature. For, taking as its boundary-stones with the level and cultivated region those that mark the tracks of the water-conduits from the Bonaly and Torduff ponds, it includes 'Bonnie Bonaly' and Swanston.

John Geddie,
The Fringes of Edinburgh (1926)

Swanston Cottage

Swanston Cottage needs no describing to those Stevenson lovers who have seen it, and yet it is a grievous thing to a stravaiging Scot that so many live to-day in Stevenson's city who have never seen this paradise with a wall. This quaint old eighteenth-century junketing house of the Edinburgh bailies, where long ago the city fathers laid primitive wooden water-pipes, and, later, built a water-house to preserve the springs in the garden. What jovial days and nights our municipal ancestors must have spent there, with the finest of Pentland water to mellow their drinks! Then those wise councillors enlarged the cottage, and robbing the old Cathedral of St Giles, at its vandal restoration, of some of its gargoyles and crockets, set them up to ornament the new-made garden. Here among the roses and gillyflowers, there came a lad in the year 1867 to dream and scribble and laze his time away in the best of all literary apprenticeships – ruminating and reading and letting his imagination rove freely, while the seven sisters of Caerketton looked down on him, through the long summer nights, where the old drove roads wind over the hills and far away. Stevenson would often moon about the grey old farmhouse standing in its 'bouquet of trees'. Here there was an added glamour in the fact that on this spot there once stood a grange of the good monks of Whitekirk. With that dreamy eye of his he saw in these very fields the rosy friars tilling the soil. He saw, too, the farm door standing open all night in the killing times to welcome many a hunted Covenanter. He saw, later still, in the 'Forty-five, Charlie's wild Highlanders surrounding Swanston in the dawn and plucking the very blankets from the bed of a little child who sat up in fear and watched the royal thieves mixing their 'braw brose' with cream from the dairy. What a fine translator of history was this lanky lad with the delicate air, who filled his lungs with the heather-scented winds of Swanston, transforming the dry-as-dust details into brave pictures and moving stories, which were to delight the hearts of later generations.

Ratcliffe Barnett, *Border Byways and Lothian Lore* (1923)

Bonaly

Two burns, beloved and sung by John Stuart Blackie, bicker down from glens in the Pentlands to meet among the roses and rhododendron bushes, beside the semblance of a border keep, added to an older building, and known as

Bonaly Tower. One burn issues from the high green Torduff embankment, flanked by filtering beds, which at one time troubled Henry Cockburn with dreams that some night it might burst and sweep him and his 'household gods' down to the sea at Leith. The other stream carves its way deeply around the side of the White Hill, until it leaves the company of the broad public path from Glencorse to enter the shady groves where the author of the *Memorials*, the inspirer and name-father of the Cockburn Association, rested from his labours of the Bar and Bench. Here he walked and talked with his literary friends and associates, or, climbing to a higher outlook, 'read *Tacitus* through from cover to cover', or looked down upon his beloved city, conceiving many schemes of restoration and improvement, including the idea of a classical school, which took shape as the Edinburgh Academy.

Into this Pentland Eden Cockburn gathered a collection of carved stones, old and new – vases, plinths, and cornices – most of which are still disposed about the grounds or are built into the house. They include the figure of Shakespeare that crowned the pediment of the old theatre in Shakespeare Square, on the site of the General Post Office, and two statues of Scottish warriors – evidently representing Bruce and his faithful follower Douglas – that are said to have formed part of the fountain in Linlithgow Palace, a claim hardly borne out by the style of the sculpture, or of the attached couplets, which run:

> I Scotland's Glorey made returne
> Victoriously at Bannockburn,

and

> My King and Country ever claimed
> Those martial deeds for which I'm famed.

It was from the hill above Bonaly, or from Torphin, that

'Grecian Williams' saw the city as the 'Modern Athens':
'Close upon the right Brilessus is represented by the
Braids; before us, in the abrupt and dark mass of the
Castle, rises the Acropolis; the hill Lycabetus joined to
that of the Areopagus, appears in the Calton; in the Firth
of Forth we behold the Ægean Sea; in Inchkeith, Ægina;
and the hills of the Peloponesus are precisely those of the
opposite coast of Fife.'

John Geddie, *The Fringes of Edinburgh* (1926)

Rullion Green

I lie here, who for Christ's interest did appear
amongst those martyred on Rullion Green,
having trudged from Dumfries through Ayr,
knowing I was unlikely to see my family again;
even then, not anticipating such slaughter
as would befall us, such numbers slain.
All to see the Episcopacy overthrown.

For days, drizzle steamed on a stew of limbs;
those who tried to flee being hewn down
in the mirk, between here and West Linton,
their death-gasps reaching me like an exhalation.
So I lie, deep in Pentland bog, my person
preserved perfectly, my spirit broken.
How many must perish, in God's name?

Stewart Conn,
Stolen Light: Selected Poems (1998)

Site of Battle

The location of the battlefield of Rullion Green, [November 28, 1666] the name of which is commemorated only in a cottage near the site, has been a subject of debate for a century and a half . . . The most detailed modern account, that offered by C. Sanford Terry in 1905, sites the whole of the action on the north-east-facing slopes overlooking the valley of the Glencorse Burn, but this does not accord with the reports given – from a Covenanter perspective – in the memoirs of the captive Sir James Turner or the Covenanter soldiers Colonel Wallace and William Veitch, or – from the government side – in Charles Maitland's eye-witness soldier's account. The location of the memorial stone at the Martyrs' Grave is partly responsible for this, it having been assumed in the past to mark the scene of the main action, while it in fact commemorates the men who fell in the first skirmish between the advance guards.

Derek Alexander et al, *History Scotland*, Winter 2001

Cramond

Where does the spring come or the year die with greater beauty than at Cramond, that fairy creek on the Forth, with its picturesque huddle of houses, just within the new city boundary of Edinburgh.

To experience the surprise of Cramond, we must approach it by the shore-road from Granton. Coming along this path, the Forth, on a lown November day at low tide can give us beauty to remember. Long level swathes of blue-grey mist: islands floating on the dim horizon, the shores of Fife beyond: restless sea-anger mellowed into a monotone of peace by the magic of distance. An autumn symphony in low, quiet tones.

Over the sea-wall at Nether Cramond you will see an old tower – the only remaining fragment of the summer palace of the Bishops of Dunkeld, and once a portion of the castle which stood near the old Roman Camp of Caer-almond. For there was here an important Roman military station, where three famous roads terminated – one leading westward to the Antonine Wall at Carriden, another going south, across the Borders by Watling Street, and a third going eastward to Inveresk. The well near-by may have been that of the Roman Camp.

To get the real glamour of Cramond, there must be no trippers about, and you must stand solitary at the Cobble Ferry, whistling for the drowsy ferryman to come down the wooden steps and take you across to the further shore . . .

For those who would walk up the waterside there are many ancient things to discover: Peggy's Mill, and the old Brig of Cramond, where Jock Howieson met King James V disguised as the Guid Man o' Ballengeich, and rescued him from some wandering gypsies who had attacked him.

Ratcliffe Barnett,
Border Byways and Lothian Lore (1923)

A canty neuk whaur Almond joins the Forth.
Ye dauner doun the brae
Wi' views o' Fife's green 'Kingdom' to the north
Ayont the wee bit bay
Whaur Cramond Island rises frae the sand,
Its 'haufway' causey raxin oot frae land.

Amang the tombs the auld kirk seems to hide
Wi' elms abune its heid.
The whitewashed biggins by the water-side
Are crouned wi' tiles o' reid,
Whaur Charron, yachtin-capped (his fee saxpenny)
Will oar ye, no' to Hades, but Dalmeny.

The Kirk, the Inn, the Ferry – a' historic,
But lang afore their day
They spak a lingo here that wasna Doric:
Professor bodies say
That ance the Romans had a muckle fort,
And diggin for its founds is a' their sport.

Noo, leggy lads and lassies sail their Hornets
Aboot the narrow reach,
While weans frae Pilton sook their ice-cream cornets
Or picnic on the beach;
And jos stravaigin on the esplanade
Can view the gaswarks through the gaithering shade.

But still the sea-birds pipe their oorie cries
Athort the Lothian mud
And still the sunset pents the evenin skies
Wi' palette maist gane wud
And aye its colours fade afore the e'en
As gloamin adds its glamerie on the scene.

Douglas Fraser,
Rhymes o' Auld Reekie (1973)

People

The City's Composition

And as you get to know something of the private life of Edinburgh you will discover that this city is not like Glasgow, not a graduated community, but a series of classes and coteries. The classes are pretty sharply divided, in speech, work and ways. The coteries consist of businessmen generally, the law, the arts and what is known as 'society'. Into the last the 'high yins' of all the coteries long to get, and there is a sort of merger in this way. Pride and poverty has always been the gibe flung at Edinburgh and its *rentiers*, and, more especially, its *rentières*. Nowadays, the *rentières* cannot but display something of their poverty to the world. Life is very hard for the indigent gentlewoman. Edinburgh, as I have said, is a city of antiquities, and many of them can be seen in Princes Street on a fine forenoon or afternoon; they may be brave, but they are pathetic. They will pass away, as a class, while the castle and Holyrood will still stand

George Rowntree Harvey,
A Book of Scotland (1949)

There is a small and exceedingly exclusive set of territorial people in Edinburgh, of the Scottish landed gentry rather than the peerage. These keep themselves very much to themselves, although they mingle occasionally with the higher legal lights. But they are certainly not consistently snobbish, although they are not especially considerate to members of the classes whom they believe to be beneath them. Out with these professional and exclusive circles the ordinary citizens of Edinburgh are just as friendly and hospitable as the people of any other British community.

Indeed, if anything, I believe them to be better 'mixers' than the inhabitants of most towns . . . Edinburgh's exclusiveness chiefly arises from the circumstances that her professional classes usually make a set of friends while at school, and adhere to these friendships through life. In any case 'snobbery' in Edinburgh is not what it was . . . I cannot recall hearing *a grande dame* snort – for nearly 20 years.

Lewis Spence,
The Weekly Scotsman, 29 September 1939

Old Edinburgh is evidentially the result of the Scots' struggle against nature, against fellow-humans, against weather and against their combined ferociousness. What other capital city short of Lhasa stands so proudly and nakedly in defiance of the elements? Mediaeval man strove to tame the elements on this ridge by raising a city in the form of a single mass of building; stone cliffs to the outside and a deep trough, an *agora* known as the Hie Gait (or High Street), a uniquely spacious marketplace sheltered by tall unbreached walls at the centre. Nippy breezes, thick clinging haars, seeping cold mists, warm azure skies and unfriendly armies were all controlled by this plan.

Edinburgh's character has never been comfortable (were comfort a concept ever congenial to Calvinists), and what Muriel Spark identified as 'the puritanical strain of the Edinburgh ethos' was as much the consequence of climate as of Calvinism. Chilly whipping winds slash at you unawares around corners, and howl up Waverly Steps . . . and lifted your Victorian bonnet on George Street to waft it to Granton. They can still hurl you willy-nilly along Princes Street at a speed to match the scudding clouds above.

Edinburgh's character best responds to winter. It needs its cracking frosts and its haars to give meaning to its tight closes and tall tenements. We read of carriages slithering athwart a snowbound Dundas Street, ministers permitting themselves the spare enjoyment of joining the Duddingston Skating Club, and of the town's teenagers taking on the college students in the celebrated snowball battles and ambushes in the dark streets and wynds only occasionally lit by the warmth of yellow light streaming from tenement windows. The winter sunrise over Arthur's Seat is, when viewed from the north, one of the great sights of the world: the black paganism of the castle to the west balanced against the serene classicism of Calton Hill to the east, silhouetted against a crimson sky. Ceaselessly, Edinburgh conveys the sensation of struggle between man and nature.

Charles McKean,
Edinburgh: Portrait of a City (1991)

Edinburgh Character

Who is there to appear for the character of Edinburgh? One knows that most cities have one pre-eminent type in fact or fancy to which one can put a name; surely the Capital of Scotland, so rich in personalty, so well adorned in fancy, so old, must have produced one person whom one can remember who *is* the place. Any Edinburgh eccentric. An Edinburgh publican. An Edinburgh sinner. A face seen in George Street. A voice heard in passing. All these and how many others triumphantly press their claims upon one's recollection. Each is indubitably and absolutely Edinburgh. Each is proudly and consciously different from the rest. They have nothing in common save their differences and the circumstances which made them, circumstances which in their completely differing ways they express. Amidst incomparable individuals how can one be pre-eminent.

There is a celebrated Edinburgh 'type' that is generally referred to as 'dour'. This character is so familiar to the readers and writers of fiction, to audiences and play-wrights, that he has become stock. His dialogue can be turned on and off at will, and can be lifted with little alteration from play to play, from book to book. 'Dour', sometimes inaccurately accompanied by 'pawky', is usually applied to Edinburgh lawyers or professional men.

There is one of our Edinburgh characters that has been very much neglected by the painters. Literature has had perforce to take note of him for the simple reason that he is too insistent in our life to be overlooked by any of us whose trade and pleasure is words. Even so, he occupies a more prominent place in factual writing such as memoirs, journalism and letters than in fiction. We all known him. We not only know him from experience of the present, we perceive his presence in the past. He is a continual figure in hearsay and reminiscence, and is always cropping up in the casual printed recollection. It is quite clear that he has been with us for a very long time. He is the Edinburgh eccentric.

Moray McLaren, *The Capital of Scotland* (1950)

A Different Nature

The character of Edinburgh and the character of Glasgow, so vivid, so complementary to each other, are in their roots as Scottish as the characters of the Highlands and the Lowlands. For nearly a century and a half they have been as important in the general pattern of the character of Scotland as even the Highlands and the Lowlands were. It is impossible to know the Scotland of to-day without savouring the difference between the quality of Edinburgh and Glasgow – and this not because they are the two largest and most important towns in Scotland; it is because the difference between them is of the essence of Scotland. The differences in the characters of the two cities may have been slightly influenced by climate and geography, but far the greatest factor in their great diversity has lain in history. Each city is most strikingly and, even for European cities, unusually shaped and influenced by its past. To this day each is strongly conscious of this and proclaims it in its way of life. Any perceptive visitor, even if he stays but for a short time, becomes aware of this, as much in the bustling modern Glasgow; as in the more obviously historic Capital of Scotland.

Moray McLaren, The Scots (1951)

Eccentrics

The Capital of Scotland is filled with strongly individual individuals, and has a larger proportion of native eccentrics than has any other town in Britain. Yet even these eccentrics, if they are of the true Edinburgh breed, conduct their eccentricities with an odd formality, in a kind of pattern of peculiarity suitable to the extravagant pattern in the appearance and background of the town. It would be too much to say that that background was itself responsible for their eccentricities, but perhaps in common with Edinburgh's long individual history and with the still lingering eighteenth-century tradition it has helped to make them possible. Imperturbability tinged with complacency, formality in expression and habit, a strong sense of individuality that runs easily to eccentricity – you will find all these qualities in all classes in Edinburgh, amongst the poor as well as the prosperous, in the public houses, small shops and wynds, and closes of the High Street in the poorest parts of the Old Town as well as in the clubs, lawyers' offices, and what remains of the drawing rooms of the New Town.

Moray McLaren, *The Scots* (1951)

Speech

Edinburgh has no easily recognisable speech of its own. Most Edinburgh men think that they talk 'educated Scots' which is an off-shot of pulpit Scots. Scottish ministers subscribe to a theory of elocution which is, on the whole, widely admired. This ministerial speech extracts the chill of locality and superimposes a kind of neutral and slightly noisy sound-complex which can be very fine and resonant or else almost meaningless. Since Edinburgh is full of churches and crammed with incumbents it would not be surprising if the voice of the Church had carried over into the general population. This, however, is a generalisation which must not be accepted too literally. One can go down to Northumberland Street, where the advocates live, and listen, on a quiet evening, to the thin voices of the Bar.

The language that the great majority of Edinburgh people speak is still almost a hundred-per-cent Scots. At least, that's what you hear in the playgrounds, in the shops, pubs, and buses, on the football terrace, and in most colloquial talk. But what you hear on the radio is 'Morningside English'; or 'Kimly Benk [Comely Bank]'; and this same stilted speech is the only kind that is countenanced in the schools. Edinburgh children really get a rotten deal. 'Keepin' a guid Scots tongue in your heid' has long been discouraged. The language of Dunbar and the makars, of Ramsay and Fergusson is curtly described as 'not English' – or worse, dismissed as 'slang'.

Everytime an Edinburgh child opens his mouth he has to make a thousand-and-one changes – 'guid' to 'good', 'heid' to 'head', 'isnie' to 'isn't', 'dinnie' to 'don't', 'ain' to 'own', 'mair' to 'more', 'aboot' to 'about', 'ken' to 'know', 'a'' to 'all', 'o'' to 'of' and 'aye' to 'always' – to say nothing of pronouncing all those 'ts' and sounding all those '-ings'. No wonder Scottish students don't feel at ease in English interviews, or in front of a microphone! This early interference with our natural speech may also explain why Edinburgh doesn't produce lively playwrights like Sean O'Casey or Brendan Behan. As it is, the only result that education appears to achieve is the complete mucking-up of the declensions of the verbs 'to do', 'to see' and 'to go'.

James T. R. Ritchie,
The Singing Street (1964)

What a lingo the Edinburgh populace had, what a pronunciation, what a queer accent and usage of voice, as compared with that perfect speech and exquisitely-delicate modulation for which the Aberdonians are famous! One picked up phrases in the streets – such as 'There it's' for 'There it is' – which betokened that one was among strangers; nay, one maintained, with conscious pride, that the very oaths heard in Edinburgh were of a poor and effeminate quality, that northern blasphemy was far superior, and that expressions which served to convey an Edinburgh carter's wrath in the last stage of articulate excitement would in Aberdeen be but the easy utterances of a moderately-vexed lassie.

David Masson,
Memories of Two Cities (1911)

Edinburgh Worthies

Edinburgh is a hotbed of genius. I have had the good fortune to be made acquainted with many authors of the first distinction: such as the two Humes, Robertson, Smith, Wallace, Blair, Fergusson, Wilkie etc. and I have found them all as agreeable in conversation as they are instructive and entertaining in their writings.

Tobias Smollett,
Expedition of Humphrey Clinker (1771)

Everybody drank too much, washed too little, swore horribly, and lived roughly. Some made long prayers, which changed their habits no whit. Despite it all, old Edinburgh was an amusing place. Life was anything but dull, everybody knew everybody else, there was much good fellowship, there was the best of claret, the best of talk, and the best of stories. The pathetic and heroic memories of the place, its nearly superb position and surroundings, kindled the imagination. There was an old and famous aristocracy, whose very names were instinct with romance. Moreover, there was high breeding, there was learning, there was genius, for in that strange city there lived during the second half of the eighteenth century men who have profoundly influenced the thought and literature of the world. Here as contemporaries were Adam Smith, the political economist; David Hume, the philosopher; Walter Scott, the future novelist. Could living London furnish such a trio? Burns and Smollett were 'residenters', though not citizens; and there were crowds of lesser and yet distinguished names: Allan Ramsay, Fergusson, Home, Blair, Henry Mackenzie, Henry Raeburn, Creech, Principal Robertson, the two Tytlers, Kames, Monboddo, Dugald Stuart, James Boswell, to name but these.

Francis Watt, *Terrors of the Law* (1902)

John Knox (1513–1572)

It seems to me hard measure that this Scottish man, now after three hundred years, should have to plead like a culprit before the world; intrinsically for having been, in such way as it was then possible to be, the bravest of all Scotchmen! Had he been a poor half-and-half, he could have crouched into a corner, like so many others; Scotland had not been delivered; and Knox had been without blame. He is the one Scotchman to whom, of all others, his country and the world owe a debt.

Thomas Carlyle,
Heroes, Hero Worship and the Heroic in History
(1840)

To those who know Knox by hearsay only, I believe the matter of this paper will be somewhat astonishing. For the hard energy of the man in all public matters has possessed the imagination of the world . . . .And yet the language of passion came to his pen as readily, whether it was a passion of denunciation against some of the abuses that vexed his righteous spirit, or of yearning for the society of an absent friend. He was vehement in affection, as in doctrine.

It was in virtue of this latter disposition that Knox was capable of those intimacies with woman that embellished his life; and we find him preserved for us in old letters as a man of many women friends; a man of the acquaintance of Mrs Mackgil, Mrs Guthrie, and some other, or all of these Edinburgh friends while he was still Douglas of Longniddry's private tutor.

Our certain knowledge begins in 1549. He was then but newly escaped from his captivity in France, after pulling an oar for nineteen months on the benches of the galley *Nostre Dame*; at this happy juncture he fell into the company of a Mrs Elizabeth Bowes, wife of Richard Bowes, of Aske, in Yorkshire to whom she had borne twelve children. From the first time she heard Knox preach she formed a high opinion of him, and was solicitous ever after of his society. Nor was Knox unresponsive. 'I have always delighted in your company,' he writes.

Robert Louis Stevenson,
Familiar studies of Men and Books (1874)

John Napier (1550–1617)

A contemporary of King James – born sixteen years before him – was the mathematician and inventor of logarithms, John Napier of Merchiston, on the southern fringe of the city. His father was only fifteen when he begot him. His father's father was killed at the battle of Pinkie. His great-grandfather, whose father, grandfather and great grandfather had all been provosts of Edinburgh, fought at Flodden. John Napier received some education at St Andrews, and by two wives had six sons and six daughters. His first work was entitled *A Plaine Discovery of the whole Revelation of Saint John*, but after its publication he seems to have busied himself with the invention of new weapons of war for use against Spain. One of these secret weapons was a mirror to burn the enemy's ships at a distance; another was a gun to engage targets round the arc of a circle; and a third appears to have been a primitive tank. According to Sir Thomas Urquhart of Cromarty the traversing gun was successfully tested against sheep and cattle.

In 1614 Napier published his *Mirifici Logarithmorum Canonis Descriptio*, and the world received the first announcement of a discovery that has been placed second only to Newton's *Principia*; perused the first table of logarithms; and heard for the first time that word which Napier had invented. As a contribution to science, in that age, it stands alone; there is no one but Napier, of British origin, who may be compared with Kepler or Galileo or Tycho Brahe. In a country whose savagery and superstition were still the commonplace of life, it is remarkable indeed to come upon a man who deliberately, and in a solitude far removed from the assistance of any congenial mind, sets himself the apparently insoluble problem of simplifying the processes of multiplication and division; and by the use of arithmetic and geometry alone, finds the one simplification that could be found.

Three years later a little book called *Rabdologia* appeared, in which a calculating device that came to be known as 'Napier's bones' was described. It was warmly welcomed by a large public that had found multiplication difficult, but his other invention, the use of the decimal point, may not have received such immediate acclaim. Napier died in 1617.

Eric Linklater,
Edinburgh (1960)

Jenny Geddes

Tradition asserts that on Sunday, the 23rd day of July, 1637 when the new Prayer Book imposed by Charles I was read for the first time, in St Giles Cathedral, an Edinburgh woman, Jenny Geddes by name, threw her stool at the officiating clergyman and shouted 'Villain, daur ye say Mass at my lug'. 'She was a brave Scotchwoman,' says Lord President Inglis; but Bishop Wordsworth counters this by dubbing her 'ignorant and fanatical'. Both are agreed, however, that the story is true. But is it? Did Jenny Geddes exist? It is notable that in none of the contemporary accounts of the riot in St Giles is any mention made of her or her exploit.

In those days, fashionable ladies did not come to church till sermon time, but sending their servants to place their folding-stools and occupy them till their arrival. Thus when the service began, the congregation consisted mainly of serving woman and women of the lower classes. As soon as the Dean opened the Prayer-Book the uproar started, and from all parts of the Church there came derisive shouts, of which the least objectionable were 'Anti-Christ', 'Beastly Bellygod', 'Woolf', and 'Craft Fox'. The congregation with clapping of their hands, curses, and our-cries, raised such an uncouth noise and hubbub in the church, that not any one could hear or be heard, though the tumult grew worse. The Dean proceeded with his reading and then someone threw a folding-stool at him, 'intending to have given him a 'ticket of remembrance', but jouking became his safeguard'. In a moment, there was a perfect shower of stools. But all of them missed the target, partly through bad marksmanship, and partly, no doubt, through the Dean's successful 'jouking'.

That is the whole story – there is no mention of Jenny Geddes, and there is no particular importance attached to the throwing of the first stool.

J. G. Fyfe, *From Scotland's Past* (1930)

Some praise the fair Queen Mary, and some the
           good Queen Bess
And some the wise Aspasia, beloved by Pericles;
But o'er all the world's brave women, there's one
           that bears the rule,
The valiant Jenny Geddes, that flung the
           three- legged stool.
With a row-dow – at them now! – Jenny fling the stool!

And thus a mighty deed was done by Jenny's
           valiant hand,
Black Prelacy and Popery she drave from Scottish
           land;

King Charles he was a shuffling knave, priest Laud
a meddling fool,
But Jenny was a woman wise, who beat them
with a stool!
With a row-dow – at them now! – Jenny fling the stool!

Verses composed and sung regularly by
Professor John Stuart Blackie. Quoted by
Rosaline Masson in 'In Praise of Edinburgh' (1912)

Lord Braxfield (1722–99)

And in this town and among these men there moved the portentous figure of Robert Macqueen, Lord Braxfield, Senator of the College of Justice, and as Lord Justice Clerk President of the Court of Justiciary, the Weir of Hermiston of Stevenson's unfinished romance. His day witnessed a social revolution. The city overran its ancient bounds . . . Braxfield removed to George Square: that was his sole concession to the newer time. He was middle-aged when the change began; he was formed by Old Edinburgh, by its wit, its learning, its prejudice, its moral and physical grime, its caustic and racy speech, and it is as a representative of Old Edinburgh that he abides to-day.

His origin was provincial. His grandfather was gardener to the Earl of Selkirk, and his father was made a lawyer that he might be Baron-Baillie to his lordship. He prospered, became Sheriff of Lanarkshire, and acquired the estate of Braxfield, near Lanark. His eldest son was first educated there, then served a full term of apprenticeship with a Writer to the Signet, during the latter part whereof he studied at the University for the Scots Bar, and at twenty-two was admitted Advocate, February 14,

1744. A lawyer and the son of a lawyer, instruments of sasine, feu charters, all the quaint terminology of Scots jurisprudence were familiar to him from his cradle. That jurisprudence derived from two sources: the old Feudal Law and the Civil or Roman Law, as these had been modified by the practice of the country during the centuries of its history. Now, of the field of Feudal Law Braxfield knew every inch, and he was well acquainted with the Civil Law in all its practical applications; so that Lord Cockburn, who cordially detested him, styles him the best lawyer of his time. In 1776, Macqueen, after some opposition on his part, for the change meant a reduced income, was raised to the Bench as Lord Braxfield . . . He died in 1799 after a long illness, so that ten years measures the time of his pre-eminence.

On the Bench his characteristics were accentuated, and, of course, more noticeable. Passable in a young advocate, a fondness for cards, for wine, for 'sculduddery', was scandalous in an elderly judge, and swearing was no longer considered 'a great ornament to the conversation of a gentleman'. Yet Braxfield out-Heroded Herod. He cursed 'without provocation, like an ensign of the last age in his teens', is the strange simile of his contemporary, Ramsay of Ochtertyre, in thought and sentiment . . . The younger men hankered after southern turns of speech, though their efforts were not over successful, for it was true of them what Braxfield said of Lord Jeffrey: 'He had tint his Scots, and gained nae English'. Also, high-flown sentiments expressed in vague and enthusiastic language – the flatulent eloquence of the *Man of Feeling* – were much in fashion. And for all this Braxfield cherished an utter hatred, a supreme contempt. He abhorred verbiage, he was ever pertinent and material. He exaggerated his Scots of set purpose; only one of his time could use the words, so expressive for wit and satire, of that dead and gone, or now degraded language, to the same fell purpose. 'He struck me as very like Robert Burns', says (again rather oddly) Ramsay of Ochtertyre, who knew both men intimately. His seemed the voice of Old Scotland protesting against a degenerate and effeminate time. Raeburn, and Raeburn at his very best – (and how good that is!) – has limned him for us, and various Knox's thought, if not Knox's words, must have been often in his mind: the world was weary of him as he was of it. Yet he, too, had his softer hour. He was a warm and attached friend, and he spared no trouble in the service of his friends. One or two of his letters, written in his clear, almost feminine hand, are preserved among the Lochnaw papers. The tome is kindly, even delicate and chivalrous.

Weir of Hermiston is professedly a resuscitation of Braxfield. Stevenson was too true an artist to repeat old anecdotes. The sayings he puts in Hermiston's mouth are such as Braxfield might have uttered; but not one of them is his.

Francis Watt, Terrors of the Law (1902)

Adam Smith (1723–90)

I was informed that a place of Commissioner of Customs in Scotland had been given to a Philosopher who for his own glory and for the benefit of mankind had enlightened the world by the most profound and systematic treatise on the great objects of trade and revenue which had ever been published in any age or any Country.

Thus Gibbon greeted the news which reached him in

London in November 1777. Smith's own account of his life in the aftermath of the publication of *WN*, and the turn of events that took him from solitude in Kirkcaldy to a busy life in Edinburgh as a Customs Commissioner, runs as follows:

> I had returned to my old retirement in Kirkcaldy and was employed in writing another Work concerning the Imitative Arts, when by the interest of the Duke of Buccleuch, I was appointed to my present Office; which though it requires a good deal of attendance is both easy and honourable.

He had anticipated, apparently, concentrating on part of that 'Philosophical History of all the different branches of Literature, of Philosophy, Poetry, and Eloquence', one of the 'two great works' which he indicated in 1785 he still had 'upon the anvil'. But the people above him had other views.

On accepting his appointment, Smith moved his household to Panmure House, the town residence of a prominent Forfarshire landed family forced to lay out nearly £50,000 in 1764 to recover the estates forfeited after the 1715 Jacobite rising. The building, which is still standing, is a plain, L-shaped rubble building, with a raised courtyard and the attractive crow-stepped gables of similar seventeenth-century houses nearby. It is to be found in Little Lochend Close on the north side of the Canongate, formerly a separate burgh and essentially the suburb of the ancient Palace of Holyroodhouse . . .

John Kay, whose engraver's shop was at the corner of Parliament Close, and who must have seen Adam Smith many times going towards the Royal Exchange opposite, on whose upper floors was the Custom-house, issued a print dated 1787 showing him in a broad-brimmed hat, wearing a light linen coat and carrying in his left hand a bunch of flowers, perhaps to ward off the notorious Edinburgh effluvia. In his right hand he grasps his cane by the middle, sloping it against his shoulder, according to Smellie, 'as a soldier carries his musket'. He also describes Smith's strange gait, his head moving in a gentle manner from side to side, and his body swaying 'vermicularly' (a nice touch from a naturalist) as if with each step 'he meant to alter his direction, or even to turn back'. Meantime, his lips would move and form smiles as if he were deep in conversation with persons unseen. Edinburgh anecdote had it that an old market-woman observing him in these oddities exclaimed: 'Heigh, Sirs!' and shook her head, to which a companion answered by sighing compassionately, then observed: 'and he is well put too', thus expressing surprise that an obviously well-to-do lunatic would be allowed to wander freely.

Ian Simpson Ross, *The Life of Adam Smith* (1995)

Sir Walter Scott (1771–1832)

This little inroad into Northern Antiquities brought me into closer intimacy with Walter Scott; at that time known to the world at large only by his poetry; but well recognized in the society of Edinburgh, even by his political adversaries, as one of its agreeable and accomplished members. I still hold in happy memory the little suppers (a meal now lost to social life) at his house in Castle Street, of which he himself was the soul and spirit . . . A little political sarcasm now and then stole into his conversation, but rarely if ever showed itself in any harsh or ungenerous personality, – a feeling alien, as I believe, to his nature, though I have heard him accused of it. Frequently too at this period, I saw him when listening with enthusiastic enjoyment to 'Lochinvar' and other of his ballads, set to music and sung to him by Miss Clephane (afterwards Lady Northampton), with the fine stories, which he ever had at hand to point and illustrate the matter of converse, whatever it might be. Many of these, as he told them, might have been transferred almost literal accompaniment of her harp. This made a picture in itself. It was the poet revelling in the musical echo of his own poetry. These are my early recollections of Walter Scott in Edinburgh.

Sir Henry Holland, *Recollections of Past Life* (1872)

Peter Mark Roget (1779–1869)

Doctor, inventor, scientific researcher, and Secretary to the Royal Society, Roget was seventy years old when he finally put together his 'word book'. This undertaking, which had been at the back of his mind for many years, is known to-day as *Roget's Thesaurus*.

Born in Soho, London, Roget was the only son of a Swiss pastor, who died when he was three years old. After hiring a series of tutors for her young son, his mother Catherine, sister of Sir Samuel Romilly (a great reforming lawyer), found that he was particularly gifted in astronomy and brought him to Edinburgh at the age of fourteen. Here Roget excelled in his studies, and after a bout of typhus fever [1797] went on to graduate in 1798 at the age of nineteen. His thesis entitled *De chemicae affinitatis legibus*, ('on the laws of chemical affinity'), was dedicated to Samuel Romilly and Dugald Stewart. After University, Roget returned to London where for a short time he became a scientific researcher for Jeremy Bentham who was devising a plan to construct a 'Frigidarium' (a building in which to hold and maintain the freshness of food longer than keeping it in standard cupboards or larders and thus prevent 'spoilage').

In 1802, while employed as travelling tutor to two boys, taking them on the 'Grand Tour' with Lovell Edgeworth (half-brother to Maria Edgeworth, authoress), Roget was detained in France as a result of Napoleon's decree that all British visitors over eighteen years of age be held as prisoners-of-war. Pleading Swiss citizenship, he managed to escape back to England with his charges and companion via Germany and Switzerland.

After a brief stay in Edinburgh he was appointed physician to the Public Infirmary in Manchester at the age of twenty-six. He went on to help found the first medical school in Manchester.

However, he had other interests which included mechanics, inventing an early form of slide-rule, which would measure the power of numbers based on logarithms. He wrote a paper on this invention which led to his becoming a Fellow of the Royal Society in 1814, and became secretary from 1827 to 1849, during which time he edited the *Proceedings* of the Society and Council, as well as preparing abstracts for the papers submitted.

After retirement, he attempted to build a calculating machine and also invented and solved chess problems, many of which were published in the *Illustrated London News* and *London* and *Edinburgh Philosophical Magazines*. Roget's interest extended to developing a pocket chessboard in 1845 called the Economic Chessboard.

Roget's Thesauras, for which he is perhaps best remembered, first appeared in 1852 under the title of *Thesauras of English words and phrases, classified and arranged so as to facilitate the expression of ideas and assist in literary composition.* It had been an ongoing project in the back of his mind for nearly fifty years and he was able to see his creation reach its twenty-eighth edition before he died in 1869. Today Roget's famous thesaurus, which was sold to Longmans, Green in 1950 by Samuel Romilly Roget (Roget's grandson), is still widely used and new editions such as the International edition and the pocket sized versions have recently emerged to help increase usage, along with on-line versions.

Edinburgh University Worthies (1999)

Thomas De Quincy (1785–1859)

So far back as early in the fifties, I more than once came across that mysterious and wonderful personality, Thomas De Quincy, a writer of marvellous and subtle originality. In the year 1854 he was living in lodgings in Lothian Street, and some of my college chums occupied apartments in the same street. In the course of our going too and fro we frequently came across a little man of humble mien, and attired in a rather broken-down and negligent fashion. He seemed to prefer taking his outdoor exercise nocturnally, for it was usually at night, and sometimes late at night, that we met the silent and solitary man wandering to and fro not far from his humble quarters. He was always alone, and communed silently with himself.

J. B. Sutherland,
Random Recollections and Impressions (1903)

David Roberts (1796–1864)

My parents moved in a very humble sphere of life, but by unwearied industry maintained and educated their family. My father, who was the second son of a small farmer near Forfar, and by trade a shoemaker, married and settled in the village of Stockbridge, near Edinburgh, where I was born, the first of five children, on the 24th October 1796. Three of these children, a sister and two brothers, died when very young, and within a short time of each other . . . At eight years of age I was sent to a school in Edinburgh, where, like other boys at that period, I was cruelly treated. This gave me a dislike to the school, and on expressing my determination to leave, it was resolved that I should be apprenticed to a trade. Long previous to this, however, I had acquired an intense love of pictures, although those which came in my way were of the humblest description, consisting of halfpenny picture-books, such as 'The Life and Death of Cock Robin', 'Little Red Riding Hood', and similar productions. Panoramas and collections of wild beasts were frequently exhibited on the Earthen Mound, the site of the Royal Scottish Academy's Exhibition; and the outsides of the wooden structures and caravans were generally decorated with representations of their contents, painted on cloth. These were sources of great attraction to me, and I was wont, on going home, to attempt to give my mother an idea of what they were by scratches on the whitewashed kitchen-wall, made with the end of a burned stick and a bit of keel.

My attitude for copying whatever attracted my attention increased, and I began to imitate such pictures or engravings as I could procure. A lady, whom I recollect with profound respect and gratitude, took a deep interest in me, and gave me drawings to copy, after which she showed my productions to Grahame, then the Master of the Trustees' Academy in Edinburgh, with a view to my becoming an artist-pupil there. Grahame, however, took the correct view of the case, and gave judicious advice, saying, that as the parents of the boy were poor, he had best be apprenticed to a house-painter, where he might still practise drawing, and learn an act by which he could earn his living. This advice was followed, and I was apprenticed for seven years to Mr Gavin Beugo.

At length, having completed my seven years' apprenticeship I went to Perth, where I was engaged as foreman by Mr Conway, a house-decorator who had come from London to paint Scoon Palace. This was in the summer of 1815, and I remained there till the spring of the following year, when I returned to Edinburgh.

At this time, in addition to the Theatre Royal, there was a Circus opened in North College Street. . . . scenery was required, and as I was at that time unemployed, a friend proposed to me that I should attempt to paint the scenes.

This was the commencement of my career as a scene-painter. I knew little of the ancient and still less of the modern masters. The scenery of Aladdin and the Forty Thieves had irresistible charms for me.

James Ballantine, *Life of David Roberts R.A.* (1866)

Robert Louis Stevenson (1850–1894)

Mr Stevenson is not to be labelled novelist. He wanders the byways of literature without any fixed address. Too much of a truant to be classified with the other boys, he is only a writer of fiction in the sense that he was once an Edinburgh University student because now and again he looked in at his classes when he happened to be that way. A literary man without a fixed occupation amazes Mr Henry James, a master in the school of fiction which tells, in three volumes, how Hiram K. Wilding trod on the skirt of Alice M. Sparkins without anything's coming of it. Mr James analyzes Mr Stevenson with immense cleverness, but without summing up. That 'Dr Jekyll and Mr Hyde' should be by the author of *Treasure Island*, *Virginibus Puerisque* by the author of *The New Arabian Nights*, *A Child's Garden of Verses* by the author of *Prince Otto*, are to him the three degrees of comparison of wonder, though for my own part I marvel more that the author of *Daisy Miller* should be Mr Stevenson's eulogist. One conceives Mr James a boy in velveteens looking fearfully at Stevenson playing at pirates.

There is nothing in Mr Stevenson's sometimes writing essays, sometimes romances, and anon poems to mark him versatile beyond other authors. One dreads his continuing to do so, with so many books at his back, lest it means weakness rather than strength. He experiments too long; he is still a boy wondering what he is going to be.

J. M. Barrie,
An Edinburgh Eleven (1889)

Sir Harry Lauder

'It is a wonderful thing, a signal honour, to be honoured in your own city. I say Edinburgh is my city – it became my city when Portobello annexed it. I believe that was 31 or 32 years ago. Anyway the honour is greater because it was my father's city, my grandfather's city, the city of romance, Edinburgh. Over its cobbled 'causeyed' streets the feet of the wild clansmen have hurried; up its shaded closes their slogans have rung. Round its grim rock wars have raged, and alike in its palaces and towers, and under its humblest roofs, poets have dreamed and lovers have sung. From its barracks men have marched to make the word freedom great and holy by the shedding of their blood. Through all its grim conflicts there has ever been the urge of the same great liberty. So Edinburgh all down history has been the centre and the symbol of things that cannot die.

> Sir Harry Lauder, speech at Ceremony of Freedom
> of City, 24 November 1927

Angela Varecchi

An interwar-years memory in the streets of Edinburgh – a rotund Angela with her travelling hurdy-gurdy pulled by a diminutive Shetland pony – and riding high a monkey.

> Leah Leneman,
> *Into the Foreground* (1993)

Ronald Selby Wright – The Radio Padre

> With pipe and specs and friendly smile,
> You'll find him down the Royal Mile
> Nearby his Kirk of Holyrood,
> Or at the Mike – perhaps as good!

The preaching of this fearless Youth,
With stern adherence to the Truth,
Allied to forceful presentation,
Quite *gets* the Forces of the Nation!

His heart is in Boys' Camps and Clubs,
And – Shorts or Cassock – naught disturbs
Our far-famed Padre with a flair
For a devout 'Questionnaire!'

C. C., *Modern Athenians* (1944)

Asa Wass

The Cowgate was then, as indeed it may still be, the home of Auld Reekie's principal rag-and-bone merchants and rag-pickers. Yet, by far the most illustrious in the former category was to be found, not in the Cowgate, but in equally salubrious surroundings in Fountainbridge. His name was Asa Wass. He was regarded as king among the rag-and-bone fraternity. No one, to my knowledge, ever actually saw Asa. For all that, he advertised regularly in our local newspapers, offering good prices for horsehair, and for scrap-metal of any description. He was almost a legendary figure among Edinburgh schoolboys. We never really doubted his existence, however, though the sign bearing his name in Fountainbridge was becoming quite illegible at this time. His premises were so well known that they needed no legible designation. I once sold to a representative of his an old lawn-mower, for sixpence. Fancy my chagrin when, in boasting of the transaction, I was assured that the handle alone was worth a shilling!

Alastair Alpin MacGregor, *Auld Reekie* (1943)

Hugh MacDiarmid (1892–1978)

I remember vividly Grieve's arrival among us. I see the little, slimly built figure in hodden grey, the small sharp-featured face with its piercing eyes, the striking head with its broad brow and great mass of flaxen curly hair. He hailed from Langholm, and had a Border accent you could have cut with a knife. I am afraid some of the city students smiled at first at the newcomer, but he very speedily established himself . . .

He was not, it must be admitted, a model student; in some subjects, frankly he had no interest. As a matter of fact he became the despair of most of his teachers. Yet none of them could help liking him. He had a most engaging ingenuousness, and I have yet to meet the infant who could look as innocent as Grieve.

Alan Bold, *MacDiarmid* (1988)

Street Characters

There were many street characters in my boyhood' days. One notable character was 'Daft Willie', sometimes called 'Cramond Willie'. He was a big man with a long black beard and always carried a basket with eggs and provisions over his arm, and he always wore a 'lum' hat and carried a stout stick, but was very inoffensive.

A different type of character, and much smaller in build was 'Daft Charlie' who was blind and played a concertina. Sometimes the boys round about would call out, 'Swing, Charlie, swing' and his stick would swing round, and woe betide anyone caught by it.

Cripple Kirsty, alias 'Burn the Bible', was a well-known character. She was an old wife, little, toothless and grandmotherly like, but very alert. When the children called after her, 'Burn the Bible,' she made them fly. How she acquired the name I do not know, but the youngsters all understood that she had burned a bible and gone daft over it.

Then there was Piper Campbell, who played his pipes at the foot of Hanover Street. He rode about in a little carriage, like a modern perambulator, drawn by two large dogs. Last but not least, in width at any rate, was a funny little man called 'Caunle Doup'. He was as broad as he was long, and was usually to be seen with a huge basket of candles resting on a leather bun on his head. He had funny little short legs and arms and a very big head, and was altogether a striking figure, and was often teased by boys. A prominent citizen of Edinburgh, unknown by the younger generation, may have suitable mention here, as he was considered a character. Professor John Stuart Blackie, an eminent Greek authority, might be seen striding along Princes Street daily, until his death in March 1895. He was a tall lithe figure, clean shaven sharp features, while underneath his jaunty billycock hat his silvery locks rested on his shoulders, and over his shoulder was thrown a shepherd check plaid. He had a thick stick which he called his 'Kail runt', and which he carried in swaggering style, sometimes over his shoulder. He was a genial old gentleman, frequently delivered lectures sometimes interspersed with Scotch songs, and it was no secret that he was 'fond o' the lasses'.

D. A. Small, *Through Memory's Window*
(unpublished memoirs 1860–1927)

Visitors

~

ROYAL VISITORS

The Prince comes into his own

The city clocks were striking noon when, on the 17th of September 1745, some eighty horsemen entered the royal park of Holyrood. As they reached the brow of a hill, their leader dismounted and looked down on the grey stone palace. A young man of twenty-five, and seemingly tall among the surrounding Highland chieftains, his short tartan coat, scarlet breeches and blue velvet bonnet marked him as '*a gentleman and a man of fashion, but not like a hero or a conqueror*'; while the star of St Andrew which glittered on his breast, and the blue ribbon he wore across one shoulder, proved him a man of rank. Charles Edward Stuart, Prince Regent of his father's kingdoms, looked down for the first time on his ancestral home . . . As he rode down to the Palace, a cannonball from the fortress struck the James V Tower and dislodged some masonry; but the incident failed to stop the Prince as he made his way to the piazza where Hepburn of Keith waited to do him homage before leading him, with a drawn sword in his hand, up the staircase which leads to the royal apartments. The king's son had come into his own again.

Sacheverell Sitwell &
Francis Bamford,
Edinburgh (1938)

Residents of Holyroodhouse

That first floor afforded an asylum for the Royal Family of France; Charles Philip Count d'Artois, brother of the ill-fated Louis XVI, arriving at Edinburgh in June 1796. Duc d'Angoulême, the elder son, followed a few days later. There the exiles found shelter until August 1799.

The apartments associated with the Bourbons were occupied between 1817 and 1822 by Major William M. Nairne, Assistant Inspector-General of Barracks in Scotland. He was accompanied by his wife, Caroline Oliphant of Gask, writer of *The Auld House* and *The Land o' the Leal*. The Nairne Barony having reverted to her husband as a result of the Attainder Enactment of 1824, Caroline Oliphant is best known as Lady Nairne.

King George IV having intimated his intention of visiting Scotland in 1822, the Crown Authorities induced the Nairnes to surrender their claim to apartments in Holyroodhouse, an annuity of £300 being granted by way of substitution.

The Bourbon dynasty being restored in 1815, Louis XVIII ascended the throne, and on his death his brother, Le Comte d'Artois, succeeded as Charles X. The events of 'The Three Days' drove the monarch back to Edinburgh, where he occupied the Palace once more between October 1830 and September 1832, the Dauphin, with his wife, spending the first winter at No. 21, Regent Terrace.

Robert T. Skinner, *Figures and Figureheads* (1931)

George IV's Visit to Edinburgh (1822)

As soon as Leith was fixed upon as the landing place, preparations for his Majesty's reception commenced in that town and along the Walk with great spirit. A triumphal arch was erected in Bernard Street, and another in Constitution Street, while from the Pier to the Palace, along the route of the royal procession, namely Leith and Leith Walk, Picardy and York Place, St Andrew's Street, Princes Street, Waterloo Place, and the Caltonhill-road, upwards of a hundred platforms and balconies were formed for the accommodation of spectators of the grand and novel scene so soon to be exhibited.

Strangers of every age and class were pouring hourly into town from every part of Scotland, by every possible mode of conveyance. Track-boats, steamboats, coaches, and carts, were arriving constantly with fresh importations of visitors, determined to gratify their curiosity with a sight of royalty. Splendid equipages were driving through the streets in all directions from morning till night; numerous groups of beautiful and elegantly dressed ladies were seen in shops or in the public walks; and to give the scene a more picturesque effect, the Celtic Society, associated some years ago for the purpose of preserving the peculiarities of the Highlanders, assumed the costumes of the clans, while the Macgregor, the Campbell, the Macdonell, the Drummond, and some of the other chiefs, not only wore the Highland garb themselves, but sent bands of their men from their native glens to the metropolis, to grace and diversify the scenes so soon to be exhibited there. Thistles, heather and oak twigs, emblems of Scotland, were brought into town in abundance . . . and were worn in the hat or upon the heart.

Anonymous

OTHER VISITORS

Robert Burns in Edinburgh

From his own correspondence we learn that he spent the first winter of his residence in Edinburgh in the house of Mrs Carfrae in Baxter's Close, Lawnmarket, first stair on the left hand going down the close, and first flat up – he and his friend John Richmond, a lawyer's clerk, sharing the same room, with its deal table and sanded floor, sleeping together in the one chaff bed, at a cost of three shillings a week. Their window looked out upon Lady Stair's Close. The tenement is still standing, though very old, and there is a tablet placed on the front of the house looking into the High Street, telling the public that the poet Burns had lodged there. That was in 1786.

Upon the strength of this [a letter of encouragement in relation to a second edition of his poems] he posted off to Edinburgh without a single letter of introduction in his pocket. This time it appears that he lodged with his friend William Nichol, one of the teachers of the High School, in the house over the pend now called Buccleuch Pend, leading into St Patrick Square. Nichol's apartments were on the top floor. At that time in this archway there was an underground public-house, which was kept by one Lucky Pringle and much frequented by Nicol and Burns.

Speaking of taverns, the one most popularly known in connection with Burns was 'Johnnie Dowie's' in Liberton Wynd, where the poet composed some of his best songs. He used to sit in a *very* small room with one or two friends

158

only; but many were the visitors who just called in to gaze upon what they called 'the coffin of the Bard'.

The next time Burns visited Edinburgh he stayed with William Cruikshank, another teacher of the High School, the house being at the south-west corner of St James' Square in the New Town. The poet's window was in the attic on the gable side looking towards the General Post Office in Waterloo Place. It was while residing here that he became acquainted with Mrs M'Lehose, and carried on that poetic correspondence with her for three months under the assumed names of 'Clarinda' and 'Sylvander'. She was living in General's Entry, Potterrow, at that time.

Mrs J. Stewart Smith,
*Historic Stones and Stories
of Bygone Edinburgh* (1924)

As for Burns, I may truly say, *Virgilium vidi tantum.* I was a lad of fifteen in 1786–7, when he came first to Edinburgh, but had sense and feeling enough to be much interested in his poetry, and would have given the world to know him; but I had very little acquaintance with any literary people, and still less with the gentry of the west country, the two sets that he most frequented. . . . As it was, I saw him one day at the late venerable Professor Fergusson's, where there were several gentlemen of literary reputation, among whom I remember the celebrated Mr Dugald Stewart. Of course we youngsters sat silent, looked and listened. The only thing I remember which was remarkable in Burn's manner, was the effect produced upon him by a print of Bunbury's, representing a soldier lying dead on the snow, his dog sitting in misery on the one side, on the other his widow with a child in her arms. These lines were written beneath:

> 'Cold on Canadian hills, or Mindens' plain
> Perhaps that parent wept her soldier slain;
> Bent o'er her babe, her eye dissolved in dew,
> The big drops, mingling with the milk he drew
> Gave the sad presage of his future years,
> The child of misery baptized in tears.'

Burns seemed much affected by the print, or rather the ideas which it suggested to his mind. He actually shed tears. He asked whose the lines were, and it chanced that nobody but myself remembered that they occur in a half-forgotten poem of Langhorne's, called by the unpromising title of 'The Justice of the Piece'. I whispered my information to a friend present, who mentioned it to Burns, who rewarded me with a look and a word.

J. G. Lockhart, *Life of Sir Walter Scott* (1837)

To Clarinda – on leaving Edinburgh

> Clarinda, mistress of my soul,
> The measur'd time is run!
> The wretch beneath the dreary pole
> So marks his latest sun.
>
> To what dark cave of frozen night
> Shall poor Sylvander hie; –
> Depriv'd of thee, his life and light,
> The sun of all his joy?
>
> We part – but, by these precious drops,
> That fill thy lovely eyes,

No other light shall guide my steps,
Till thy bright beams arise!

She, the fair sun of all her sex,
Has blest my glorious day;
And shall a glimmering planet fix
My worship to its ray?

Robert Burns, *Poems* (1787)

Frédéric Chopin (1809–1849)

Whenever the tramcar is about to bear me northward across the Water o' Leith at the Canonmills of Edinburgh, my eyes are unconsciously diverted along Warriston Crescent, the first opening on the right thereafter, and but a stone's throw beyond the water's edge. With his music flowing through my mind, I always imagine that one day I may see Chopin afoot upon this crescent's pavement, or perhaps turning in, languidly, at Number 10, assisting himself up the few steps to the front door by means of the railing.

A century ago – on the evening of the 4th of October, 1848, to be precise – Frédéric Chopin gave a piano recital in the Hopetoun Rooms.

This venue for such occasions has disappeared long since. On the site of the Hopetoun Rooms now stands the Mary Erskine School for Girls, one of the four schools administered by that ancient and admirable institution, the Company of Merchants of the City of Edinburgh, commonly designated the Merchant Company. Until recently, this school, situated in Queen Street, was known as the Edinburgh Ladies' College, or, more colloquially, as Queen Street. The school hall is believed to occupy substantially the site of the room in which Chopin played.

Warriston Crescent, a fine example of the architecture of the period, remains exactly as it was a hundred years ago, when Chopin's visit brought it brief fame. At the time, it was one of Edinburgh's more fashionable streets. It is a *cul-de-sac*, consisting of a gentle curve of fifty solid, identical, symmetrical houses, each having one storey, a basement, and a deep area to the front. It overlooks some elms and plane trees, a bowling-green, and the back gardens of the adjacent Howard Place. From the upper windows of Number 10, one sees easily the back of 8 Howard Place, where, two years after Chopin's visit, was born that gloriously elusive lad, Robert Louis Stevenson.

Alasdair Alpin MacGregor, *Scotland's Magazine,*
October 1948

Dorothy Wordsworth (1771–1855)

Thursday, September 15th – . . . Arrived at Edinburgh, a little before sunset. As we approached, the castle rock resembled that of Stirling – in the same manner appearing to rise from a plain of cultivated ground, the Firth of Forth being on the other side, and not visible. Drove to the White Hart in the Grassmarket, an inn which had been mentioned to us, and which we conjectured would better suit us than one in a more fashionable part of the town. It was not noisy, and tolerably cheap. Drank tea, and walked up to the Castle, which luckily was very near. Much of the daylight was gone, so that except it had been a clear evening, which it was not, we could not have seen the distant prospect.

Dorothy Wordsworth,
Recollections of a Tour made in Scotland (1803)

Edward Topham

I have continued in this City ever since you last heard from me, and find it so agreeable that I foresee it will be with difficulty I shall prevail on myself to leave it. The inhabitants have so much civility and hospitality, and the favours I receive are so many, that it would argue a want of acknowledgement, and that I am unworthy of the good opinion they are so kind to entertain, did I wish to hasten my departure . . . I find here everything I can wish; and must own, I never spent my time more to my satisfaction.

Edward Topham,
Letters from Edinburgh (1776)

Benjamin Franklin (1706–1790)

Joys of Prestonfield, adieu!
Late found, soon lost, but still we'll view
Th'engaging scene – oft to these eyes
Shall the pleasing vision rise.

Hearts that warm towards a friend,
Kindness on kindness without end,
Easy converse, sprightly wit,
These we found in dame and knight.

Cheerful meals, balmy rest,
Beds that never bugs molest,
Neatness and sweetness all around
These – at Prestonfield we found.

Hear, O Heaven! A stranger's prayer!
Bless the hospitable pair!
Bless the sweet bairns, and very soon
Give these a brother, those a son!

Verses (1759)

William Thackeray (1811–1863)

Lately I saw that Melville column rising over Edinburgh; come, good men and true, don't you feel a little awkward and uneasy when you walk under it? Who was this to stand in heroic places? And is yon the man whom Scotchmen most delight to honour?

W. M. Thackeray,
Roundabout Papers (1863)

Andrew Carnegie (1835–1919)

That the travellers were delighted with Edinburgh, that it more than fulfilled all expectations, is to say but little; and those who saw it for the first time felt it to be beyond all that they had imagined. Those of us who knew its picturesque charms were more than ever impressed with its superiority over all other cities. Take my word for it, my readers, there is no habitation of human beings in this world so fine in its way, and its way itself is fine, as this, the capital of Scotland.

Andrew Carnegie,
An American Four-in-Hand in Britain (1883)

Everyday Life

~

Edinburgh's Glorious Literary Period

The high place which Edinburgh held among the cities of
the earth it owed exclusively to the intellectual standing
and high literary ability of a few distinguished citizens,
who were able to do for it greatly more in the eye of
Europe than had been done by its Court and Parliament,
or than could have been done through any other agency, by
the capital of a small and poor country, peopled by but a
handful of men. . .

During the last quarter of a century one distinguished
name after another has been withdrawn by death from
that second great constellation of Scotchmen resident in
Edinburgh to which Chalmers, Sir Walter Scott, and Lord
Jeffrey belong; and with Sir William Hamilton the last
group may be said to have disappeared. For the future,
Edinburgh in recollection over the times when she stood
highest in the intellectual scale, and possessed an influence
over opinion co-extensive with civilized man . . .

Lord Cockburn came into life just in time to occupy the
most interesting point possible for an observer. He was
born nearly a year before Chalmers, only eight years after
Scott, and about fourteen years before Lockhart. The
place he occupied in that group of eminent men to which
the capital of Scotland owed its glory was thus, chrono-
logically, nearly a middle place, and the best conceivable
for observation. He was in time too to see, at least as a
boy, most of the earlier group. The greatest of their
number, Hume, had, indeed, passed from off the stage;
but almost all the others still lived. Home, Robertson,
Blair, Henry, were flourishing in green old age at a time
when he had shot up into curious observant boyhood; and
Mackenzie and Dugald Stewart were still in but middle

life. It is perhaps beyond the reach of philosophy to assign adequate reasons for the appearance of one period rather than another of groups of great men . . . Nor can it be told why Humes, Robertsons, and Adam Smith should have appeared together in one splendid group, to give place to another group scarce less brilliant, though in a different way. It is greatly easier to say why such talent should have found a permanent centre in Edinburgh. Simple as it may seem, the prescriptive right of the capital to draft to its pulpits the *elite* of the established clergy did more for it than almost aught else.

Hugh Miller, *Essays* (1862)

The Pooters

The tasteful suburban villa was almost unknown in those days, and houses were built with hideous blind windows, more or less disguised, in order to evade the obnoxious window tax. For every window exceeding eight in number in each dwelling-house or other building a tax had to be paid. This window tax, which had been imposed in 1695, continued with varying fluctuations until 1851, when it was abolished, and the inhabited house duty substituted for it.

These were the days when the best room was garnished with artificial flowers, made of wax and often of wool, placed under glass shades; when antimacassars were spread all over the chairs and sofas in a room, and the decoration of a drawing-room table consisted of volumes of 'Elegant Extracts', the 'Beauties of English Poetry', 'Poetical Keepsakes', 'Friendship's Offering', 'Forget-me-Nots', and 'Literary Souvenirs', generally school prizes or gifts handsomely bound, with gilt edges, and placed at regular intervals round the table, to be looked at but not to be disturbed, or, if so, to be replaced in their wonted regularity.

J. B. Sutherland,
Random Recollections and Impressions (1903)

Mode of Life

The staple food for dinner in town and country was barley-broth, called and spelled *broath*. It was made of beef, generally salt, and was thickened with barley. In those days there were no barley-mills, so the barley was bruised in a mortar and then rubbed in a coarse cloth to husk it. Cabbage was also largely used, as other vegetables were little cultivated. In some old books we read of *cabbie-claw*, codfish dressed with a sauce made of horse radish and eggs. Friar's chicken was a dish which had descended from monastery cooks, and was considered a dainty. It was made of chicken cut in pieces and cooked with eggs and parsley and cinnamon. Cockie-leekie was then, as now, a favourite dish, and was reserved for company. It was made with a well-fed young cock, boiled with leeks and prunes, which seems to point to a French origin. Roast meat was very little used; pigeons and moorfowl were roasted on the spit or baked in 'pot ovens', which may be seen to this day in herds' houses in the moorland solitudes of Dumfriesshire and Galloway. Knives and spoons were used at table, but, up to the time of the Union, forks were rarely provided. The ordinary dinner-knife was called by the odd name of a Jockteleg, from its inventor, 'Jacques de Liége'. When the use of forks became more common, people of any position always carried a leather case with a knife and fork, and sometimes also a spoon. At the end of a meal these were carefully wiped, put in the case, and returned to the owner's pocket . . . Silver cups, or 'tassies' as they were called, were used by the better classes, and pewter drinking-cups by working people. Even in the eighteenth century glasses were very little used.

The changes of the dinner hour in different generations are very curious. In the fourteenth century kings and nobles dined at eleven o'clock, and supped at five. Mary, Queen of Scots when she lived at Holyrood dined at one o'clock, and we read that she was at supper, between five and six on 9th March 1566, when Rizzio was murdered.

In the eighteenth century in Edinburgh, one was the common dinner hour for all, 'gentle or simple'; by the beginning of the nineteenth century it had crept on to two or even three o'clock; and from 1850 onwards, for a good many years, 4.30 or five was a very usual dinner hour. Now, dinner is really what was our ancestors' supper. In the eighteenth century people began the day much earlier, as in the days of small dark rooms, lighted merely by candles, people liked to get the benefit of all the daylight they could. The men of the house had a morning dram, over which they said 'grace'; breakfast was between seven and eight, and consisted of porridge, collops of beef or mutton, oatcakes or barley bannocks, washed down by draughts of strong ale.

M. G. Williamson, *Edinburgh: A Historical and Topographical Account of the City* (1906)

Cleanliness

This city is placed in a dainty, healthful, pure air, and doubtless were a most healthful place to live in, were not the inhabitants most sluttish, nasty and slothful people. I could never pass through the hall, but I was constrained to hold my nose; their chambers, vessel, linen and meat – nothing neat, but very slovenly. . . . . The people . . . fetch not fresh water every day, but only every other day, which makes their water much worse (especially to drink), which, when it is at best, is bad enough. Their houses of office are tubs or firkins placed on end, which they never empty until they be full, so as the scent thereof annoyeth and offendeth the whole house. . . . . Their houses, halls and kitchens have such a noisome taste – a savour, and that so strong, as it doth offend you so soon as you come within their walls; yea, sometimes when I have light from my horse, I have felt the distaste of it before I have come into the house; yea, I never came to my own lodging in Edenborough, or went out, but I was constrained to hold my nose, or to use wormwood or some such scented plant.

The pewter, I am confident, is never scoured . . . only sometimes, and that but seldom, they do slightly rub them over with a filthy dish-clout, dipped in most sluttish, greasy water. Their pewter pots, wherein they bring wine and water, are furred within, that it would loathe you to touch anything which comes out of them.

Sir William Brereton, *Travels* (1844)

Off-Putting

The Lodgings are as nasty as the streets, and wash't so seldom that the dirt is thick eno' to be par'd off with a Shovel; every room is well scented with a close stoole, and the Master, Mistress and Servants lye all on a flour, like so many Swine in a Hogsty. This, with the rest of their sluttishness, is no doubt the occasion of the Itch, which is so common amongst them. We had the best lodgings we could get, for which we paid £3, 5*s*. Scots, being about 10*d*. a night English, and yet we went thro' the Master's Bed chamber and the Kitchen and dark Entry, to our room, which look't into a place they call the close, full of Nastinesse. 'Tis a common thing for a Man or woman to go into these closes at all times of the day to ease nature.

Joseph Taylor,
A Journey to Edenborough in Scotland (1705)

Tavern Life

The Playhouse, St Cecilia's Concert Hall and the Assembly Rooms, routs, ridottos and occasional balls at Holyrood provided entertainment for the refined circles of Edinburgh, but most of the menfolk hankered after pleasures of a heartier sort. Professional and business men, after pitting their keen wits and sharp tongues against each other during the day, plunged into the evening hours of relaxation with unfailing gusto. Where could such men find better diversion than in the numerous cosy little taverns at which they were more at home than in their own houses? Even the shopkeeper, closing at night the shutters of his tiny booth in the Krames, made straight for his favourite 'howff', since at home, in the small crowded rooms, his good wife would be at the noisy task of stowing the bairns away to bed – an unattractive scene for a tired business man. So, till the tuck of drum at ten o'clock, he could be seen night after night with the same cronies in his accustomed place at Fortune's or Douglas's or Dowie's tavern, supping on minced collops, brandered beefsteaks or rizzared haddock, relishing his wine or whisky or humbler 'tippenny ale' and sharing in the rowdy chorus of gossip and jest.

All classes and types mingled in the taverns which therefore present a striking cross-section of the city's life. In their free and easy good fellowship were united lords and lawyers and men of letters, hard-drinking and hard-headed, fitter to match wits with Falstaff than to muddle their pates with Tony Lumpkin.

Marie W. Stuart, *Old Edinburgh Taverns* (1952)

The Oyster Cellar

There is, however, a species of entertainment, different indeed from yours, but which seems to give more real pleasure to the company who visit it, than either Ranelagh or the Pantheon. The votaries to the shrine of pleasure are numerous; and the manner is entirely new. As soon as the evening begins to grow late, a large party form themselves together, and march to the Temple; where, after descending a few steps for the benefit of being removed from profaner eyes, they are admitted by the good Guardian of it; who, doubtless, rejoices to see so large and well-disposed a company of worshippers. The Temple itself is very plain and humble. It knows no idle ornaments, no sculpture or painting; nor even so much as wax tapers – a few solitary candles of tallow cast a dim, religious light, very well adapted to the scene. There are many separate cells of different sizes, accommodated to the number . . . who attend in greater or smaller parties, as the spirit moves them.

In plain terms, this shrine of festivity is nothing more than an Oyster-cellar, and its Votaries the First People in Edinburgh . . . The large table was covered with dishes full of oysters and pots of porter. For a long time, I could not suppose that this was the only entertainment we were to have, and I sat waiting in expectation of a repast that was never to make its appearance . . .

The bill for entertaining half a dozen very fashionable women, amounted only to two shillings a-piece. If you will not allow the entertainment an elegant one, you must at least confess it is cheap.

Edward Topham, *Letters from Edinburgh* (1776)

Other Entertainment

In the Victorian era the citizens of Auld Reekie took their enjoyments simply; places of amusement were comparatively few.

Some kind of light entertainment seemed to be desired by the menfolk, and the power of good and catchy songs was revealed in the many 'free-and-easies' which sprang up, mushroom-like, throughout the city. Almost every public-house that could boast of a back room large enough had a piano, and particularly on a Saturday night, smoking concerts, or as they were more familiarly termed, 'free-and-easies' were held.

The frequenters . . . were chiefly of the commercial class – shopkeepers and clerks, with a sprinkling of beard-less middies, and spurred horse-soldiers from Jock's Lodge in their scarlet tunics and gold braidings.

The comic songs sung were usually those that had just become popular in the London music-halls, while sentimental and patriotic ditties never failed to receive the well-deserved encores.

J. Wilson McLaren,
Edinburgh Memories and Some Worthies (1926)

Extra-Mural Activities

In my youth, there was only one famous brothel in Edinburgh – long since closed and gentrified – run by the celebrated madame, Dora Noyce in the New Town's Dublin Street.

This place held a fascination for generations of pubes-cent teenagers. It was a staple of adolescent smut. An enduring landmark in the sexual geography of Edinburgh. Playground wiseacres talked knowledgeably about it even though they had never been anywhere near. Which as why, as 14-year olds, I and a friend organised an expedition to boldly go where no-one had gone before.

It was the time of the General Assembly of the Church of Scotland. This was no accident, of course. Legend had it that Dublin Street was at its busiest then. I half expected to see queues of men with dog-collars snaking along the street.

But there was not a dog-collar in sight when we turned

the corner from St Bernard's Crescent into the most notorious street in Edinburgh. Indeed, as far as we could see, there was nothing there at all, apart from those cheerless black New Town facades. No red light; no guilty-looking men in macs; no floozies with come-hither stares. Only a man mending a Vauxhall Victor. The only screwing that was going on was on its carburettor.

Iain MacWhirter, *The Scotsman*,
1 August 1996

The Kirk's Approach

Nine unfortunate young women. 'Very naked and meagre beings' made an *amende honorable* through the streets of Edinburgh, the hangman attending them, while drums beat to the tune of 'Cuckolds-come-dig'.

The Courant and Mercury, July 1736

And a Comment

'The tuck of the drum made everyone run to his doorstep to gaze on the locksman (hangman) leading a woman, stripped to the waist, through the streets, at certain stations to flog her with his lashes, before taking her to jail . . . Such penalties . . . wonderfully relieved the monotony of burgal existence.'

H. G. Graham, *The Social Life of Scotland in the Eighteenth Century* (1899)

Earlier Society

Somewhere about the year 1750 a society called the *Sweating club* made its appearance. The members resembled the Mohocks and Bullies of London. After intoxicating themselves in taverns and cellars in certain obscure closes, they would sally at midnight into the wynds and large thoroughfares, and attack whomsoever they met, snatching off wigs and tearing up roquelaures. Many a luckless citizen who fell into their hands was chased, jostled, and pinched, till he not only perspired with exertion and agony, but was ready to drop down and die of sheer exhaustion.

In those days, when most men went armed, always with a sword and a few with pocket-pistols, such work often proved perilous; but we are told that 'even as late as the early years of this century it was unsafe to walk the streets of Edinburgh at night, on account of the numerous drunken parties of young men who reeled about, bent on mischief at all hours, and from whom the Town Guard were unable to protect the sober citizens'.

James Grant, *Old and New Edinburgh* (1880)

A 'Stock' Society

Clubs in the eighteenth century sense, where congenial spirits met once a week and combined chicken-broth with discussions on trade and the fine arts . . .

Adam Smith managed (at the same time) to be a member of certain clubs in Edinburgh, in particular, the Select Society, which also discussed economic questions, though perhaps with a bias in favour of agriculture. He was also an original member of the Edinburgh Poker Club,* a designation which may convey a wrong impression in these degenerate days. The Club derived its name from the fact that – as its members hoped – it was designed to be an instrument for stirring opinion by keeping the poker of agitation in active exercise. It is probable that these clubs played quite a peculiar part in the development of Adam Smith . . .

Perhaps there are less agreeable forms of education than that which consists of inbibing instruction along with chicken-broth.

Sir Alexander Gray, *Adam Smith* (1948)

'The Crochallan Fencibles'

A favourite house for the last years of the bygone century was *Douglas's*, in the Anchor Close, near the Cross, a good specimen of those profound retreats which have been spoken of as valued in the inverse ratio of the amount of daylight which visited them. You went a few yards down the dark narrow alley . . . you entered the hospitable mansion of Dawney Douglas, the scene of the daily and nightly orgies of the Pleydells and Fairfords, the Hays, Erskines, and Crosbies of the time of our fathers. Alas! How fallen off is now that temple of Momus and the Bacchanals!

The gentle Dawney had an old Gaelic song called Crochallan, which he occasionally sung to his customers. This led to the establishment of a club at his house, which,

* Editor's Note: The Poker Club eventually became the renowned 'New Club' in 1787

with a reference to the militia regiments then raising, was called the Crochallan Corps, or Crochallan Fencibles, and to which belonged, amongst other men of original character and talent, the well-known William Smellie . . . Smellie, while engaged professionally in printing the Edinburgh edition of the poems of Burns, introduced that genius to the Crochallans, when a scene of rough banter took place between him and certain privileged old hands, and the bard declared at the conclusion that he had 'never been so abominably thrashed in his life . . . '

He described Smellie as coming to Crochallan with his old cocked hat, grey surtoat, and beard rising in its might. The printing-office of this strange genius being at the bottom of the close, the transition from the correction of proofs to the roaring scenes at Crochallan must have been sufficiently easy for Burns.

Robert Chambers,
Traditions of Edinburgh (1825)

Rutherford's Bar

Last night as I lay under my blanket . . . all of a sudden I had a vision of Drummond Street. It came on me like a flash of lighting: I simply returned thither, and into the past. And when I remember all I hoped and feared as I pickled about Rutherford's in the rain and the east wing; how I feared I should make a mere shipwreck, and yet timidly hoped not; how I feared I should never have a friend, far less a wife, and yet passionately hoped I might; how I hoped (if I did not take to drink) I should possibly write one little book etc, etc. And then now – what a change! I feel somehow as if I should like the incident set

upon a brass plate at the corner of that dreary thoroughfare for all students to read, poor devils, when their hearts
are down.

Robert Louis Stevenson, *Letters of R. L. S* (1899)

The Caddies

The Cross [a handsome octagonal building in the High
Street surmounted by a pillar bearing the Scottish
Unicorn] was the peculiar citadel and rallying point of
a species of lazzaroni called *Caddies* or *Cawdies*, which
formerly existed in Edinburgh, employing themselves
chiefly as street-messengers and valets-de-place. A ragged,
half-blackguard-looking set they were, but allowed to be
amazingly acute and intelligent, and also faithful to any
duty intrusted to them. A stranger coming to reside
temporarily in Edinburgh, got a caddy attached to his
service to conduct him from one part of the town to
another, to run errands for him; in short to be wholly at
his bidding.

'Omnia novat,
　　Graeculus esuriens, in cælum, jusseris, ibit'

A caddy *did* literally know everything – of Edinburgh;
even to that kind of knowledge which we now expect only in
a street directory. And it was equally true that he could
hardly be asked to go anywhere, or upon any mission, that
he would not go. On the other hand, the stranger would
probably be astonished to find that, in a few hours, his
caddy was acquainted with every particular regarding himself, where he was from, what was his purpose in

Edinburgh, his family connections, and his own tastes and dispositions. Of course for every particle of scandal floating about Edinburgh, the caddy was a ready book of reference.

R. Chambers, *Traditions of Edinburgh* (1825)

The Fisherwives of Newhaven

One of the most picturesque sights upon the streets of Edinburgh in my young days was the fishwife of Newhaven. The women were a class entirely by themselves, retaining a garb not worn elsewhere and showing by their appearance that they were not of the race to whom they sold their fish. It was an appearance of which they had no cause to be ashamed. What racial stem they came from I know not, and leave it to the learned in folklore to inform the inquirer. But they were splendid specimens of humanity, clear-complexioned, bright-eyed, and while strong and vigorous, carrying heavy burdens, they were neat-handed, and their small feet, always in well-made shoes, might have been envied by many a lady of what are called the refined classes. Wearing red and white, or blue and white short striped petticoats, and dark blue panniered skirts with a bright handkerchief round the neck, the younger girls bareheaded, and the head covered in the case of the older women by a cap that seemed to indicate a relation with Normandy or Brittany, they were a most charming feature of life on the streets. Strong and healthy, they carried their 'creel' with its basin-shaped basket above it, and bore their heavy load by the strap crossing the forehead, walking two miles from the fishing station, and climbing many a stair to sell their fish, as the song says: 'New drawn frae the Forth.' 'Caller herrin' – 'Caller cod' were called sonorously during the forenoon, and 'Caller ow-oo' at night, when the oysters were offered for sale.

Sir John H. A. Macdonald,
Life Jottings of an Old Edinburgh Citizen (1915)

Stallholders

Among customs now abolished were the open stalls for vending sweetmeats and fruit in various parts of the town. One of the most famous of these was the stall of Sarah Sibbald at the foot of the North Bridge, at the corner of Shakespeare Square, where the Theatre Royal stood, both square and theatre being now swept away to make room for the General Post-Office, which occupies the site of the theatre and the whole area of what was the Square. Sarah was a well-known public character, and her vested interest in the site of her stall was so well recognised that at the time the alterations for the new Post-Office were begun, a site was provided for her close by, which she continued to occupy until her death . . .

Another character somewhat similar was Gundy Jock, who had a stall near the gate of St John's Episcopal Church, in the Lothian Road. His wares consisted of sweeties of the period, gundy, sugar bools, and 'parliament', a cake compounded of flour and treacle with coloured 'sweeties' known at the time as Glasgow jam, springled on the top. He was a tall raw-boned Highlander, and wore a conspicuous tartan cloak down to his heels in cold or wet weather. His parliament cakes, gingerbread, and gundy were very popular among the youths of the time.

J. B. Sutherland,
Random Recollections and Impressions (1903)

Not Catering for All

In 1587, Robert Vernour, skinner, having been admitted a Gild brother, became bound: 'to observe and keep the laws and consuetudes of burgh concerning the Gild brether hereof, and to desist and cease from all trade and occupation in his own person that is not comely and decent for the rank and honesty of a Gild brother; and that his wife and servants shall use and exercise no point of common cookery outwith his own home, and, namely, that they shall not sell nor carry meat dishes or courses through the town to private houses, hostilare houses, or any other parts outwith his own house under whatsoever colour or pretence, or pass to bridals nor banquets within or without this burgh to the occupation of common cookery, or yet to be seen in the streets with their aprons or serviettes as common cooks uses to do,' under pain of losing the freedom of the city and of the Gild brotherhood for ever.

J. D. Marwick, *Edinburgh Gilds and Crafts* quoted by
I. F. Grant, *The Social and Economic
Development of Scotland* (1971)

The Lamplighters

There were nearly sixty of them in Edinburgh, and they swarmed out of their crevices at dusk and swept through the city in a systematic raid on the streets, closes, wynds and parks. Beginning as always with the ornamental lamps outside the Lord Provost's home, they clambered quickly to the heights of Calton Hill, coursed down the gilded esplanade of Princes Street, curled through the courteous crescents of the New Town and sallied into the sooty recesses of the Old Town labyrinths, regulating themselves by the church bells and shirking only those darker tendrils of the Cowgate from which even the light recoiled. In less then two hours they knitted together a jewelled chain of lights that on clear evenings resembled an inverted cosmos of sparkling stars, and on nights of dense fog – when sea mist merged with chimney smoke, locomotive steam and noxious emissions from overcrowded graves – helped enclose the city in an enormous glowing lampshade. They were the 'leeries' – the lamplighters – and they were rarely seen in the sun.

Anthony O'Neill,
The Lamplighter (2003)

Some Lounging Shops of Old Edinburgh

The only great lounging bookshop in the New Town of Edinburgh is Mr Blackwood's. . . This shop is situated very near my hotel, so Mr Wastle carried me into it almost immediately after my arrival in Edinburgh; indeed, I asked him to do so, for the noise made even in London about the Chaldee MS., and some other things in the *Magazine*, had given me some curiosity to see the intrepid publisher of these things, and the possible scene of their concoction. Wastle has contributed a variety of poems, chiefly ludicrous, to the pages of the *New Miscellany*, so that he is of course a mighty favourite with the proprietor, and I could not have made my introduction under better auspices than his . . .

The length of vista presented to me on entering the shop has a very imposing effect, for it is carried back, room after room, through various gradations of light and shadow, till the eye cannot distinctly trace the outline of any object in the farthest distance. First there is, as usual, a spacious place set apart for retail business, and a numerous detachment of young clerks and apprentices, to whose management that important department of the concern is entrusted. Then you have an elegant oval saloon, lighted from the roof, where various groups of loungers and literary *dilettanti* are engaged in looking at, or criticising amongst themselves, the publications just arrived by that day's coach from London. In such critical colloquies the voice of the bookseller himself may ever and anon be heard mingling the broad and unadultered notes of its Auld Reekie music; for, unless occupied in the recesses of the premises with some other business, it is here he has his usual station. He is a nimble, active-looking man, of middle age, and moves about from one corner to another with great alacrity, and apparently under the influence of high animal spirits. His complexion is very sanguineous, but nothing can be more intelligent, keen, and sagacious than the expression of the whole physiognomy; above all, the grey eyes and eyebrows, as full of locomotion as those of Catalani. The remarks he makes are, in general, extremely acute – much more so, indeed then those of any other member of the trade I ever heard upon such topics. The shrewdness and decision of the man can, however, stand in need of no testimony beyond what his own conduct has afforded – above all, in the establishment of his Magazine (the conception of which, I am assured, was entirely his own), and the subsequent energy with which he has supported it through every variety of good and ill fortune.

J. G. Lockhart,
Peter's Letters to His Kinsfolk (1819)

Childhood shops

There wasn't nearly such a variety of toys and games in
the shops, though of course there was a blissful penny
drawer in the arcade where I sometimes went: this had
divisions each holding different penny toys: small wooden
dolls or animals, tops, marbles, puzzles, single lead soldiers.
That was the best place of all when it came to shops. But
in Prince's Street, which must have been then partly
unspoiled, there was Maule's at the corner by Charlotte
Square, where Binns is now, which had 'ballies', round
shells into which one's bill and money were put to whizz up
on to an overhead rail along which they trundled to a central
desk and then back. How deplorable if two purchases were
made at the same counter so that both went into one
'ballie'! Jenner's, however, had a lift. Duncan and Flockart
had blackcurrant jujubes which made a cold into a treat
and there was also the hairdresser where my mother,
before her time with short hair which indeed became her
well, had it brushed with a rotary machine.

Naomi Mitchison, *Small Talk* (1973)

Jenners

One hundred and thirty-two years ago what appeared to
be a major catastrophe happened in the lives of two
drapers assistants. Charles Jenner and Charles Kennington were dismissed by their Leith Street employers for
attending Musselburgh races during working hours. With
experience as their stake and faith on their side, they
embarked on a more serious gamble – they set up their

own drapery business at No. 47 Princes Street. The address has remained the same although the growth of the business has been spectacular and its success needs no eulogy.

The Royal warrant was awarded to Jenners by King George V in 1911 and again by the present Queen in 1954 for the supply of furnishing materials. After Kennington's death in 1863, Jenner continued to run the business until his retirement 18 years later.

In November 1892 occurred the great fire clearly visible from Fife when the entire shop was destroyed . . . business was transferred and reopened in the Rose Street factory within five weeks.

At the same time began the erection of the magnificent six storey neo-Baroque building which still houses much of the selling space and the administrative offices of the company.

Due to the growth of the business and the addition of new departments, Jenners has had to extend to almost double its size. However, the directors have resisted the temptation to modernise the original 1895 frontage to the detriment of one of Europe's finest streets.

It is a monument of civic dignity and grace.

The Edinburgh Tatler, November 1970

Childhood Streets

The sights and sounds and smells of Edinburgh crowded in upon my senses day after day and year after year. To this day I cannot hear the whirr of a lawnmower without being taken back at once to a summer afternoon in

Millerfield Place – how childhood memories seem to cluster around summer! – with Mr Fyfe (his son is now Lord Chancellor) at the bottom of the street cutting the grass in his front garden and the shouts of boys coming up from the Meadows; nor can I see lilac or laburnum without remembering those quiet Edinburgh streets between Marchmont and Blackford Hill where the heavy blossomed trees leaned over the stone garden walls and the air was hung with a scented quietness and it seemed as though the sun stood still in the sky and time was arrested forever; nor see a horse-drawn cart without hearing again the rattle of early morning milk-traps or the heavy clatter of vans drawing cases of Leitch's lemonade or Dunbar's mineral waters or sacks of coal along the uneven paving of Melville Terrace. A chalk mark in the street brings back the girls playing 'peevers' on the Edinburgh pavements, or skipping to their traditional chants, or counting out for some game in weird rhymes. And the traditional chanting of Hebrew prayers brings back the Meadows and Lauriston Place and the Vennel and the old synagogue in Graham Street (pulled down over twenty years ago) with its mixed congregation of Yiddish-speaking immigrants and native-born Edinburgh Jews with their strong Edinburgh accent even in the singing of Hebrew hymns.

David Daiches,
Two Worlds (1957)

In place of Shank's Pony

How did one get about the streets of Edinburgh a hundred
years ago . . . Usually one walked. The alternative to that
was to hire a sedan chair. What a delightful conveyance
that was! In the 'Sixties the distances were becoming too
great. The sedan chair's day was over. But even as late as
the 'Seventies some chairmen were still to be found fallen,
alas from their high estate.

The 'Forties saw the 'Noddy' and the 'Minibus'. Fearsome contraptions these! The 'Noddy' was not unlike the
hansom-cab, but decidedly more dangerous to life and
limb. Coming down a steep hill – and Edinburgh can
provide these in plenty – the chances were that you might
fly out on to the horse's neck. One stumble settled the
matter; you flew.

The 'Minibus' was also two-wheeled, square-shaped and
side-seated. Your luggage preceded you into the interior;
climbing a steep hill, it was up to you to keep it there. But
the moment of arrival was the test; as the driver went in
for the engaging practice of backing his 'Minibus' smartly
against the kerb, and delivering you like a load of coal,
your luggage a-top. These two inventions of the devil
made a deep impression on the Edinburgh mind. Hansoms
were looked on askance; it was 1878 before anyone had
the temerity to apply for a licence for them. The 'Growler',
on the other hand, was popular from the first. They were
one of the reasons why Princes Street had to be widened.
Drawn up in ranks, the horses' noses well out into the
middle of the road, they provided a fine entertainment for
the passers-by, racing each other to capture a fare, and
exchanging the customary abuse. Yes, four-wheelers were
alright; they might 'coup', to be sure, but it was that

backward or forward slide that Edinburgh folk had learned to know and to dread.

Mary G. Grierson,
A Hundred Years in Princes Street (1938)

The Tram Ride

Sometimes as a special treat my grandfather might take me on a tram ride to the Leith Docks to see the ships, for ships and sea voyages had already fired my imagination. I loved the Edinburgh trams, the yellow slatted wooden seats, the whine and rattle, as they gathered speed, the driver's low-pitched bell to shoo people out of the way. I was intrigued too by the exotic-sounding destinations which they and some of the corporation buses displayed: Portobello and Balerno, Ratho, Joppa and Bo'ness. Ours was the Granton tram which knew when it reached the North British Hotel to go left down the Leith Walk and not straight on to Portobello or right up the South Bridge – though just *how* it knew I never discovered. At the docks my grandfather would grease the palm of some loitering tar to show us round his vessel, and there I encountered for the first time the powerful, indefinable smell of ships, a blend of paint and polish and filtered air, ropes and fuel oil and the salty sea, for me a lifelong, psychological aphrodisiac. Here I would peer down alleyways and through scuttles, visit cabins and wireless rooms and galleys that spoke of worlds elsewhere. And when I had had my fill we took the tram home, stopping off at Alfresco's in the Leith Walk for a banana split or a knickerbocker glory.

Ludovic Kennedy, *On my way to the Club* (1989)

Victoria Day

One of the most exciting nights of our year was bonfire night. I think even the grown-ups quite enjoyed it. Most people associate bonfires with Guy Fawkes, but our biggest bonfire was in mid May, to celebrate Victoria Day. Two great advantages of this were that the weather was usually reasonable and I could regard the big night as a kind of celebration of my birthday, May 19th. All over Edinburgh the skies were aglow with fires blazing at crossroads and on any patch of waste ground.

There was so little traffic at that time that the police allowed us to spend days building up our mountain of junk in the roadway. We used to go round the doors collecting anything that would burn. We must have burnt many an old piece of furniture which today would fetch a good price in the trendy second-hand furniture shops.

On the night, the grey street would be transformed into a wonderland of sparks and shadows. Excited faces would reflect the red glow as catherine wheels whirred and rockets whooshed into the dark sky. Dogs yelped as bangers exploded and wood cracked loudly in the fire. Sometimes, if it was windy, sparks would be blown unexpectedly into an open window and the curtains would begin to smoulder. Then the climax of the night would be the noisy arrival of a fire-engine.

As the night wore on and the bonfire sagged into a flattened heap of embers, some of us would risk a scorching to bury potatoes in the ash. They were rarely properly cooked but that mixture of earth, charcoal and hard potato tasted magnificent. Eventually we would be called home with our hands and mouths blackened and our hair and clothes reeking like a kippery.

Howard Denton, The *Happy Land* (1991)

Hogmanay

When a citizen of Edinburgh says to another on the last day of the year, 'Are you going to the Tron to-night?' he is not inquiring about attendance at a religious service. The Tron is the focal point of Edinburgh's New Year celebrations. On the night of Hogmanay, the 31st of December, it is a public rendezvous and thousands gather on the streets outside. Why this should be is a matter of conjecture. The Tron is not old as age is understood in Auld Reekie. It was built quite recently, in 1647, and its most momentous experience was when the steeple collapsed during a great fire that swept away a large part of the High Street in 1824.

The Tron is equipped with four large clocks, one on each side of the steeple. It is probably this convenience that makes it a New Year meeting place. Further up the High Street is the Cathedral Church of St Giles, the most important of Edinburgh's historic churches, St Giles has no clock, but it has a chime, a well-known and soft cliché of bells at every quarter. It is unusual for a Presbyterian church to have a chime and this may partly explain why St Giles is regarded by sterner worshippers as regrettably 'high church' in its ritual. The fact remains that the capital's chief church, with its happy crown of Gothic stone, is neglected on Hogmanay. The grimmer Tron, without a chime, is a more fitting background for saturnalia.

Neil MacCallum, *It's an Old Scottish Custom* (1951)

Laundries

In the 1930s, few people in Morningside, or indeed Edinburgh, possessed electric washing machines. There were some of a mechanical, handle-turning type, heated underneath by a gas ring but there were certainly no spin dryers. During the weekly washing, shirt or blouse cuffs, collars, etc. were first rubbed with soap and water to remove excess soiling, using a ribbed scrubbing board. After washing, the clothes were then put through a hand wringer (the Acme type was popular) which was fixed onto the joint in the sink between the washing-up section and the deeper washing tub. After the excess water had been pressed out, my mother took the clothes down three flights of stairs to the back green where each household had its own clothes' ropes tied to heavy iron poles. There was some amicable, and sometimes less amicable, protocol involved. Monday was the commonest washing day, one traditional reason being that there was sufficient of Sunday's lunch left over to save cooking on washing day. However, on account of the drying green's limited capacity, not all housewives could do their washing on that day, which meant that a weekly schedule had to be agreed. Usually the person who had lived in the stair for the longest time got Monday. On whatever day was allocated, the ladies of the stair would go down early and hang out their ropes to book a place, occasionally creating mild friction if someone put up too much rope. At No. 3 Maxwell Street, and also in other stairs, there were cellar-type wash-houses with a tub and a boiler but I cannot recall these ever being used. Fitted to the ceiling in the kitchen-cum-living room of our house was a long pulley which our mother used either to air the clothes or to dry them when the weather was too wet to put them out in the back green.

An alternative, or addition, to the weekly wash was to use the bagwash services of St Cuthbert's Co-operative Society or other local laundries, many of which were in the Marchmont area. Braid Laundry had a leaving and collection service at No. 265 Morningside Road.

Charles J. Smith, *Looking Back* (2000)

A Wedding Custom

Further down, where the tenements were higher still, with those curious clotheshorses sticking out of the windows, a crowd had gathered about a taxi standing at a dark little doorway. It was a wedding, and I was just in time to see the pair drive off. There was a cheer, some confetti, heads poked out of a hundred windows, and then a shower of coppers from the taxicab . . . Never have I seen so many human beings – mostly boys and girls; it is true – in so small a space.

J. B. Priestley,
Sunday Despatch, 19 May 1929

Funereal Ways

The hearse was all black and the sides covered with pleated black cloth, and the roof had a huge black plume in the centre and one at each corner. The coffins were covered with black cloth, and were trimmed round the top, sides and ends with black enamelled embossed metal which the undertakers termed 'lace'; all the mountings were jet black, a depressing sight. The horses were handsomely caparisoned with silver-plated harness and there was a nodding black plume above each horse's head. The chief mourners had deep bands of crape on their silk hats with usually a great bow or hanger behind. They had white weepers from one to two inches wide stitched to the cuff of the coat. The weepers and hatbands were worn on Sundays for a month, or longer, after the funeral.

Walking funerals were quite usual in all classes of the community, and infantile mortality was then very high. The undertaker's man could, in the case of the funeral of an infant or young child, be seen striding along, wearing a top hat and a long black cloak, beneath the voluminous folds of which he carried the little coffin, and behind him walked the mourners.

No women attended funerals. In well-to-do families two funeral services were held, at the same time, for men in the dining-room, for women in the drawing-room – this required two ministers.

There was a prayer at the open grave – usually far too long, considering that all stood bare-headed, whatever the weather.

We stood till the earth was filled up to the surface, and the turfs laid thereon – this probably to avoid all risk of the gravediggers getting a chance to abstract the body.

The heathen folly of flowers had not yet appeared.

D. A. Small,
Through Memory's Window
(unpublished memoirs 1860–1927)

Communications

Some few facts relating to the city at this time throw a side-light upon the state in which society then existed. For example, on Thursday the 9th May 1734, it was announced in the *Caledonian Mercury* that 'a coach will set out towards the end of the week for London, or any place on the road, to be performed in nine days, or three days sooner than any other coach that travels, for which purpose eighty stout horses are stationed at proper distances.' Gentlemen and ladies are promised to be carried 'to their entire satisfaction'.

W. M. Gilbert (Ed.),
Edinburgh in the Nineteenth Century (1901)

Railways

The first passenger railway in or near Edinburgh, opened in 1831, was called the 'Innocent Railway'. The station was called St Leonard's, and it is still used as a Coal Depot. The railway was constructed principally for conveying coals from Dalhousie and Dalkeith to Edinburgh, but carried passengers also. The train consisted of a 'Dandy' coach, and sometimes behind it an open truck for the fishwives and their creels. There was only one set of charges, and it was left to the conductor to find suitable seats for the passengers. The start from St Leonard's was through a long tunnel which had a steep gradient, down which the 'train' ran by its own momentum. When it arrived at the foot of the tunnel near Samson's Ribs, it had a horse attached to it and started off. The driver had a boy as assistant, whose duty it was to attend to the points on the way. It was a very leisurely journey, the carriages stopped at any place to take up or set down passengers, and when the driver met a carriage coming in the opposite direction, he would stop so that the drivers might have a 'crack'. There was a branch line to Fisherrow. On the return journey the trains were drawn up, through the long tunnel by a rope winding on a drum in St Leonard's Station.

Until the late 'sixties, the North British Railway Station was just like a country station of the present day, with two lines of rails only. The Edinburgh and Glasgow Railway was opened in February 1842, but at that time the Edinburgh terminus was at Haymarket. When the railway was run through the gardens to the Waverley Station in 1847, the train emerged from what looked like a long, dark tunnel, the old Waverley Bridge.

The trains from London – in 1860 a 12 hours' journey – arrived opposite where Lindsay's Fruit Warehouse is, and the only carriage entrance was by Market Street, underneath a huge arch in a high wall, part of which may still be seen at the Suburban Station. There were three flights of stairs from the North Bridge leading down to the station. A stone stair where the Scotsman stair is; exactly opposite, a long wooden stair; near the Post Office, a short stair leading down to a paved walk where one could revel in the steam and smoke coming up from the railway engines and the fumes of chemicals from Duncan Flockhart's Stores, and a stair from Princes Street, now called the Waverley Steps.

D. A. Small,
Through Memory's Window
(unpublished memoirs 1860–1927)

Railways are not yet obsolete in their present form, but they are already obsolescent . . . It is sad that, under the exciting influence of what once upon a time seemed the last word in human transport, the railways were allowed to defile Edinburgh. However, the citizens at that time were bewitched by the novelty of them, and so the defilement was complacently accepted as the price that must be paid for progress.

Sir Compton Mackenzie,
Edinburgh Evening News, 26 October 1959

The Scotsman

It was while the Crimean War was in progress, during the years 1854–5, that papers were cheapened and were more widely in circulation. The duty on newspapers was reduced from 4*d*. to 1*d*. in 1836, and the duty on advertisements was abolished in 1853. These modifications gave the first impulse to an improved and larger issue; and when in 1855 the stamp on newspapers was totally abolished, there sprang up quite a crop of cheap papers all over the country . . .

The five leading newspapers of that day were *The Scotsman, The Edinburgh Advertiser, The Courant, The Caledonian Mercury*, and *The Witness*, each representing the political or ecclesiastical parties of the day. *The Courant* and *The Advertiser* were Tory and Established Church papers, while *The Witness* was an out-and-out Free Church paper . . . *The Edinburgh Advertiser* was an ably conducted paper of excellent literary qualities; but the Tory Party being weak in Scotland, it died from want of financial support. *The Caledonian Mercury*, which claimed to be the oldest newspaper in Scotland, was a Whig paper, but somewhat unstable in its principles. In its later days it was feeble, and its literary qualities indifferent, while it greatly lacked enterprise. It ceased to exist in 1867, though its name lingered in connection with *The Weekly Scotsman*, with which it merged, for a few years longer. *The Courant* continued to struggle on until 1886, when it, too, died in spite of great efforts and many monetary sacrifices on the part of its supporters to keep it going. Of the five papers I have named, *The Scotsman* alone survives and flourishes. The secret of its success is not difficult to discover. It has from first to last been under able management, and has been conducted with great enterprise under editors of the highest reputation. Above all, it has followed a plain consistent line of genuine liberal principles, and its steady adherence to a frank and straightforward policy in matters political, social, and ecclesiastical, combined with its excellent literary qualities, have secured for it the confidence of a very extensive section of the community, and insured for it a permanency of existence, while its contemporaries I have named have disappeared.

J. B. Sutherland,
Random Recollections and Impressions (1903)

In Adversity

~

The Christmas Phoenix

A new Edinburgh was gradually rising upon a black and white carpet of snow and cinder. From St David's Tower the ridge, with its black ruins dappling the white drift, looked not unlike a chessboard, or one of those tiled floors of which the monks down in the Abbey were so proud. Richard of England had indeed left the folk a bonny-like midden-mount where he had found a king's town. But they had buckled to the redding-up with a cheerful stolidity which had amazed their French allies, and already by the Yule half of the charred and trampled burrows-toun had been rebuilt – fine new timber houses, some of them with galleries, going up in the High Street and Lawnmercat.

It had been a struggle to re-edify St Giles by Cristhenmas, 1385. English Dick's soldiers had done their worst upon the thick whitewashed walls, and had fired the thatch. Edinburgh, almost habituated as she was to sudden raid, could not readily forgive the damage to her braw new kirk, over whose roof only five-and-twenty years had passed. But John of Gaunt had at least spared Holyrood. The Abbey had once given him shelter in banishment for a fortnight, and he would not do it scaith. He was e'en so neighbour-minded that he had actually halted his army outside the burgh to give the folk a chance to carry off the thatched roofs of their houses before he made entry with blazing torches.

That was, every decent man would admit, the spirit in which war should be waged.

Lewis Spence, *The Scotsman,* 23 December 1939

Eve of Flodden – 1513

Early they took Dun-Edin's road,
And I could trace each step they trode:
Hill, brook, nor dell, nor rock, nor stone,
Lies on the path to me unknown.
Much might it boast of storied lore;
But, passing such digression o'er,
Suffice it that the route was laid
Across the furzy hills of Braid.
They pass'd the glen and scanty rill,
And climb'd the opposing bank, until
They gain'd the top of Blackford Hill.

Blackford! on whose uncultured breast,
Among the broom, and thorn, and whin,
A truant-boy, I sought the nest,
Or listed, as I lay at rest,
While rose, on breezes thin,
The murmur of the city crowd,
And, from his steeple jangling loud,
Saint Giles's mingling din.
Now, from the summit to the plain,
Waves all the hill with yellow grain;
And o'er the landscape as I look,
Nought do I see unchanged remain,
Save the rude cliffs and chiming brook.
To me they make a heavy moan,
Of early friendships past and gone.

Sir Walter Scott, *Marmion* (1808)

Flodden

Forasmuch as there is a great rumour now lately risen within this town, touching our Sovereign Lord and his army, of which we understand there is come no verity as yet; wherefore we charge strictly and command in our said Sovereign Lord the King's name, and in that of the Presidents, for the Provosts and Baillies within the burgh, that all manner of persons, townsmen within the same, have ready their arms of defence and weapons for war, and appear therewith before the said Presidents at the tolling of the common bell, for the keeping and defence of the town against them that would invade the same. And we also charge that all women, and especially vagabonds, that they pass to their labours, and be not seen upon the streets clamouring and crying, upon the pains of banishing of their persons without favour, and that the other women of the better sort pass to the kirk and pray, when time requires, for our Sovereign Lord and his army, and the townsmen who are with the army: and that they hold them at their private labours if the streets within their houses as becometh.

Municipal Proclamation issued
on 10 September 1513

After Flodden

News of battle! – news of battle!
Hark! 'tis ringing down the street:
And the archways and the pavement
Bear the clang of hurrying feet.

News of battle! who hath brought it?
News of triumph? Who should bring
Tidings from our noble army,
Greetings from our gallant King?

. . .

The elders of the city
Have met within their hall –
The men whom good King James had charged
To watch the town and wall.
'Your hands are weak with age,' he said,
'Yours hearts are stout and true;
So bide ye in the Maiden Town,
While others fight for you.
My trumpet from the Border-side
Shall send a blast so clear,
That all who wait within the gate
That stirring sound may hear.
Or, if it be the will of Heaven
That back I never come,
And if, instead of Scottish shouts,
Ye hear the English drum, –
Then let the warning bells ring out,
Then gird you to the fray,
Then man the walls like burghers stout,
And fight while fight you may.
'Twere better that in fiery flame
The roofs should thunder down,
Than that the foot of foreign foe
Should trample in the town!'

W. E. Aytoun,
Lays of the Scottish Cavaliers (1849)

Another Sacking

1547 – Henry VIII put 10,000 soldiers on board his fleet, pretending to transport them to France; but the admiral, having private orders, lands them a little above Leith, which they plunder, and march to Edinburgh; sack and burn a great part of it; and for three days they ravish the country round the city; burn several noblemens' castles; return to Leith and set it on fire; embark, and with their spoils, sail for England.

Robert Stevenson,
Annals of Edinburgh (1839)

Mary's Reign

During the troubled years of Mary of Guise's regency and her daughter's reign, blood had flowed freely in the streets of Edinburgh. She had known sieges and want, and had learnt to live in momentary expectation of danger. When Kirkcaldy of Grange held the Castle for Queen Mary, and Lennox in the Canongate summoned a parliament in King James's name, things were not easy for the citizens. Cannon from the Calton Hill and the Pleasance battered them continually, and the gates were well closed and guarded. And even then their safety depended on the merest accident.

One morning, in the August of 1571, Thomas Barrie came down to the Netherbow as the grey light of dawn was stealing up the street. He had spent the night in the city, but now wished to return to his house in the Canongate. The busy citizens were just beginning to stir, and people were gathering outside the gate for the day's marketing in the town. Barrie passed out and sauntered down the road. Six millers were approaching, their horses laden with meal-bags, making for the Netherbow. Nothing odd in that; but as Barrie glanced this way and that, he saw the glint of armour in the shadow of the close-heads, and quickly turned back. The heavy gates of the Netherbow were shut fast and bolted, just as the six millers reached them, and the city was saved for a time. 'The eternall God', said an old diarist, 'knowing the cruell murther that wold have bene done and committit upoun innocent pover personis of the said burgh, wold not thole (permit) this enterpryse to tak success.' For the millers were six of Lennox's soldiers, with instructions to drop the meal-bags in the gateway as it opened to admit them, so that the army, hidden in the closes, might pass in and have the city at their mercy.

Flora Grierson, *Haunting Edinburgh* (1929)

The Murder of Rizzio

But I saw more to-night. The crouching man was as visible as the lady whose gown he clutched. He is a little swarthy fellow, with a black pointed beard. He has a loose gown of damask trimmed with fur. The prevailing tints of his dress are red. What a fright the fellow is in, to be sure! He cowers and shivers and glares back over his shoulder. There is a small knife in his other hand, but he is far too tremulous and cowed to use it. Fierce faces, bearded and dark, shape themselves out of the mist. There is one terrible creature, a skeleton of a man, with hollow cheeks and eyes sunk in his head. He also has a knife in his hand. On the right of the woman stands a tall man, very young with flaxen hair, his face sullen and dour. The beautiful woman looks up at him in appeal. So does the man on the ground. This youth seems to be the arbiter of their fate. The crouching man draws closer and hides himself in the woman's skirts. The tall youth bends and tries to drag her away from him. So much I saw last night before the mirror cleared. Shall I never know what it leads to and whence it comes? It is not a mere imagination, of that I am very sure. Somewhere, some time this scene has been acted, and this old mirror has reflected it. But when – where?

A. Conan Doyle,
'The Silver Mirror', *Strand Magazine* (August 1908)

∾

Lament of the Queen's Maries

'O ye mariners, mariners, mariners,
That sail upon the sea,
Let not my father nor mother to wit,
The death that I maun die!'

When she came to the Netherbow Port,
She laughed loud laughters three;
But when she cam' to the gallow's foot,
The tear blinded her e'e.

'Yestreen the Queen had four Maries,
The night she'll ha'e but three;
There was Marie Seton and Marie Beatoun
And Marie Carmichael, and me'.

Anonymous

Montrose

They brought him to the Watergate,
Hard bound with hempen span,
As though they held a lion there,
And not a fenceless man.
They set him high upon a cart –
The hangman rode below –
They drew his hands behind his back,
And bared his noble brow.
Then, as a hound is slipped from leash,
They cheered the common throng,
And blew the note with yell and shout,
And bade him pass along.

It would have made a brave man's heart
Grow sad and sick that day,
To watch the keen malignant eyes
Bent down on that array.
There stood the Whig west-country lords,
In balcony and bow;
There sat their gaunt and withered dames,
And their daughters all a-row.
And every open window
Was full as full might be
With black-robed Covenanting carles,
That goodly sport to see!

But when he came, though pale and wan,
He looked so great and high,
So noble was his manly front,
So calm his steadfast eye;–
The rabble rout forbore to shout,
And each man held his breath,

For well they knew the hero's soul
Was face to face with death.
And then a mournful shudder
Through all the people crept
And some that came to scoff at him
Now turned aside and wept.

W. E. Aytoun,
Lays of the Scottish Cavaliers (1849)

The Castle and Oliver Cromwell

It was the fourth day of September 1650, and in Edinburgh prevailed a panic such as had not been since the days of Flodden. Tidings had come of the disastrous fight at Dunbar, and with stupefied amazement the citizens heard of the total rout of the Scottish army on the preceding day at the hands of Cromwell. The news was hard to credit. All through the month of August, Cromwell and his army, from their headquarters at Musselburgh, had tried to enter Edinburgh, but in vain . . . the Scots had foiled every attempt he made, until, on 31st August, baffled and disappointed, the great English soldier had been obliged to give orders to retire to Dunbar, 'to be near our sole friends in this country, our ships.' Thither Leslie had followed him, and in Edinburgh news of a crowning victory was complacently awaited. And now in place of victory the citizens were told of a defeat more shameful and complete than any other ever sustained by Scottish troops. The Scots numbered twenty-two thousand, the English eleven thousand men; yet, 'after a hot dispute for about an hour' (as Cromwell writes), 'we routed their whole army; killed near three thousand, and took ten thousand prisoners,

211

their whole train of artillery being about thirty pieces, and
near two hundred colours. And I believe, though many of
ours be wounded, we lost but above *thirty* men!' Well has
Carlyle termed this battle 'Dunbar Drove'.

Edinburgh was now defenceless, and on the 7th September Cromwell and his victorious troops were in
possession of the city. The wounded were placed in Heriot's
Hospital, and the soldiers quartered mostly in Holyrood
Palace, while Cromwell himself found a lodging in the
Earl of Moray's house in the Canongate, from which centre
for the next seven months he directed the operations
throughout Scotland against King Charles II.

J. N. Ogilvie,
Castle Memories (1911)

The Forty-five

The hackney-coachman, who had his own residence and his
stables in the Canongate, was desirous to return to that
suburb through the Netherbow Port, which then closed the
head of the Canongate. The man was known to the waiters
or porters, as having been that night engaged in the
services of the magistrates, and, as a matter of course,
they opened the gate to let him go home. The leaves of
the gate had no sooner unfolded themselves, than the
Camerons rushed in, and secured and disarmed the few
watchmen. With the same ease they seized on the city
guardhouse, disarming such soldiers as they found there.
Colonel O'Sullivan despatched parties to the other military
posts and gates about the city, two of which were occupied
with the same ease and without a drop of blood being spilt.
The Camerons, in the dawn of morning, were marched up

to the Cross, when the Castle, now alarmed with the news of what had happened, fired a shot or two expressive of defiance. These warlike sounds waked such of the citizens of Edinburgh as the tumult of the Highlanders' entrance had not yet roused, and many with deep anxiety, and others with internal exultation, found that the capital was in the hands of the insurgents.

Sir Walter Scott,
Tales of a Grandfather (1828)

Prince Charles

About noon on this important day [the 17th of September], Charles Edward prepared to take possession of the palace and capital of his ancestors. It was at that time, when, winding his march round by the village of Duddingston, to avoid the fire of the Castle, he halted in the hollow between Arthur's Seat and Salisbury Crags. As Charles approached the palace by the eastern access, called the Duke's Walk, he called for his horse, as if to show himself to the populace, who assembled in great numbers, and with loud acclamations. The young Adventurer had begun his march on foot, but the immense crowd with which he was surrounded, many of whom pressed to touch his clothes, or kiss his hand, almost threw him down. He again mounted his charger as he approached the palace, having on his right the Duke of Perth, on his left Lord Elcho, the eldest son of the Earl of Wemyss, who had joined him a few days before, and followed by a concourse of chiefs and gentlemen. The personal appearance of the Chevalier was as prepossessing, as the daring character and romantic circumstances of his enterprise were calculated to excite the imagination. His noble mien, graceful manners, and ready courtesy, seemed to mark him no unworthy competitor for a crown. His dress was national. A short tartan coat, a blue bonnet with a white rose, and the order and emblem of the thistle, seemed all chosen to identify himself with the ancient nation he summoned to arms . . .

The possession of Edinburgh threw a gleam of splendour upon Charles Edward's fortunes, but can scarcely be said to have produced very important consequences. King James VIII was proclaimed at the Cross. At this ceremony the heralds and pursuivants were obliged to assist in their official dresses, and the magistrates in their robes. A great multitude attended on this occasion, and made the city ring with their acclamations. The gunners of the Castle were disposed to give a different turn to this mirth, by throwing a bomb, so calculated as to alight near the Cross, and interrupt the ceremonial. Fortunately this act of violence, which might have endangered the lives of many of King George's good subjects, whom mere curiosity had drawn to the spot, was prohibited by General Guest. At night there was a splendid ball at Holyrood, where might be seen a great display both of rank and beauty, the relatives of the gentlemen who were in arms.

Sir Walter Scott,
Tales of a Grandfather (1828)

The Call to Arms – 1914

For some months – until indeed conscription came – the recruiting tramcar was one of the features of our street life. The best meetings were usually held at Waterloo Place. But all over the city recruiting gatherings were held.

W. M'P.,
Edinburgh Evening News, 18 February 1939

Zeppelin at Midnight

On a sleepy Sunday back in 1916, the quiet around the port of Leith was shattered by a loud explosion – a bonded warehouse had been bombed and the blaze was already illuminating nearby Edinburgh . . . there was a Zeppelin abroad.

The date was April 2, the time, ten minutes to midnight.

A warning had been received as early as nine o'clock. Road and rail traffic had been halted, but many houses were still lit by gas and black-out precautions left much to be desired. The night, moreover, was calm and clear; the Capital was a sitting target, and unlike major English coastal towns, Edinburgh had no anti-aircraft defence – though a squad of willing riflemen were assembled on the Castle ramparts.

By 11.55 several more bombs had been dropped around Leith, causing substantial damage, but the airship was now moving towards the centre of Edinburgh.

Unbelievably, people was pouring out on to the streets so as not to miss the excitement.

At midnight, a bomb landed in East Claremont Street,

causing only slight damage, but countless windows were shattered by the blast and numerous bystanders injured by flying glass.

Shortly after midnight, a black cigar-shape was spotted over St Andrew Square. By now everyone could hear the soft, low-pitched whirr of the airship's engines.

At 12.05 the raider reached Lauriston Place, where it dropped at least one bomb together with a number of incendiaries. The back of the Royal Infirmary had a narrow escape from one bomb, but all its windows on the western side were shattered by another.

George Watson's College received a direct hit, wrecking the ground and first floors, and not far away, at No. 39 Lauriston Place, a Doctor McLaren had a rude awakening.

A bomb dropped through his ceiling and exploded in his pantry on the ground level, having passed through four storeys, narrowly missing his startled daughter.

Shortly after, McCallum's Bonded Store just off Nicolson Square was hit and went up in flames immediately – a sore loss. But in nearby Marshall Street, there was a much greater tragedy: a bomb dropped on the pavement directly outside a crowded close and killed five and wounded many more . . . Next on the list was St Leonard's, where two more died before the raider moved off towards Causewayside, Marchmont and then back north.

At around 12.20 the Castle came under attack, but the bomb-aimers were unlucky and the Grassmarket took the brunt. The White Hart and Gothenburg hotels on the north side were wrecked, while on the south side the Corn Exchange was extensively damaged. There was barely a window left unbroken in the entire area.

At 12.25 the airship moved off in a westerly direction, bombing first Lothian Road and then an area around the Water of Leith.

Then, just after 12.30, the attack ended – the raiders had run out of bombs.

Ten people, including three children, lay dead, 11 were seriously injured. Many more had cuts or concussion . . .

One month later, on the night of May 2, came a hurried message indicating that an airship had crossed the coast at Berwick and could be expected over Edinburgh within two hours. . . . This time the bombs were jettisoned harmlessly over agricultural land to the south. Edinburgh was denied its chance of revenge and the enemy never returned.

J. C. Alexander,
Edinburgh Evening News, 2 May 1987

War Memorial

England's national memorial, the Cenotaph, noble as it is, was the outcome of a chance. The first anniversary of Armistice Day fell to be commemorated. A solemn observance was ordained to take place in Whitehall. A focal point was needed. The Cenotaph was designed in an evening by Sir Edwin Lutyens and set up hurriedly in lath and plaster . . . A year passed and the Cenotaph arose again in stone.

The Shrine that crowns Edinburgh Castle is of another sort . . . So long ago as January, 1918, the Government indicated that Edinburgh Castle would not be needed for any large body of troops after the war. The War Cabinet was willing that the peak of this rock, round which Scottish life and history had surged for centuries, should be dedicated to the purposes of a War Memorial and ultimately develop into a treasure house for the national history of Scotland.

The old barracks which formed the north side of Crown Square were built in 1755. The south front was altered and the interior remodelled about 1870.

This block occupies nearly the same site as the Chapel of St Mary, founded by David the First, rebuilt by David the Second about the middle of the fourteenth century, and afterwards used as a magazine and armoury, until demolished to make way for the barracks. It is impossible that any part of the old chapel walls can be incorporated into the existing structure. The old stones were, however, utilised. In height and length this building corresponds roughly with the old chapel, and to this extent preserves the ancient outlines of the Castle, though the form is entirely different. But the retention of the old rubble walls is a very precious feature of the Memorial, for they were built of rude and noble stones richly various in their red and brown and golden hues.

Sir Lawrence Weaver,
The Scottish National War Memorial
at the Castle Edinburgh (1927)

∼

Edinburgh's Loss

In May 1915 . . . a train of recruits, mainly from Mussel-burgh and Leith, was involved in Britain's worst rail disaster at Quintinshill, Gretna Green, when on their way to the Front. No fewer than 214 of the total 227 death-toll were Royal Scots. Their remains were buried at Rosebank Cemetery, Pilrig, with full military honours, and their graves are marked by a pink sandstone cross of Celtic design . . .

The war diary of the 1st City of Edinburgh Battalion of the Royal Scots records 628 casualties in the first week of the Battle of the Somme in 1916, leaving virtually no Edinburgh men left in that unit.

Sandy Mullay,
The Edinburgh Encyclopedia (1996)

1939 – October 16th

We chatted idly for five minutes or so, during which there was not much to do except watch a number of Blenheims flying in and out of the clouds overhead as they made their way up the river towards Edinburgh. 'Hang on while I ring Ops to find out what's happening,' announced Douglas, sliding down the bank and disappearing into the Mess, only to re-emerge seconds later as if catapulted from a gun. 'For Christ's sake get a move on – these aren't Blenheims – they're ruddy Germans!

Belting over the Forth towards the bridge I suddenly experienced severe turbulence and noticed I was circled by numerous puffs of dark smoke and looking over the side saw it was coming from the aircraft carrier *Furious* which was clearly living up to her name and letting fly at me with everything she's got! From the amount of excited shouting going on in my earphones it was clear that the boys had got stuck into a real fight and I was anxious not to be left out of it. However by the time I had extricated myself from the unwelcome attentions of the Royal Navy and reached the Forth Bridge, the sky was empty except for one twin-engined aircraft I spotted climbing rapidly towards a bank of cloud to the east of Edinburgh. I managed a short burst at extreme range just as it was disappearing from view, praying inwardly it was not one of ours, as it still looked awfully like a Blenheim . . .

Now that the dust has settled it appears that an unknown number of Ju 88s was caught near the Forth Bridge and that bombs have been dropped. So far, three enemy aircraft have been accounted for . . . Certainly a Ju 88 and a Heinkel 111 were seen to crash into the sea and I have just heard that the pilot of one has been fished out and taken to the Naval Hospital at Rosyth. It seems we have been the first fighter squadron to go into action, although I hear 603 Squadron was also in the air at the time.

Air Vice-Marshal Sandy Johnstone,
Spitfire into War (1986)

∽

St Valery – 1940

What happened that fateful June in France to impose upon Scotland what seemed to be a tragedy that bore echoes of Flodden and caused grief in so many hearts and homes.

Ernest Reoch,
The St Valery Story (1965)

General Charles De Gaulle, the leader of the Free French Forces, was in Edinburgh yesterday . . .

'I felt at home five minutes after my arrival in Edinburgh,' the General said. He spoke at the City Chambers of the understanding and friendship which Frenchmen had always found in Scotland, and disclosed that the comradeship sealed on the battlefield of Abbeville in May-June 1940 between the French armoured division which he commanded and the 51st (Highland) Division played its part in the decision which he made to continue the fight by the side of the Allies. 'You know where stands the

real France, and you maintain confidence in her future . . .
If the roses of France are to-day bloodstained, yet they
crowd lovingly around the thistle of Scotland.'

The Scotsman, 24 June 1942

A Coup at the Left Luggage

Between 6 and 7 a.m. on the morning of the 30th
September 1940 two people entered the little railway
station of Buckpool near Buckie, Banffshire, and asked
for tickets for London. This early morning request, plus
the fact that their clothing appeared to be damp up to the
knees, aroused the suspicions of the porter . . . After
questioning, the inspector came to the conclusion that
they were in fact German agents.

Since such agents previously must have landed from the
sea, the aid of coastguards, wardens and others was enlisted
to search the beaches. At one point a pair of heavy working
men's boots was discovered and this gave someone the
impression that there might be a third suspect about.

[In Edinburgh] A comb-out of the city was ordered . . .
We made inquiries at Waverley Station, and all the porters
were questioned. While this was going on, two of my
officers searched the left-luggage office and came across a
case with a whitish irregular mark, from which they were
sharp enough to deduce the case had been standing in salt
water. . . . The case was opened, and inside was found a
wireless transmitting set of German manufacture.

Someone was going to come to collect the case – an
enemy agent might be armed and dangerous. I decided
that a porter would be least noticeable in the close vicinity
of the office and borrowing a porter's uniform I took on the

task myself . . . At about 9 p.m. a man in foreign type clothing came down the nearby steps from Princes Street, approached the left-luggage office, hesitated for a second or two, then strolled on some fifteen yards and stood at a corner of one of the kiosks, intently watching the left-luggage office. The suspect himself approached and handed the ticket and said 'Now please'.

The porter went to get the luggage, the suspect retreating with his back towards the paling and the kiosk, and standing with his left hand hidden in his trouser pocket, arm apparently rigid. Clearly he was armed. I sauntered up to him. As he watched me, I gestured with my hands as if to someone behind him – an old trick. When he half-turned to see who was there, I sprang forward and gripped his wrist. I can assure you it was no light grip. I wrenched, and his hand was jerked out of the pocket, grasping a Mauser automatic pistol, fully loaded. I hung on to him until my assistants arrived.

William Merrilees, *The Short Arm of the Law* (1966)

[Robert Petter was executed, after an Old Bailey trial on August 6th, 1941. The boots belonged to a local fisherman!]

The Score

In 1946 Edinburgh's Chief Constable reported that, in the six years of war, the city had experienced 105 air attack alerts, 15 of which proved to be genuine, bringing about the deaths of 20 citizens, with injuries to a further 210. Two land-mines, 47 high explosive bombs, and more than 600 incendiaries had rained down.

Sandy Mullay, *The Edinburgh Encyclopedia* (1996)

Another Scoreboard

Before the war a whole range of what were termed 'Vulnerable Points' had been identified. These VPs, as they were known, included Drem Airfield, Turnhouse Airfield, Drone Hill radar station and, for some reason, the East Manse at Linlithgow . . .

An enormous number of blockhouses were constructed to defend these and other locations. The fact that this was done with scant regard for the safety of road users is clear from a survey conducted by Edinburgh police in 1942. Many of them had the effect of creating blind corners on busy main roads, particularly hazardous in the blackout. One blockhouse in Colinton Road, outside Redford Barracks, was directly responsible for an accident which killed two and injured four. By the time of the police survey 155 accidents attributable to the presence of blockhouses had taken place in which 55 people had been injured. At least 40 such accidents had taken place at the corner of Lothian Road and Princes Street, injuring 17. Despite this, and with invasion not even a remote possibility, as late as 1943 the military were most reluctant to sanction the removal of many of these hazards. For some unspecified reason, early in 1944, the army sought permission to erect even more pillboxes in the city.

Andrew Jeffrey, *This Present Emergency* (1992)

The Home Guard

The birth of 1941 found the Company confined by bitter weather to indoor training at Morningside School. This, and the night guards at Company H.Q., comprised the sole material occupation of eager spirits during weekdays in that bleak period; but on Sundays – mostly in the afternoons in those days – the Company always paraded at Company H.Q. Snow and sleet were bad indeed if they prevented some sort of training or exercise on the Braids or in Trench Field. However, this period was almost wholly devoted to musketry, map-reading, bayonet-fighting, lectures and for the tougher souls, a little practice in unarmed combat under the guidance of C.S.M. Goodall who had lately returned from a course in this 'rough stuff'.

A Home Guard unit like 'C' Company, drawn as it was from a cross-section of a residential district of a large city, was naturally fortunate in the wealth of instructional talent at its disposal. Most of the Officers and N.C.O.s were qualified to instruct in musketry, drawing on the experience of 1914–1918, or Territorial service.

The Watch on the Braids (1946)

Jubilation in the Streets

In pleasing sunshine last night celebrations in the streets of Edinburgh were continued and showed no signs of having diminished in enthusiasm. As on the previous night Princes Street was the rendezvous of the general revelry, and presented a colourful scene with flags and bunting on the north side blowing and flapping in the breeze, and the green sward of the Gardens opposite alive with crowds and multi-coloured groups of people sprawling in the sun.

Around the bandstand an audience of several thousand listened to a relay of the Usher Hall service and joined in some of the singing.

As the evening advanced, Princes Street itself became more and more congested and the overflow surged into the Gardens, with the result that confusion reigned at some of the exits where hundreds were pressing their way in and out. At the floral clock a Canadian Army sergeant was responsible for a pedestrian jam – and he did not know it! He lay sound asleep among the shrubbery, and hundreds of people elbowed their way to have a glimpse at him.

When dusk fell, celebrations became noisier, and with the Gardens crowds rapidly thinning out, the Mound and Princes Street became more densely crowded. Squibs, whiz-bangs, and other rocket-like fireworks were brought into operation, and the 'bangs' which broke into the singing and dancing crowds went on until well after midnight.

Edinburgh Evening News, May 1945

AN EVEN DARKER SIDE – CRIME

They Rest in Grange:

'She was buried close to Lovers' Lane, says the doctor in his diary, and there she still lies. If you wander into Grange Cemetery and take the path to the left, you will see by the wall two little yew trees at the head of a grave marking the resting place of a Mrs Taylor and her daughter, Mary Jane, both of whom died within a month of each other in the year 1865 – the year when Lister discovered antiseptics. Round that grave centres one of the great murder trials of last century.

Had you in those days looked into the chemist's shop at 46 Clerk Street – which is still to-day a chemist's – you might have observed a little lady entering rather frequently as she walked into town from her house at No. 1 Lauder Road, where she and her husband, Michael Taylor, had recently moved from 22 Minto Street. She was ordering a drug known as Batley's solution, of which she took fairly large quantities.

In February 1865 her visits ceased for she went to Glasgow to look after her daughter Mary Jane who was married, outwardly very happily to a Dr Edward William Pritchard. Mrs Pritchard had, since autumn, been ill with stomach trouble, but was being well looked after by her doctor husband. Soon after her arrival at the Pritchard's Sauchiehall Street home, Mrs Taylor also took severely ill, and on 25th February she died. It was unfortunate, her son-in-law pointed out, that such a fine old lady should have visited the chemist so often to have her little bottle filled with an opium solution. Amidst many signs of sorrow she was brought back to her resting-place in the Grange.

Meanwhile her daughter showed no signs of improvement. While Dr Pritchard was seeing to Mrs Taylor's funeral in Edinburgh, another doctor saw her, and while he was inwardly convinced that she was being slowly poisoned he had no evidence which would allow him to interfere. On Saturday, 18th March, Mrs Pritchard also died and her death certificate was signed by her husband.

On Monday, Dr Pritchard again visited Edinburgh to make arrangements for her funeral, but while he was absent from Glasgow things had moved swiftly. As a result of an anonymous letter to the Fiscal, probably from the doctor who had had his suspicions, he was arrested at Queen Street Station as he stepped from the train.

At the trial it was discovered that Dr Pritchard's qualifications were very vague and doubtful. His purchases of poison were far above those of the ordinary doctor. On circumstantial evidence he was convicted in the High Court at Edinburgh, and before his execution he confessed fully to the deaths of the two ladies who lie 'close to Lovers' Lane'.

John Gray,
The Southside Story (1962)

Eugene Marie Chantrell

The grave can be easily found. It also lies in Grange Cemetery situated on the south walk on the right after going through the tunnel. Her name – Elizabeth Dyer, later Mrs Chantrell, has not been inscribed on the stone, but it contains names of the Dyer family.

Poor Elizabeth Dyer. Little did she think when she went as a young girl from her home at 5 Buccleuch Place to Newington Academy in Arniston Place (now 3 Newington Road) that she was to become the central figure in another of the murder sensations of the century. In 1867, while attending Newington Academy, Elizabeth Dyer became infatuated with a Frenchman named Eugene Marie Chantrell, who was one of her language teachers and had recently come to Edinburgh to seek his fortune.

Chantrell was born in Nantes in 1834. In his younger days he was a brilliant student, but left France and went to America. He became an outstanding success as a teacher and was the author of several French textbooks. He taught Latin, German and Greek. Handsome and elegant with a dark moustache, it is not surprising that his infatuated pupil was unable to resist his advances and the couple were married when Elizabeth was only sixteen. After the marriage Chantrell and his wife settled in a comfortable house at 81a George Street, but Mrs Chantrell was most unhappy. Chantrell treated her very badly and made her life a misery. He threatened her with pistols and often struck her.

In 1887 Chantrell insured his wife for £1000, which was a very large sum in those days. On New Year's day, 1878, Mrs Chantrell became very sick. The following morning the maid heard moans in the wife's bedroom and found her unconscious. She was immediately removed to the Royal Infirmary where she died. It was subsequently established that Mrs Chantrell had died from narcotic poisoning, possibly morphia. On 7th May, 1878, Chantrell was charged with murder and found guilty after a trial lasting 4 days. In spite of vigorous attempts by a number of well-known opponents of capital punishment to obtain a reprieve, Chantrell was subsequently executed in the Calton

Jail. This was the first execution carried out in the Calton Jail in private. All previous executions in Edinburgh had been carried out in public mainly at the Market Cross.

John Gray, *The Southside Story* (1962)

Dr Knox

In the early 1820s the great houses in Newington were being built and frequently in the evening the residents in Newington Place would hear sounds of music and merriment coming from No. 4 (now No. 17, Newington Road,) which for many years was the home of the celebrated Edinburgh anatomist, Dr Robert Knox. Dr Knox was a jovial host and his sister, Miss Mary Knox, was hostess to the numerous dinner and evening parties, at which her brother entertained the eminent personalities of the period.

On 12th February, 1829, however, there was no merriment in Newington. The streets were deserted and the windows shuttered. About a week earlier Burke had been publicly hanged in a vicious atmosphere before a crowd of 30,000. Burke, who had been engaged in the notorious trade of body snatching, had been convicted of a number of murders in the West Port with the intention of selling the corpses to the anatomists of Surgeons' Hall for dissection. Dr Knox, who was one of the greatest anatomists of his day, was suspected (quite wrongly) by the Edinburgh mob of complicity in the murders and for some days after the execution he was subjected to a series of unprovoked assaults by groups of hooligans.

On 12th February matters came to a head. Early in the day a mob assembled in the Calton and marched up the Bridges to Newington carrying an effigy of the Doctor which was hung by the neck from a tree in Newington with a bonfire lit below. The effigy was later torn in a thousand pieces by the frenzied crowd. In these days the houses in Newington Road had no shops in front and the garden of the Doctor's house and the adjacent street were packed with people screaming that the Doctor was a murderer.

Later in the evening the crowds reassembled in many parts of Edinburgh, and about 7 o'clock the mobs swarmed into Newington Place. This time the mob was in an ugly mood. The Doctor's house was attacked and a fusilade of stones smashed every pane of glass in the building.

The situation was now serious and Dr Knox knew that he endangered not only his own life but that of his friends by remaining in the house. Fortunately, his features were not well-known to the ordinary people of Edinburgh and with a military cloak concealing a sword, pistols and a highland dirk, Dr Knox left the house by the back door, slipping through the mob and thus safely reached the house of his friend, Dr Adams in St Patrick Square. Meanwhile the City Guard had arrived and the mob was dispersed, about 20 being apprehended.

Although this ended a day of rioting in Newington the scars left on the house by the stones can be seen to this day. A Committee of Investigation subsequently cleared Dr Knox from any suggestion of complicity with the murders but the Doctor never felt that his undoubted ability was fully recognised in Edinburgh and he spent the last 20 years of his life in London where he died in December, 1862. The house in Newington Road was sold by his sister in 1855.

John Gray, *The Southside Story* (1962)

Burke and Hare

> Up the close and doon the stair
> Ben the hoose wi' Burke and Hare,
> Burke's the butcher, Hare's the thief,
> Knox the boy who buys the beef.

Four scurrilous lines but an accurate enough summing up of the murders in the West Port of Edinburgh during 1827 and 1828. . . . The West Port Murders is the most famous murder case in Scottish legal history, and one which is still talked of in whispers . . . . For several generations children went in fear of them just as those of earlier generations had been terrified by the Black Douglas. To win perfect obedience Victorian mothers had only to threaten, 'Behave, or Burke and Hare will get you'.

Children adopted the legend themselves for one of their street rhymes. They would chant:

> Burke and Hare
> Fell doon the stair
> Wi' a body in a box
> Gaun to Doctor Knox.

Mary Docherty, indeed, went up the close, and down the stair into the house of Burke and Hare. Fifteen others preceded her – some of them well-known figures in the city and others poor creatures whose names were not known to their murderers and who were hardly even missed.

Hugh Douglas,
Burke and Hare – The True Story (1973)

Deacon Brodie

When two o'clock struck the excitement became intense . . .
Soon afterwards the great bell of St Giles began to toll
slowly and solemnly. Then a door on the platform opened,
and the executioner and his assistant appeared, and were
greeted with yells that seemed almost to shake the solid
foundations of the houses. But these yells suddenly died
away, and gave place to silence, as a clergyman stepped on
to the platform, and was immediately followed by Smith,
then Brodie, while warders and guards brought up the rear.

Brodie was dressed in a full suit of new black clothes of
fashionable make, and his hair was dressed and powdered.
Smith, who seemed half dead already, presented a striking
contrast to his fellow-prisoner. He was attired in the
habiliments of the grave – white shroud trimmed with
black. His face was ghastly, his eyes sunken and filled with
shrinking fear. Brodie, on his part, might have come to a
wedding instead of to his own execution. He was blithe
and merry, and, looking out over the vast sea of upturned
faces, he smiled and waved his hand. Then, turning to
Smith, he said:

'Cheer up, man! It's a leap in the dark, but what does it
matter?'

Smith groaned, and, glancing at the gibbet, he shuddered.

'Why, what a fellow you are!' cried the Deacon. 'We are
the chief actors in a grand tragedy, and look at the
magnificent audience we have got. Conduct yourself like a
man.'

But George's manhood left him; he was a pitiable object
of cringing dread.

In pursuance of the scheme formed by Degravers,
Brodie had succeeded in bribing Jock Ramsay, a chief

warder of the Tolbooth, to approach the executioner with a view to getting the rope shortened.

Brodie had been informed by Ramsay that the executioner had been duly feed, and as he glanced at the rope intended for himself, it seemed to him too long, and he whispered to the hangman, 'Can't you shorten it?'

This the man undertook to do, and it led to considerable delay. . . . At last all was ready. Then Brodie clapped the trembling Smith on the back, saying with a loud guffaw:

'Now, George Smith, you are the first in hand.'

Brodie saw that the fall he would have would be exceedingly short, while the drop that Smith would get would certainly dislocate his neck . . . The ropes were then adjusted, and the two criminals were swung off into space . . . Not more than fifteen minutes elapsed before Brodie's body was cut down and delivered up to two of his own workmen, who were waiting.

Dick Donovan,
Behind the Mask (1901)

Captain Porteous

When the painful procession was completed, and Wilson, with the escort, had arrived at the scaffold in the Grassmarket, there appeared no signs of that attempt to rescue him which had occasioned such precautions . . . But there was no attempt at violence. Wilson himself seemed disposed to hasten over the space that divided time from eternity. The devotions proper and usual on such occasions were no sooner finished than he submitted to his fate, and the sentence of the law was fulfilled.

He had been suspended on the gibbet so long as to be

totally deprived of life, when at once, as if occasioned by some newly-received impulse, there arose a tumult among the multitude. Many stones were thrown at Porteous and his guards; some mischief was done; and the mob continued to press forward with whoops, shrieks, howls, and exclamations. A young fellow, with a sailor's cap slouched over his face, sprung on the scaffold, and cut the rope by which the criminal was suspended. Others approached to carry off the body, either to secure it for a decent grave, or to try, perhaps, some means of resuscitation. Captain Porteous was wrought by this appearance of insurrection against his authority into a rage so headlong as made him forget, that, the sentence having been executed, it was his duty not to engage in hostilities with the misguided multitude, but to draw off his men as fast as possible. He sprung from the scaffold, snatched a musket from one of his soldiers, commanded the party to give fire, and, as several eye-witnesses concurred in swearing, set them an example by discharging his piece, and shooting a man dead on the spot. Several soldiers obeyed his command or followed his example; six or seven persons were slain, and a great many more hurt and wounded.

Sir Walter Scott, *Heart of Midlothian* (1818)

Captain John Porteous

Edinburgh, July 20, 1736
The above assize having inclosed, did choice Sir John Inglis of Cramond to be their Chancellor, and James Davidson, bookseller in Edinburgh, to be their clerk; and having considered the indictment at the instance of Duncan Forbes of Culloden, Esq. his Majesty's Advocate

for his Highness's interest, against John Porteous, late one of the Captain-Lieutenauts of the City Guard of Edinburgh, pannel, with the Lord Justice-Clerk and Lords Commissioners of Justiciary their interlocutor thereupon, and depositions of the witnesses adduced for proving thereof, the pannel's own judicial confession, and depositions of the witnesses adduced for the said John Porteous, pannel, his exculpation, they all in one voice found it proven, that the said John Porteous, pannel, fired a gun among the people assembled at the place of execution, and time libelled; as also, that he gave orders to the soldiers under his command to fire; and upon his and their so firing, the persons mentioned in the indictment were killed and wounded; and found it proven, that the pannel and his guard were attacked and beat by several stones of a considerable bigness, thrown amongst them by the multitude, whereby several of the soldiers were bruised and wounded. In witness whereof, our said Chancellor and Clerk, in our name, have subscribed these presents, day and place foresaid. *Sic subscribitur*

Jo. Inglis, Chancellor.
James Davidson, Clerk.

The Lord Justice Clerk and Lords Commissioners of Justiciary, having considered the verdict of assize returned against John Porteous, pannel, of this date, they, in respect thereof, by the mouth of John Dalgleish, dempster of Court, decerned and adjudged the said John Porteous to be taken from the Tolbooth of Edinburgh, upon Wednesday the eighth day of September next to come, to the Grass-market of Edinburgh, the common place of execution of the said burgh, betwixt the hours of two and four of the clock of the afternoon of the said day, and there to be hanged by the neck upon a gibbet, by the hands of the executioner, until he be dead; and ordained all his moveable goods and gear to be escheat and be inbrought to his Majesty's use, which was pronounced for doom. *Sic subscribitur,*

And. Fletcher.
Ja. Mackenzie.
Da. Erskine.
Wa. Pringle.
Gilb. Elliot.

Criminal Trials (Companion Volume) Edinburgh (1818)

The Gallows

In former times, England had her Tyburn to which the devoted victims of justice were conducted in solemn procession up what is now called Oxford Road. In Edinburgh, a large open street, or rather oblong square, surrounded by high houses, called the Grassmarket, was used for the same melancholy purpose. It was not ill chosen for such a scene, being of considerable extent, and therefore fit to accommodate a great number of spectators, such as are usually assembled by this melancholy spectacle. On the other hand, few of the houses which surrounded it were, even in early times, inhabited by persons of fashion; so that those likely to be offended or over deeply affected by such unpleasant exhibitions were not in the way of having their quiet disturbed by them . . .

It was the custom, until within these thirty years (1818) or thereabouts, to use this esplanade for the scene of public execution. The fatal day was announced to the public, by the appearance of a huge black gallows-tree towards the eastern end of the Grassmarket. This ill-omened apparition was of great height, with a scaffold surrounding it, and a double ladder placed against it for the ascent of the unhappy criminal and the executioner. As this apparatus was always arranged before dawn, it seemed as if the gallows had grown out of the earth in the course of the night, like the product of some foul demon; and I well remember the fright with which the schoolboys, when I was one of their number, used to regard these ominous signs of deadly preparation.

On the night after the execution, the gallows again disappeared, and was conveyed in silence and darkness to the place where it was usually deposited, which was one of the vaults under the Parliament House, or Courts of Justice. This mode of execution is now exchanged for one similar to that in front of Newgate,– with what beneficial effect is uncertain. The mental sufferings of the convict are indeed shortened. He no longer stalks between the attendant clergy, dressed in his grave clothes, through a considerable part of the city, looking like a moving and walking corpse, while yet an inhabitant of this world; but, as the ultimate purpose of punishment has in view the prevention of crimes, it may at least be doubted whether, in abridging the melancholy ceremony, we have not in part diminished that appalling effect upon the spectators which is the useful end of all such inflictions, and in consideration of which alone, unless in very particular cases, capital sentences can be altogether justified.

Sir Walter Scott, *The Heart of Midlothian* (1818)

Reviving a hanged man

13th September 1766:
At Glasgow, obtained first criminal client – John Reid – accused of being by 'habit and repute' a common thief and of having stolen one hundred and twenty sheep from a farm in Peeblesshire. This offence, if proved, as a capital offence. Trial on 15th December. Verdict one of 'not proven' which result met with the severe disapproval of the judges who each stated that the verdict was contrary to clear evidence.

15th July 1774:
I went in the afternoon to the prison and conferred with my old client John Reid (again charged with sheep-stealing.)

1st September, 1774:
Mr Hay and I went for a walk to Heriot's Garden, and I dined with him. He had Dr Monro and several more company with him, and it was concerted that we should get information from the Anatomical Professor as to the recovering a hanged person, which would be useful to Reid. Harry Erskine was there and talked so much that it was long before we could get Dr Monro set upon the subject. He said in his opinion a man who is hanged suffers a great deal; that he is not at once stupefied by the shock, suffocation being a thing must be gradual and cannot be forced on instantaneously; so that a man is suffocated by hanging in a rope just as by having his respiration stopped by having a pillow pressed on the face, in Othello's way, or by stopping the mouth and nostrils, which one may try; and he said that for some time after a man is thrown over he is sensible and is conscious that he is *hanging*; but that in three minutes or so he is stupefied.

He said that it was more difficult to recover a hanged person than a drowned, because hanging forces the blood up to the brain with more violence, there being a local compression at the neck; but that he thought the thing might be done by heat and rubbing to put the blood in motion, and by blowing air into the lungs; and he said the best way was to cut a hole in the throat, in the trachea, and introduce a pipe. I laid up all this for service in case it should be necessary. He told me that ten or twelve of his students had, unknown to him, tried to recover my clients Brown and Wilson, but had only blown with their own breaths into the mouths of the *subjects*, which was not sufficient.

Hugh M. Milne,
Boswell's Edinburgh Journals 1767–86.

The Last Hanging

As you walk on the south side of the Royal Mile, close to the junction with George IV Bridge, and directly facing the former Sheriff Court, glance at the edge of the pavement and there you will see three brass blocks in the shape of an 'H'.

At one time there was a plaque on the adjacent wall explaining their significance, but it was removed some years ago and never replaced. In fact this 'H' marks the spot, then at the head of Liberton's (or Libberton's) Wynd, where on 21 June 1864, George Bryce of Ratho was hanged for the murder of a young nursemaid. It was the last public hanging in Edinburgh.

James U. Thomson,
Edinburgh Curiosities (1996)

Donald Merrett

'We are getting on quite well, and like Edinburgh in spite of the really appalling climate,' wrote Mrs Merrett on 26th February, to her banker at Boscombe, 'and Donald has taken to life at the 'Varsity.' And again, on 4th March, 'Donald is doing well at the University, and is quite settled down to the life here.'

The flat at 31 Buckingham Terrace was in one of those modern reconditioned houses which have suffered the fate gradually overtaking the West End mansions of Edinburgh in being, like Cæsar's Gaul, divided into three parts. It occupied the first flat above the street . . . There was no accommodation for servants, so Mrs Merrett had to employ a daily maid. The person appointed to the office was a Mrs Henrietta Sutherland.

On the morning of Wednesday, the 17th, Mrs Sutherland was twice in the sitting-room and on the last occasion she left Mrs Merrett seated at the table writing, with the open bureau behind her on the right. Merrett was then sitting in the recess on the other side of the room reading a book. The time was about 9.40. She got a pailful of coals from the cellar in the hall, and went into the kitchen to make up the fire. Just as she was bending down to the grate she heard a shot, followed immediately by a scream and the thud of a falling body. Some seconds later she heard Merrett coming towards the kitchen and a sound of books falling in the hall. On reaching the kitchen, he said, 'Rita, my mother has shot herself.'

'She seemed quite all right this morning,' said the maid; to which he replied that he had been wasting his mother's money and she had 'quarrelled' him about it; he thought she was worried over that.

240

In the Infirmary Mrs Merrett had recovered consciousness. Mrs Merrett asked Sister Grant, who was attending her, 'What has happened? Why am I here?' – it was so extraordinary; she could not understand it. The sister answered that she didn't know; could not Mr Merrett tell her? She said 'She was sitting writing at the time, when suddenly a bang went off in her head like a pistol.' 'Was there not a pistol there?' asked the sister; upon which the patient, in great surprise, exclaimed, 'No; was there?' Asked further whether she was certain she was writing when this occurred, Mrs Merrett answered, 'Yes; quite sure. Donald can tell you; he was standing beside me, waiting to post the letter.'

Nine months were to elapse before anything definite was done to cast a doubt upon the question of Mrs Merrett's suicide. On 27th November there was presented to the Sheriff of the Lothians and Peebles a petition setting forth 1) that John Donald Merrett had murdered his mother, and 2) that he had 'uttered as genuine' – presented for payment – 29 cheques upon her bank account . . .

On Tuesday, 1st February, the trial began. The jury returned their verdict on the first charge, murder, by a majority, Not Proven; [The vote, according to information supplied to the author was 5 for Guilty and 10 for Not Proven. So no single member of this jury of fifteen saw his or her way to find the pannel Not Guilty.] on the second charge he was found guilty and sentenced to twelve months' imprisonment.

William Roughead,
Notable British Trials – John Donald Merrett (1929)

Cologne, Tuesday. – A man identified by German police as John Ronald Chesney was found shot dead in a secluded wood near here today.

Chesney was the husband of Mrs Isobel Veronica Chesney, who with the mother, self-styled 'Lady' Mary Menzies, was found dead in the gloomy old Victorian mansion in Montpelier Road, Ealing last week.

The description of the man the Yard wished to interview gave three names by which he had been known, Ronald Chesney, John Donald Milner, and John Donald Merrett.

Investigations established that Mrs Chesney had been forcibly drowned in her bath. Lady Menzies had been strangled.

The Scotsman, February 1954

Jean Brash

One of the most successful artists of the tender sex that ever appeared in Edinburgh was the well-known Jean Brash. I knew her very well, but, strange as it may appear, her ladyship always contrived to keep out of my hands. The house she occupied in St James's Square was a 'bank of exchange', regularly fitted up for business. In the corner of a door-panel of every bedroom, there was a small hole neatly closed up with a wooden button, so as to escape detection. Then the lower panels were made to slide, so that while through the peephole she could see when the light was extinguished, she could by the opened panel creep noiselessly in on all fours and take the watch off the side-table or rifle the pockets of the luckless wight's dress. She made occasionally great catches, having once 'done' £400; but she was at length 'done' by the paltry sum of 7s. 6d. I have heard that she is still alive in Australia, and married, perhaps driving, like a pastoral Arcadian, 'the yowes to the knowes'.

James M'Levy, *The Sliding Scale of Life* (1861)

The Douglas Cause

It was not only in criminal cases that the people of Edinburgh were wont to take such vehement interest as led to disorder.

No civil suit has ever caused such fiery excitement in the capital, or, indeed, in Scotland generally, as what became known as 'the Douglas Cause'. Lady Jane Douglas, daughter of the second Marquess of Douglas, became betrothed to the Earl of Dalkeith, afterwards second Duke of Buccleuch; but the match was broken off through the intrigues of the Duchess of Queensberry. Thereafter Lady Jane lived for many years at Drumsheugh House, on the outskirts of Edinburgh, until 1746, when, being forty-eight years of age, she secretly married Colonel, afterwards Sir John, Stewart, a former lover with whom she had parted ten years previously owing to a misunder-standing. Stewart being practically a penniless soldier, Lady Jane concealed her marriage, fearing lest her brother, third Marquess and the first Duke of Douglas, with whom she was on bad terms, should stop her allowance. She quitted Scotland with her husband, and they travelled on the Continent as Mr and Mrs Gray. In 1748, being then in her fiftieth year, she gave birth to twin boys in Paris, and wrote to her brother, the duke, of the fact. He refused to believe her, stopped her allowance and, when she returned to London, declined to receive her. In 1752 Lady Jane brought her children to Edinburgh, where one of the boys died, and she herself died in the following year. Meanwhile the Duchess of Douglas had been exerting all her influence over the duke to persuade him to sift the case of his sister to the bottom. She succeeded; the duke became convinced that his surviving nephew, Archibald, was his sister's legitimate son, revoked the existing entail of his great estates and settled them upon him. On the duke's death in 1761, Archibald was at once served heir to the estates, in spite of the opposition of the heir male, the Duke of Hamilton, upon whom the inheritance would have devolved could Archibald have been proved to be, as was alleged, the child of a French woman fraudulently represented as Lady Jane's.

Next, the Duke of Hamilton raised an action in the Court of Session to prove his claim. The trial began in 1762 and ended in 1767, by the fourteen judges being equally divided in opinion, Lord President Dundas giving the casting vote against Archibald Douglas. People of all classes in Edinburgh had hotly espoused the Douglas cause; before the close of the trial the Duke of Hamilton's family had to leave the city, so great was the uproar, and the apartments which he occupied in Holyroodhouse as Hereditary Keeper of the Palace were broken into and plundered by the mob. Douglas's guardians then appealed to the House of Lords, where, after eighteen months further litigation, the judgment of the Court of Session was reversed, Archibald Douglas being declared to be the son of Lady Jane Stewart and rightful heir to the Douglas estates. When tidings of the reversal reached Edinburgh, there was a renewal of rioting. It is said that James Boswell, the obsequious biographer of Samuel Johnson, being a perfervid partisan of Douglas, headed the mob that broke the windows of his father, Lord Auchinleck, who had cast his vote for Hamilton.

The Rt. Hon. Sir Herbert Maxwell,
Edinburgh: A Historical Study (1916)

And Joy

~

PASTIMES

So-called Sport

In 1763 – There was no such diversion as public cock-fighting in Edinburgh.

In 1783 – There were many public cockfighting matches, or *mains*, as they are technically termed; – and a regular cockpit was built for the accommodation of this school of gambling and cruelty, where every distinction of rank and character is levelled.

In 1790 – The cockpit continued to be frequented.

Sir John Sinclair,
The Statistical Account of Scotland (1791)

Dancing

The dancing assemblies of Edinburgh were for many years, about the middle of the last century, under the direction and dictatorship of the Honourable Miss Nicky Murray, one of the sisters of the Earl of Mansfield. Much good sense, firmness, knowledge of the world and of the histories of individuals, as well as a due share of patience and benevolence, were required for this office of unrecognised though real power; and it was generally admitted that Miss Murray possessed the needful qualifications in a remarkable degree, though rather more marked by good-manners than good nature. . . .

The Assembly Room of that time was in the *close*, where

the Commercial Bank was afterwards established. First there was a lobby, where chairs were disburdened of their company. . . . The dancing-room opened directly from the lobby, and above stairs was a tearoom. The former had a railed space in the centre, within which the dancers were arranged, while the spectators sat round on the outside; and no communication was allowed between the different sides of this sacred pale. The lady-directress had a high chair at one end. . . . The arrangements were of a rigid character, and certainly tending to dullness. There being but one set allowed to dance at a time, it was seldom that any one person was twice on the floor in one night. The most of the time was spent in acting the part of lookers-on; which threw great duties in the way of conversation upon the gentlemen. These had to settle with a partner for the year, and were upon no account permitted to change, even for a single night.

Robert Chambers,
Traditions of Edinburgh (1825)

St Cecilia's Hall was the only public resort of the musical, and besides being our most selectly fashionable place of amusement, was the best and most beautiful concert-room I have ever seen. And there have I myself seen most of our literary and fashionable gentlemen, predominating with their side curls, and frills, and ruffles, and silver buckles; and our stately matrons stiffened in hoops and gorgeous satin; and our beauties with high-heeled shoes, powdered and pomatumed hair, and lofty and composite head-dresses.

All this was in the Cowgate! the last retreat nowadays of destitution and disease. The building still stands, though raised and changed, and is looked down upon from the South Bridge, over the eastern side of the Cowgate Arch. When I last saw it, it seemed to be partly an old clothesman's shop and partly a brazier's.

Lord Cockburn,
Memorials of his Time (1856)

Beaus and Belles

Then the Assembly Close received the fair –
Order and elegance presided there–
Each gay Right Honourable had her place,
To walk a minuet with becoming grace.
No racing to the dance, with rival hurry –
Such was thy sway, O famed Miss Nicky Murray!
Each lady's fan a chosen Damon bore,
With care selected many a day before;
For, unprovided with a favouite beau,
The nymph, chagrined, the ball must needs forgo
But previous matters to her taste arranged,
Certes, the constant couple never changed;
Through a long night, to watch fair Delia's will,
The same dull swain was at her elbow still.

Sir Alexander Boswell,
Edinburgh or the Ancient Royalty (1810)

The Plaza

Ballroom dancing has undergone a complete metamorphosis during the last fifty years. When the bulldozers moved in to demolish the Plaza Ballroom, Edinburgh lost a building that spanned half a century of changing fashions in entertainment.

The Plaza opened its doors as a palais de dance in 1926 and for many years it was one of the most popular centres in Edinburgh for dinner parties, private functions, wedding receptions and public dances.

It stood on the corner of Morningside Road and Falcon Avenue and it was the brainchild of Mr Charles Jones who started in the motor business in Peebles. He had sold his Peebles garage and moved to Lothian Road in Edinburgh in the early 1920s and as the business expanded he looked around for a new site in the city. He found the ideal spot in Morningside and prepared plans for a brand new motor showroom to be named, quaintly, 'Jones Motor House' . . .

In 1926 Mr Jones had strong competition: the *Evening News* in September carried adverts for about a dozen established dance halls including The Palais, Maxine's and the Marine Gardens. There were also nineteen cinemas, five live theatres and several skating rinks. To break into such a crowded market the Plaza would have to be good.

Elizabeth Gasciani, *The Scots Magazine*

GOLF

Bruntsfield Links

Amongst others, I was shown one particular set of golfers, the youngest of whom was turned four score. They were all gentlemen of independent fortunes, who had amused themselves with this pastime for the best part of a century, without having ever felt the least alarm from sickness or disgust, and they never went to bed without having each the best part of a gallon of claret. Such uninterrupted exercise, co-operating with the keen air from the sea, must without all doubt, keep the appetite always on edge, and steel the constitution against all the common attacks of distemper.

Tobias Smollett,
The Expedition of Humphrey Clinker (1771)

The Golf Tavern

The 'Golf Tavern' among the quaint old buildings of Wrights' Houses on Bruntsfield Links continues to draw patrons from the short-hole course, thus carrying on its long connection with the game . . . The 'great house' [erected by James Brownhill] immediately became a meeting-place for the Royal Burgess Golfing Society, its tavern function being proved by a clause in the lease of 1717 which exempted this 'Golfhall' from paying duty on foreign wines.

251

The members remained 'thirled' to this clubhouse from 1792 till 1877, with a break of three years owing to a quarrel with the landlady, who took umbrage on suspecting that they had transferred their patronage elsewhere when in reality they had been kept away by the severe winter. To escape her wrath it was necessary to remove to the east end of the Links where Anthony Gorrie's became the 'Golf-house Tavern' and play had to begin from this new quarter. Neither party in the dispute could have been happy, especially the deserted landlady who had to watch her whilom patrons playing past her windows, so eventually peace was made and the club returned to its true home in April 1830.

Marie W. Stuart,
Old Edinburgh Taverns (1952)

FOOTBALL

Heart of Midlothian Football Club

Many people think of the 'Jam Tarts' as having been at Tynecastle from time immemorial, but, in fact, that is not the case. The Hearts were founded in 1874 by a group of young footballers, whose other Saturday passion was attending the Heart of Midlothian dance hall. The hall was in Washing Green Court (later known as Holyrood Square) off the South Back of the Canongate, near the present-day high-rise flats in Dumbiedykes Road. The dance hall took its name from the Heart of Midlothian (the old Tolbooth of Edinburgh) beside St Giles Cathedral, and the football club is said to have taken its name (with the hyphen in the word Mid-lothian) from the dance hall. In establishing their own football club, the lads were greatly influenced by watching an exhibition match at Bonnington between Queen's Park Football Club and Clydesdale Football Club in December 1873. The match was played by Association Football rules which the new Heart of Midlothian Football Club adopted in 1874. When the club was first established it had no ground of its own, but used the Meadows along with several other clubs, including its arch-rival, Hibernian . . .

After securing their own ground, first at Powburn (where they beat Hibs!)and then Powderhall, Hearts made the big move to Gorgie in February 1881. The first ground, built on the site of the present-day Wardlaw Street and Place, was opened on 9th April 1881. Hearts did not remain at 'old' Tynecastle Park for long, the last match being on 27th

February 1886. New Tynecastle, on the north side of Gorgie Road, was opened on 10th April 1886 when Hearts beat Bolton Wanderers 4–1, cheered by a crowd of 5,500 fans.

Malcolm Cant, *Gorgie and Dalry* (1995)

Tynecastle

I never get doun tae Tynecastle thae days
It's a guid lang while nou sen I've been
I never get doun tae Tynecastle thae days
– tho they're sayin they hae a guid team
　　But the team that I mind
　　is the team o langsyne
when we swept aa the prizes awa
　　an the boys in maroon
　　were the pride o the toun
the best lads that e'er kicked a baw!
　　I'm thinking o Parker an Broun an Big Tam . . .
Aw, the thousands that cheered them aa on!
An my thochts haud them yet
　　For I'll never forget
　　　　My Bauld
　　　　　An My Wardhaugh
　　　　　An My Conn.

Donald Campbell, *Rhymes 'n Reasons* (1972)

Tommy Walker – Footballer

From Tynecastle to Hampden Park, from Pittodrie
                            to Wembley,
Our 'Tommy' is a hero; for all know at each assembly
That when 'Tommy Walker's' mentioned, it's not
                Just football that they mean:
Nor fitness, goals, and cheering crowds – but
                 Sportsmanship *that's clean.*

Yes, it's 'Tommy this' and 'Tommy that'
When the game begins to play:
But it's 'Captain Thomas Walker'
In Rangoon or in Bombay.

                 R. S. W., *Modern Athenians* (1946)

MORE PASTIMES

Rugby – England versus Scotland

It was the day of the England and Scotland Rugby match . . . All Edinburgh was in a ferment. Football is, and always has been, the national game of Scotland among those who affect violent exercise, while golf takes its place with the more sedately inclined. There is no game so fitted to appeal to a hardy and active people as that composite exercise prescribed by the Rugby Union, in which fifteen men pit strength, speed, endurance, and every manly attribute they possess in a prolonged struggle against fifteen antagonists. There is no room for mere knack or trickery. It is a fierce personal contest in which the ball is the central rallying point. That ball may be kicked, pushed, or carried; it may be forced onwards in any conceivable manner towards the enemy's goal. The fleet of foot may seize it and by superior speed thread their way through the ranks of their opponents. The heavy of frame may crush down all opposition by dead weight. The hardiest and most enduring must win.

Even matches between prominent local clubs excite much interest in Edinburgh and attract crowds of spectators. How much more then when the pick of the manhood of Scotland were to try their strength against the very cream of the players from the South of the Tweed.

A. Conan Doyle,
The Firm of Girdlestone (1890)

The Royal Patent Gymnasium

Canonmills Loch had been drained just after the trains began running through Scotland Street Station, and marble works were later built on that corner of the haugh, continuing to use the mill lade which still exists to the north of the haugh. The marshy land of the Meadow was also completely drained in 1860, and by the time passenger trains stopped carrying people by this route, a new and exciting venture had been created on this site: John Cox's Royal Patent Gymnasium.

John Cox was a member of the Cox family of Gorgie, which had made its wealth out of the manufacture of gelatin. He was a great philanthropist and this particular venture of his was designed to provide the people of Edinburgh with somewhere to exercise and enjoy themselves at an affordable price of 6*d*. for adults and 3*d*. for children under twelve. Mr Cox invented various original contraptions which were examined and passed with high praise by the British Association, and with these and other more common amusements, the gymnasium might seem to us more like a funfair than a gymnasium. However, the momentum for each apparatus came from human power and was designed to aid the development of a healthy physique-movement, assisted by eight paddle-wheels which were turned by people on board the boat. It must have been an amazing sight, not to mention the novel experience for those on board.

'Chang' was a giant seesaw named after a much publicised Oriental giant. One hundred feet long by seven feet wide, it was supported on a central iron axle twenty five feet above the ground. The seesaw had a capacity of two hundred people who were held in place by high, strong mesh wire. When a few passengers were transferred from one end to the other the contraption was set in motion, taking the lighter end as much as fifty feet in the air, and causing the figure of a 'fearsom looking' giant attached to the top of the framework to swing like a pendulum. Doors at the centre of the long beam were opened only at 'appropriate times', so as to control the movement, and tanks of ater at each end absorbed the shock of the end plunging downwards. But even so the 'ride' must have been somewhat jerky.

Less novel amusements were provided in the way of stilts, springboards, vaulting poles, bowls, quoits, and curling on a special curling pond. The Gymnasium also provided various events, mostly for summer amusements, with bands and shows in the showhall to the south-east of the site.

Juliet Rees, *Once Upon A Haugh* (1991)

Childhood Games

The gardens in Charlotte Square were the meeting place of the neighbourhood. From half-past eleven onwards, the children were turned out to play there, unless it was raining. They were taken across the road by a nurse or a governess, or an unwilling elder sister, and left until called in for lunch. Isa took Marjory, and she felt very proud. Everyone must see how beautiful her cousin was. According to custom, Isa left her at the gate. . . . Once inside, she was claimed by her own set. Sets were as rigorously observed here as in the grandest drawing-room. At first, this had puzzled her, for at home she had played with her sister and the children next door and thought no more about it. Here in Edinburgh it was very different. She was expected to play with the children whose parents visited her aunt, a system she hated at once.

Oriel Malet, Marjory Fleming (1946)

Peevers

During the last thirty or forty years this game appears to have evolved newer and more varied forms of play. Peevers [hop-scotch] – also called 'Peeverie Beds', or 'Peeveries, or 'Beds' – may be described as a hopping-game requiring a pattern of chalked beds or boxes over which the 'peever' [Fr: *pierre*] is pushed by a hopping foot – according to agreed rules. The 'peever' is usually an empty round tin box (very often an old boot-polish tin), or it may be a piece of tile. A favourite material at one time was marble – which was coaxed from the nearest monumental mason's. Occasionally the peever was made of slate. Or it might be an old bung from a barrel. Long ago the glassworks turned out glass peevers – there's an example made of Holyrood glass, in the Huntly House Museum. The boxes or beds for peevers are chalked on the pavements, and very often the asphalt in certain streets provides an ideal surface for playing on. In some parts of peevers the player walks instead of hopping, and sometimes the peever is carried. Girls love drawing out the beds, their numbering carries a personal touch especially the figure one, which is laced with loops and finely placed. A Edinburgh street wouldn't look the same without this gay and lively geometry.

James T. R. Ritchie, Golden City (1965)

Poole's

An institution that for several years, at Christmas-time, held Edinburgh audiences enthralled was Poole's Myriorama, staged in the Synod Hall. This type of entertainment, now almost obsolete, was intermediary between the magic lantern and the cinematograph. It consisted of the most ambitious representations of anything from active volcanoes to naval battles, all of which were produced in 'flats' of cardboard, canvas, or plywood. The subtle use of lighting and of bright colours certainly cooperated in some realistic displays. Who has forgotten the dreadnought that, to the patriotic strains of *Rule, Britannia*, steamed across the stage against a fixed back-cloth, with great waves undulating so irresistibly in the foreground that you felt at any moment the sea-blue canvas containing them might burst with ridiculous consequences? Naval scenes were always a distinctive feature of the Myriorama. For these, two hefty lads were employed, each season, behind the scenes, in order to supply the war-vessels with the necessary motion. After much practice, they acquired the knack of pushing the great, lumbering things across the stage, one at a time, and at an even speed. For all their skill and heaving prowess, nevertheless, a pause or a jerk, a stagger or a sudden burst of acceleration, occasionally disturbed the illusion, and brought forth from the audience a chorus of disapproving groans. A third employee, likewise concealed, but always in synchrony, pulled Christmas crackers with furious diligence, to represent the firing of the dreadnought's guns. This was made to appear the more real by the puffs of smoke now seen to emerge from its bulwarks. Meanwhile Mr Poole, standing in evening dress by the side of the stage, gave us a running commentary, referring at intervals to some written matter spread under a reading-lamp that, to picturesque advantage, set off his fine head and shoulders.

Do you wonder that we regarded the Poole family and its Myriorama as an integral part of our Edinburgh life?

Alasdair Alpin MacGregor,
The Turbulent Years (1945)

~

The Music Hall in Edinburgh

Music hall began in the capital in 1861 when stockbroker Wm. Paterson took over the Dunedin Hall. He transformed the structure which had housed circuses into the Alhambra Music Hall, but within a year the property was deemed unsafe and closed. Undeterred at this rebuff, Paterson opened his new Alhambra on the opposite side of Nicolson Street. Renamed Royal Princess, it failed to pay its way and petered out in 1886 to be revived as the La Scala cinema in 1912. Along the road, Charles Hengler literally folded his tent to house the Southminster Music Hall as a circus in 1863. Gutted by fire in 1875, it was rebuilt as the Queen's Theatre with J. B. Howard, who was to found Howard & Wyndham theatrical enterprises, in control until 1880 when James Newsomes' Hippodrome and Circus emerged on the site destined to house Britain's first Empire Theatre twelve years later.

Adam House at 5 Chambers Street was the location of the Gaiety Music Hall in 1875. The hall with a reputation for risque fare was leased by Herbert Moss who bought adjacent shops and the University Hotel above the theatre. Artistes on the Moss circuit, most journeying from London halls, certainly earned their corn, having to put on an extra turn at the Kirkgate Hall every Saturday. Horse drawn cabs whisked them to Leith after their twice nightly routine at the Gaiety. On moving round the corner to his first Empire in 1892, Moss closed the Gaiety, which was retitled the Operetta House presenting cine-variety before going over to films exclusively.

J. H. Littlejohn,
The Scottish Music Hall 1880–1990 (1990)

Theatre Royal

In every distant clime Great Britain knows,
The Thistle springs promiscuous with the Rose.
While in all points with other lands she vied,
The stage alone to Scotland was denied:
Mistaken zeal, in times of darkness bred,
O'er the best minds its gloomy vapours spread;
Taste and religion were suppos'd at strife,
And 'twas a sin – to view this glass of life!

When the Muse ventur'd the ungracious task,
To play elusive with unlicens'd mask,
Mirth was restrain'd by statutory awe,
And tragic greatness fear'd the scourge of law.

James Boswell,
Prologue at the Opening of the
Theatre Royal, Edinburgh, 1769

Fire – 1865

On the bitterly cold and windy afternoon of Friday, January 13, 1865, occurred the disastrous fire which completely destroyed the Edinburgh Theatre Royal of that time. Six lives were lost in the catastrophe, including that of George Lorimer, Lord Dean of Guild, who died in the act of attempting to save a trapped man.

Through the carelessness of a gasman, whose duty it was to light the jets illuminating the canvas scenery, the props were set ablaze, and soon the entire stage was burning furiously. The fire, which began about four o'clock, was fanned by fierce gusts of wind, and by five o'clock the whole theatre was a roaring inferno.

Foremost among those quickly on the scene was George Lorimer. One of the most outstanding and successful building contractors of the period, he had been born and bred in the Capital . . . Adjoining the blazing building was the Roman Catholic edifice, St Mary's Catholic Church, and at the height of the blaze, part of the doomed structure fell suddenly on the church roof, and crashed into the vestry, killing one man and burying a labourer, Thomas Henry Leeke, aged 26, up to his waist.

The horrified crowd outside could hear him shrieking above the din: 'For God's sake, try and save me.' At the head of those who immediately rushed in to the rescue of the unfortunate young man was the Dean of Guild, although his friends had tried to hold him back . . . The fears of Lorimer's intimates proved too well founded, for, a minute or so afterwards, the greater part of the north gable wall of the theatre fell with a resounding crash on the church, burying him and several others, including Leeke.

Edinburgh Evening News, 4 April 1959

Pantomime

Christmas and New Year in Auld Reekie were sombre affairs compared with the present day. Entertainments at that time were on a limited scale, and undoubtedly the pantomime season was eagerly looked forward to by young and old. Carnivals, variety theatres, Palais-de-Danses, and palatial picture-houses were unthought of. At the Theatre Royal London 'stars' for many months in the year drew the intellectual patrons; and at the Princess's, in Nicholson Street, the stock company produced national and melodramatic plays, a revival of which would undoubtedly be of a more educative nature than the 'problem' monstrosities of the present day.

J. Wilson McLaren,
Edinburgh Memories and Some Worthies (1926)

Festival

It certainly affords much matter of reasonable regret, that in Scotland, a country distinguished for its learning, and good taste in poetry and general literature, Music in the liberal sense of the term, should be so little cultivated and so mush less understood. The reason for this is not that the people of this country are less sensible to music than their neighbours; but that not being generally aware of the full scope of the art, its real dignity, and its true principles, music is too often considered by them as merely an amusement, of little interest, and of still less importance.

George Farquhar Graham, an account of the first
Edinburgh Musical Festival 1815 (1816)

Roots

The Edinburgh International Festival of Music and Drama was first discussed over a lunch table in a restaurant in Hanover Square, London, towards the end of 1944. Rudolf Bing, convinced that musical and operatic festivals on anything like the pre-war scale were unlikely to be held in any of the shattered and impoverished centres for many years to come, was anxious to consider and investigate the possibility of staging such a Festival somewhere in the United Kingdom in the summer of 1946. He was convinced and he convinced my colleagues and myself that such an enterprise, successfully conducted, might at this moment of European time, be of more than temporary significance and might establish in Britain a centre of world resort for lovers of music, drama, opera, ballet and the graphic arts. Certain preconditions were obviously required of such a centre. It should be a town of reasonable size, capable of absorbing and entertaining anything between 50,000 and 150,000 visitors over a period of three weeks to a month. It should, like Salzburg, have considerable scenic and picturesque appeal and it should be set in a country likely to be attractive to tourists and foreign visitors. It should have a sufficient number of theatres, concert halls and open spaces for the adequate staging of a programme of an ambitious and varied character. Above all it should be a city likely to embrace the opportunity and willing to make the festival a major preoccupation not only in the City Chambers but in the heart and home of every citizen, however modest. Greatly daring but not without confidence I recommended Edinburgh as the centre and promised to make preliminary investigations.

Harvey Wood in George Bruce,
Festival in the North (1975)

If Lord Rosebery had not won £12,000 on the horses there would never have been an Edinburgh Festival. When Rudolph Bing had the idea in 1947 so many scoffed. Here was a city without an opera house, only one brothel and the weather was terrible. But Rosebery thought it would save having to take his wife to Glyndebourne so often and they'd have friends up for hunting and shooting in August anyway, so he told them to take the £12,000 he won on the horses as seed money. To think the fate of the Edinburgh Festival rested on the result of the 3.30 at Musselburgh

Richard Demarco, *The Scotsman*,
20 April 2001

A Festival Programme

Edinburgh during the Festival could become a three-week obsession. Blue Skies, roseate sunsets over the castle, balmy air, and the sound of streetwise jazz or distant pipes would create an unreal, almost fairytale atmosphere which released the capital's latent Europeanism. Visitors from Glasgow, Perth or Dundee (hastening along those pre-motorway dangerous three lane roads) would speed to a concert in Leith Town Hall at eleven o'clock in the morning; followed by an exhibition over lunch, and a 2.00 p.m. performance. A further exhibition at 4.00 might lead to a Fringe event at 5.00; a bite in the Luckpenny or Henderson's at 6.00 (with a quick glance at the art on the walls) in time for a major performance at 7.30; a quick drive south to soak up the chill atmosphere of floodlit Roslin chapel with its thick smell of candlewax and musty antiquity and then back to the Footlights review at 10.45; before joining the crowd thronging up the High Street to the Traverse for a late late and risqué . . . A pre-dawn drive home, a few hours' sleep, and back in time for the following morning's concert.

Charles McKean,
Edinburgh: A Portrait of a City (1991)

A Festival Highlight

What more breathtaking entry to a play than to walk from the Mound up the stairs to the Assembly Hall in the Old Town where 'The Thrie Estaits', Sir David Lindsay's medieval riot of Scottish satirical and panoramic comedy, has been given on several occasions? The fretted skyline proclaims the ancientry of the piece; and then there is a vast open platform with ample scope for the pageantry and blaze of colour in Tyrone Guthrie's vital massing of crowd-tumult.

Ivor Brown, *Summer in Scotland* (1952)

Usher Hall

The customary conversation
Gives way to applause
For the Orchestra. Then
A roar, as Karajan
Takes the stand. He raises
His baton; the strings sweep in.

During the interval, we remain
Seated. Two Edinburgh ladies
Behind us complain:
'Such Teutonic discipline
Breeds perfection,
Not Art.' Their companion agrees.

At the end they join in,
As the ovation goes on
And on. What has changed their tune?
We overhear: 'Weren't the Chorus
Superb!' 'As one voice.'
'And that lace, on Muriel's dress.'

Stewart Conn, *Choral Symphony*

Out of Season

Ye may talk of Bach and Mozart,
Ye may talk of Harold Pinter;
Ye may think this town is culture's crown –
Have ye been here in the winter?

Anonymous

Festival Club

The auld Assembly-rooms whaur Scott
foregethert wi his fiers,
nou see a gey kenspeckle lot
ablow the chandeliers.

Til Embro drouths the Festival Club
a richt godsend appears;
it's something new to find a pub
that gaes on sairvian beers
Eftir hours
in Embro to the ploy.

Jist pitten-out, the drucken mobs
frae howffs in Potteraw,
fleean, to hob-nob wi the Nobs,
ran to this Music Haa,
Register Rachel, Cougait Kate,
Nae-neb Nellie and aa
stauchert about among the Great,
what fun! I never saw
the like,
in Embro to the ploy.

Robert Garioch, *Embro to the Ploy* (1949)

Military Tattoo

At that moment a great roar came from the Esplanade;
the crowd clapped and cheered, then silence fell over the
Esplanade. The powerful searchlights swung to the high
wall of Half Moon Battery. A line of soldiers stood to
attention. In a sudden brilliant flash the bugles went to
their mouths. A hush fell over the arena, all eyes turned
towards the great, curved bastion.

The buglers sounded a magnificent fanfare, which
reached out from the Castle over the ancient city. In

perfect unison the bugles filled the night with their call. Then they stopped. The lights went out. There was darkness. The fanfare was over. The crowds burst into enthusiastic clapping. The Military Tattoo had started.

Owen John, *Festival* (1978)

Pillars of the City

PARLIAMENT

The Union Impending

In [Andrew] Fletcher's opinion no form of union that
could be devised would secure what was Scotland's chief
concern, namely her independence. Again, therefore, he
produced a scheme of 'limitations' by which succeeding
rulers should be bound to accept the will of the people as
expressed by its representatives. Fletcher's proposal gave
rise to prolonged and obstreperous debate, but the sense
of the House gradually declared itself in favour of the
Government measure. By a trick of destiny the measure
was introduced by the Earl of Mar, who was subsequently
to repent his action, sword in hand. Under the significant
title, 'Act for a Treaty with England', it answered to the
full all the desires of Anne's advisers.

P. Hume Brown,
History of Scotland (1899)

Preliminaries

The history of the negotiations which followed, the bribes
in money and advancement offered by the English and
accepted by the Scots, and the manner in which the
Scottish commissioners placed their personal gain before
both the honour of their nation and the wishes of those
whom they were supposed to represent, makes one of the
most sordid incidents in the whole history of Scotland.

273

Not less than £20,540 17*s*. 7*d*. was necessary to purchase their consent to the proposals; and, while the Duke of Queensberry as Lord High Commissioner received the vast sum of £12,235, it cost only £11 2*s*. to overcome the scruples of Lord Banff . . .

When the gist of these proposals became known in Edinburgh, the people were roused to a wild pitch of fury. Not only were they resentful at the way in which the commissioners had signed away the birthright of their country, but they foresaw that the removal of the Government from their city to London would deprive them of the chief part of their trade. As the twelve great wagons containing the 'Equivalent Money' were escorted through the streets to the Castle by a troop of cavalry, curses and reproaches followed their passing; and, when it became known that all but a hundred thousand pounds was being paid in the form of bills drawn on London, the fury of the citizens increased a hundredfold. Though the wagons reached the Castle in safety, they were not allowed to leave the city. Scarcely had they left the fortress on their return to England than the mob had overwhelmed the guards, breaking up and burning the vehicles which had carried this Judas money to the capital.

Sacheverell Sitwell & Francis Bamford,
Edinburgh (1938)

Act for a Treaty with England

I. That the Two Kingdoms of England and Scotland shall upon the First day of May which shall be in the year One thousand seven hundred and seven, and for ever after, be united into one Kingdom by the name of Great Britain; and that the Ensigns Armorial of the said United Kingdom be such as Her Majesty shall appoint, and the Crosses of St George and St Andrew be conjoined in such manner as Her Majesty shall think fit, and used in all Flags, Banners, Standards and Ensigns, both at Sea and Land . . .

III. That the United Kingdom of Great Britain be represented by One and the same Parliament, to be stiled, the Parliament of Great Britain . . .

XXII. That by virtue of this Treaty, of the Peers of Scotland at the time of the Union, Sixteen shall be the number to sit and vote in the House of Lords, and Forty-five the Number of the Representatives of Scotland in the House of Commons of the Parliament of Great Britain.

Acts of the Parliaments of Scotland

Representation

Of all the matters that had to be handled by the Commissions the question of representation in the United Parliament was that which most sorely tried their mutual forbearance. On the one hand, the sensitive patriotism of the Scots led them to make demands which could not be justified by measure and line; while, on their side, the English insisted on regarding the question as a purely business transaction. The arrangement proposed by the English Commissioners: a representation of thirty-eight, they maintained, would be an ample recognition of Scotland, seeing she was to contribute only a fortieth of the national taxation. But this was a point of view which did not commend itself to the Scots; what they saw was that Scotland was giving up her national assembly, and that a contingent of thirty-eight would be impotent in the

United Parliament. As a concession to their insistence, the English Commissioners at length agreed to raise the number to forty-five – an offer which the Scots were given to understand would be rejected at the risk of the whole Treaty. Even more unsatisfactory to the Scots, and especially to the nobles of their number, was the ultimatum of the English with regard to representation in the House of Lords. Sixteen in all – this was the sum total that was adjudged to be a fair representation of the nobility of Scotland in the prospective British House of Peers.

P. Hume Brown, *History of Scotland* (1899)

Last Riding of the Parliament

The whole of the three estates assembled on horseback before the Palace, their horses richly caparisoned, when they dismounted and entered. Having paid their respects to the king, they remounted, and were marshalled thus: first came two pursuivants, next two trumpeters, preceding the borough members two by two, each cloaked and attended by one lacquey. Four keepers of the Courts of Justice followed, and then came the barons, wearing their mantles, in double file, each attended by two lacqueys, wearing velvet coats over their liveries, upon which were embroidered their masters' badges. Next followed the principal officers of state, and after these the nobles two and two, lords and viscounts having each three lacqueys, earls four, marquesses six and dukes eight.

Sir Andrew Agnew,
Hereditary Sheriffs of Galloway (1893)

Passing of the Treaty

The last Scottish Parliament met for its last session on the 3rd of October 1706. The month of October was spent in preliminaries to the great contest that was to decide the fate of the Treaty. After an intermittent struggle of nearly three months, the Treaty of Union received the final sanction of the House. On the 16th of January the Commissioner touched the Act with the royal sceptre. It is more than probable that certain sums of money were spent in procuring the support of influential persons for the Union. That bribery carried the Union, however, would be a contention absurd on the face of it. If one thing is apparent from the correspondence of the Scottish statesmen who were mainly responsible for its accomplishment, it is that they were profoundly convinced of its necessity in the interest of both kingdoms.

On the 6th of March, from her throne in the House of Lords, the Queen gave the royal assent to the measure in the presence of Lords and Commons; and on the 19th amid a salvo of guns from the Castle the 'exemplified' Act was read to the Scottish Parliament and ordered to be recorded. As the Chancellor Seafield handed the Act with his signature affixed to the Clerk of the House, he is said to have exclaimed. 'Now, there's ane end of ane auld song.'

P. Hume Brown,
History of Scotland (1899)

∾

The Bells Ring Out

It is said that when the Act of Union, the political alliance joining together Scotland and England, came into force on 1st May 1707, somebody broke into the tower of St Giles and played upon its bells, the old Scottish folk-song, 'Why should I be sad on my wedding day?'

Marr and Kellie Papers, May 1st 1707

The Union

In many respects the whole history of Scotland since the end of the seventeenth century appears overshadowed by one event, the Union of Parliaments, which erased the formal Parliamentary independence of Scotland, reduced her to the status of a 'region' in the new hybrid kingdom of Great Britain, created an Anglo-Scottish common market that was the biggest customs-free zone in Europe, and provided access to one of the largest empires of the world. 1707 is a watershed that seems to split our view of the past into two distinct halves. [Nevertheless, Union did not fall like a bolt from the blue. It marked only a stage, though certainly an important one, in the long story of Scotland's absorption into a wider Britain, a process that began in the middle of the eleventh century when Malcolm Canmore married an English wife, and in many ways is not complete even to-day, when people still worship in a Church of Scotland and stand trial before the High Court of Justiciary.] . . . The most important political consequence of Union might seem to be the extinction of Scottish Parliamentary interdependence. But what in fact was lost? Scotland never had had the bold traditions of Parliamentary initiative which, in England, had been so richly developed from the reign of Elizabeth onwards. James VI and Charles I kept Parliament caged behind the Lords of the Articles, so that it never dared to promulgate anything offensive to the Crown. On the signature of the National Covenant in 1638 it escaped for a time, but Cromwell's victory nipped that venture in the bud. After 1660, the Parliaments of Charles II and James VII proved capable of moments of restive and even strenuous criticism, but they never actually seized initiative from the Crown on any important point. Down to 1689, therefore, Parliament was only a little more than a solemn rubber stamp.

T. C. Smout,
A History of the Scottish People 1560–1830 (1969)

The Stone of Scone

Shortly before midnight we arrived in Edinburgh. A thin freezing rain was falling, and the streets gleamed wickedly under the lights. . . . Up there on the hill the Scottish Estates had met and passed legislation far in advance of their time. The General Assemblies had come together and dethroned a Queen and made a King and driven out an invader. John Knox had walked these very streets, and Montrose had gone quietly to his death in the shadow of buildings which still stood. The Covenant of 1638 had been signed in Greyfriars Churchyard on the other side of the hill, and, no less important, the Covenant of 1949 had been launched in the Assembly Hall, which I could see as I drove along Princes Street As I looked up at that close mass of Scottish history I thought that we too might have played our part. We might have done something to bring nearer the day when, with great joy and pageantry, the King drove up the Royal Mile to open the Scottish Parliament, while the crowds cheered and the guns of the half-moon battery roared salute. Perhaps we had done something to quicken our dead capital. I did not know, but I knew that we would go on trying until death closed our eyes.

Ian R. Hamilton,
No Stone Unturned (1952)

The New Beginning

The referendum was held on 11 September 1997. It asked two questions: the first on the basic principle of a Scottish parliament, the second on whether such a parliament should have tax-raising powers . . . The outcome of the referendum was incontrovertible: 74.3 per cent of those who voted supported the re-establishment of a Scottish parliament; 63.5 per cent agreed that it should have tax-varying powers. The referendum had triumphantly endorsed what the late John Smith had called 'the settled will of the Scottish people' . . . So the Scottish parliament rose from the ashes of the past like a phoenix . . . But all the early stutterings, all the uncertainties and concerns, pale into insignificance compared with the magnitude of this new chapter of a nations's story, which the people of Scotland are now beginning to write . . .

On 1st July, 1999, almost three centuries after 'the end of an auld sang' in 1707, Her Majesty the Queen opened the new devolved Scottish Parliament in its temporary Edinburgh home, the Assembly hall of the Church of Scotland. She presented to the parliament a silver mace, symbol of authority for the new politics of Scotland; on its head are inscribed the opening words of the parliament's founding statute – *There shall be a Scottish Parliament.*

Magnus Magnusson,
Scotland: the Story of a Nation (2000)

Scottish Parliament

What used to be the Scottish Parliament – as if that ever had much to do with open government, with its carefully selected party lists and craven protection of vested interests . . . No expense had been spared when the place was built on a site previously occupied by a brewery. Fluids of various kinds were apparently a major interest of the architect – it did rain a lot more then, I suppose. In addition to the boat design, there were pools of water placed inside and outside the structures to reflect the walls and sky . . . The Parliament chamber itself was decorated with as many native Scottish materials as the designers could think of – granite slabs, red sandstone facings, tapestries spun in the Outer Hebrides, chandeliers of Cairngorm quartz and the like.

Paul Johnston, *Water of Death* (1999)

THE COUNCIL

Lord Provost of Edinburgh

The office of chief magistrate is synonymous with that of
the Lord Mayor of London. Previous to this date the chief
magistrate of Edinburgh was styled *Alderman* but he is
now honoured with the title of *Lord Provost*. John de
Quhitness is the first on record, who filled the office of chief
magistrate, under the title of *provost*. He, in 1296, together
with eleven burgesses of the city, signed the Ragman Roll,
and swore allegiance to Edward I of England, as superior
lord of the kingdom of Scotland. Within the bounds of the
city, he has the precedency of all the great officers of state,
and the nobility; walking on the right hand of the king, or
of his majesty's commissioner and representative. He had a
jurisdiction in matters of life and death, now in desuetude,
and previous to the union, was an officer in the Scottish
parliament, colonel of the city regiment of trained bands,
and captain of the city company of fuzileers, while in
existence. He is high sheriff, coroner, and admiral, within
the city and liberties, and in the town, harbour, and
roadstead of Leith. He is president of the convention of
royal burghs, and of the town council, a justice of the peace
for the county, &c., and enjoys the privileges of having a
sword and mace carried before him, while walking in any
procession.

Robert Stevenson, *Annals of Edinburgh* (1839)

The Perils of Office

The tenure of office [of Alexander Wilson – 1735] was cut short in consequence of the Porteous Riot. Provost Wilson and his Council seem at first to have thought that they were competent to deal with the matter themselves. They met the 'audacious iniquity' of the riot by a reinforcement of the Town Guard with three companies of train bands and proceeded unperturbed to the elections in September 1736, when Wilson was re-elected. The new Council awarded a pension of £10 sterling to Porteous's widow, with which she avowed herself content. But the Regent, Queen Caroline, and the Government thought otherwise, and Provost Wilson with the four bailies were summoned to London. The Provost was imprisoned, and not admitted to bail for three weeks. But ultimately the bill brought in to disable Wilson from holding office in future, to destroy the Netherbow Port, and to abolish the Town Guard, was modified to the extent of accepting the Provost as scape-goat and awarding £2000 to the widow. On the return of the magistrates from London, a public reception was arranged for them, which Wilson evaded, returning to his home by side streets. The Town Council, deliberating as to the liability for expenses, settled that the bailies should be repaid, but that the Lord Provost need not be reimbursed for the cost of his own defence and imprisonment. He was replaced by Archibald Macaulay and, debarred from all public office, and lived as a private individual till his death in 1740.

Marguerite Wood,
The Lord Provosts of Edinburgh: 1296–1932 (1932)

The High Constables

The title of High Constables was assumed in 1805 to avoid confusion with the regular police, and in 1810 the town council authorised the society to call itself that of the High Constables of the City of Edinburgh . . . In 1857 the society was recognised by Act of Council setting the number of constables at one hundred and fifty-six, twelve from each of the thirteen municipal wards . . . Some of their duties were grim enough, such as stopping the throwing of dead cats at celebrations of the King's Birthday, and attendance at public executions, for instance at that of three people accused of murdering a policeman in the Hogmanay riots of 1811.

Regularly they took part in processions on important public occasions.

As the city expanded the society expanded according to the increase in the number of municipal wards. Leith had its own High Constables before the port town became amalgamated with Edinburgh in 1920.

The Canongate, like Leith, had its own High Constables. In their case they had separate existence from early in the seventeenth century until 1856. Their last separate appearance was at the celebrations at the close of the Crimean War.

Albert Mackie,
Scottish Pageantry (1967)

The Professions

For its survival as a recognisable though decapitated entity, Scotland was primarily indebted to those provisions in the Treaty of Union which preserved its church and its courts of law, its clergy and its advocates; and in alliance with them was the invincible temper of Edinburgh which – as may well be thought – simply refused to recognise that it had been deprived of its *raison d'être*, and continued to exist in stubborn denial of its altered status. There was, however, a long, unhappy period – some twenty-five years or so – before it became evident that Scotland and its capital city had not been mortally wounded, and the pains of traditional poverty were, at first, aggravated by fiscal innovation and the new conditions of life . . . Before its remarkable advance to the prosperity and comfort of the latter part of the eighteenth century, it had to endure a good deal of humiliation, a period of doubt, and a season of anxiety.

Eric Linklater, *The Survival of Scotland* (1968)

Edina! Scotia's darling seat!
　All hail thy palaces and tow'rs,
Where once beneath a monarch's feet
　Sat Legislation's sov'reign pow'rs!
. . .
Here Justice, from her native skies,
　High wields her balance and her rod;
There Learning, with his eagle eyes,
　Seeks Science in her coy abode.

Robert Burns, *Poems* (1787)

THE CHURCH

The Disruption

[8th June, 1843]

Dr Welsh, Professor of Church History in the University of Edinburgh, having been Moderator last year, began the proceedings by preaching a sermon before his Grace the Commissioner in the High Church, in which what was going to happen was announced and defended. The Commissioner then proceeded to St Andrew's Church, where the Assembly was to be held. The streets, especially those near the place of meeting, were filled, not so much with the boys who usually gaze at the annual show, as by grave and well-dressed grown people of the middle rank. According to custom, Welsh took the chair of the Assembly. Their very first act ought to have been to constitute the Assembly of this year by electing a new Moderator. But before this was done, Welsh rose and announced that he and others who had been returned as members held this not to be a free Assembly – that, therefore, they declined to acknowledge it as a Court of the Church – that they meant to leave the very place, and, as a consequence of this, to abandon the Establishment. In explanation of the grounds of this step he then read a full and clear protest. It was read as impressively as a weak voice would allow, and was listened to in silence by as large an audience as the church could contain.

As soon as it was read, Dr Welsh handed the paper to the clerk, quitted the chair and walked away. Instantly, what appeared to be the whole left side of the house rose to follow. Some applause broke from the spectators, but it checked itself in a moment. 1933 members moved off, of whom about 123 were ministers, and about 70 elders. Among these were many upon whose figures the public eye had been long accustomed to rest in reverence. They all withdrew slowly and regularly amidst perfect silence, till that side of the house was left nearly empty. They were joined outside by a large body of adherents, among whom were about 300 clergymen. As soon as Welsh, who wore his Moderator's dress, appeared on the street, and people saw that principle had really triumphed over interest, he and his followers were received with the loudest acclamations. They walked in procession down Hanover Street to Canon-mills, where they had secured an excellent hall, through an unbroken mass of cheering people, and beneath in-numerable handkerchiefs waving from the windows. But amidst this exultation there was much sadness and many a tear, many a grave face and fearful thought: for no one could doubt that it was with sore hearts that these ministers left the church, and no thinking man could look on the unexampled scene and behold that the temple was rent, without pain and sad forebodings. No spectacle since the Revolution reminded one so forcibly of the Covenanters,

Lord Cockburn, *Journal* (1874)

The Edinburgh Mode

One outstanding difference I perceived between religious life in Auld Reekie and that of the Highlands was that I now heard less of eternal damnation, of an infuriated and avenging God and more of the sort of God one might like to meet in Heaven. The prospect of my being there with Him one day certainly brightened on reaching the Lowlands. The Day of Doom, the inevitability of which I had accepted without question since cradle days, now appeared less imminent. For the mental relief this brought, I felt truly thankful. It was comforting to be able to join in public worship in an atmosphere not so charged as heretobefore with the fumes of brimstone. For the first time in my life, it would seem, I was in the way of hearing a little more about the God of Love, and corresponding less about the God of Vengeance. Auld Reekie then, as ever, was much given to sermons, but these had a touch of charity about them. Furthermore, they had a contributory virtue in their being less protracted than those to which, in childhood, I had been subjected.

For all that, churches and the precincts and premises appurtenant thereto were held in much greater veneration in Auld Reekie than to-day. When we arrived but a few years before the Great War, there was raging a controversy as to whether it was seemly to use church-halls for badminton and amateur dramatics and suchlike. The Roman Catholics, taking a more metallic view of the church's function in this connection, had long been letting its properties for cold cash. That, in itself, was sufficient to intensify any logomachy in our ultra-Calvinist city. The sterner brethren especially those of the Free Church, refused to countenance such a 'carry-on'. They questioned the legality even of soirees and cantatas on church premises. About this time, Coleridge-Taylor's *Hiawatha* was enjoying a considerable measure of popularity among guilds and choirs; and it was a usual occurrence to find half a dozen dramatic societies connected with the city surfeit of kirks all rehearsing feverishly. Vying with the other in its performance, despite the disapproval of the purists who, interested primely in the propagation of the

Gospel through such channels as the Sunday-school and the Bible-class, held out against this monstrous desecration of sanctified stone and lime. The purists, in the end, were routed completely, since the churches, never able to withstand for long the temptation of the bawbees, found it commercially advantageous to let their halls, especially at this time, when musical and dramatic societies, springing up all over the city, were experiencing difficulty in finding premises in which they could display their talent not too expensively.

Notwithstanding, the religious life of the city proceeded apace; and the clamour of competing bells remained a resounding feature of its Sabbath. Right from the pious purlieu of Morningside to the sea's edge at Leith or Granton, they could be heard, announcing, in challenging tones, a score of incongruous orthodoxies. Inwardly fortified by the matutinal bacon-and-eggs, male representatives of all denominations trooped out in frock-coats and top-hat or Sunday bowler, followed a pace or two behind by their womenfolk and bairns. Umbrellas were always an indispensable adjunct, even in midsummer sunshine; and a pair of gloves, worn but infrequently, dangled, from the hand with conventional precision. One would as readily have gone to church without umbrella or gloves as without trousers in those days. God had to be worshipped in correct habit. Upon this He insisted. Nowadays, so few disport any of these formal appurtenances that the clergy is glad to welcome us without them. So serious, indeed, has been the decline in church attendance that one minister actually announced in staid Auld Reekie (though not without incurring the displeasure of a section of his congregation) that he did not mind if young men came to church in plus-fours, so long as they had the decency to leave their golf-clubs outside.

Alasdair Alpin MacGregor, *Auld Reekie* (1943)

The Edinburgh Sunday

Th' approach of Sunday still I can't but dread,
For still old Edinburgh comes into my head,
Where on that day a dreary gloom appears
And the kirk-bells ring doleful in your ears.
Enthusiastics sad, how can you thus employ
What your Redeemer made a day of joy?
With thankful hearts to your Creator pray,
From labour rest, be cheerful and be gay
Let us not keep the Sabbath of the Jews;
Let generous Christians Christian freedom use.

James Boswell, *Boswell in Holland* (1952)

A Jewish Sabbath in Edinburgh

There were some things, of course, that one did not talk
about to one's school fellows, because they would never have
understood. And, while at home we never called Saturday
'Saturday' but always *Shabbos* (the Hebrew for Sabbath in
the 'Ashkenazi' pronunciation used by most European Jews
before the 'Sephardi' pronunciation of the Palestinian
Jews came to be associated with the Zionist movement
and with modern Hebrew culture), I was always careful to
say 'Saturday' at school. Only once do I remember making
a mistake in vocabulary, and that was because I did not
know that the Hebrew word *yomtov* (festival) was not
current English usage. I was taking off my coat in the
school cloakroom and chatting to a red-headed boy named
Cunningham. It was one of the intermediate days of
Passover, when we could go to school though of course we

still ate only *Pesachdick* food. Cunningham offered me a sweet – it was a red jujube, as I clearly recall, though the incident happened in 1920 – and, momentarily forgetting that it was Passover and that I could not eat any food that had not been specially prepared under rabbinical auspices, I popped it into my mouth. A second after I had done so, I realised what I had done, and hastily spat it out on to the floor. Cunningham watched in amazement, and I tried to explain: 'It's a Jewish *yomtov*, when we can only eat unleavened bread and specially prepared food that hasn't been near any leavened.' It was the utterly bewildered look on Cunningham's face that first taught me that *yomtov* was not a regular English word.

This was an exceptional incident, which accounts for it having stuck so clearly in my memory. Normally I had no difficulty at all in living in two worlds at once; both seemed to be satisfactorily related to the physical environment of Edinburgh. The synagogue in Graham Street – it had once been some sort of a chapel and had been made over – was in a decayed but fascinating part of the city; behind it the old streets tumbled down into the Grassmarket and Johnston Terrace and the southern, precipitous side of Edinburgh Castle, and the approach from the east was by a picturesque narrow lane known as the Vennel, flanked by part of the old city wall. Many years later when I was a student at Edinburgh University, my father's efforts resulted in the building of a fine new synagogue in a less run-down part of the city, and though like everyone else I hailed the new building with satisfaction, the move was for me a disturbing break with my childhood and coincided (whether by chance or not I am not sure) with a far-reaching revaluation on my part of the relation between the two elements in my background.

But in 1919 I was untroubled by any conflict of beliefs or

loyalties . The streets and meadows and hills of Edinburgh represented the timeless world, while my religion, with its fixed times and seasons, its recurring sabbaths and feasts and fasts, each with its own synagogue and domestic ritual, was a world strictly divided into temporal units. On Saturday nights we would watch until three stars appeared in the sky, and then we knew that the sabbath was over – *shabbos* was 'out', as we put it – and one could strike a match or play the piano or revert to any of the usual weekday activities, even if my father, holding a lighted torch of twisted tapers, had not yet formally announced the change with a blessing over a glass of warm milk and a sniff at the silver spice-box whose comforting odour was supposed to console one for the departure of the Princess Sabbath.

David Daiches, Two Worlds (1957)

A Victorian Chestnut

One Sunday evening, a visitor to Edinburgh is picked up by a 'carmine-headed lassie'. While she is preparing to bed with him he whistles an air. She turns to him 'in an agony of holy terror' and cries: 'Jist button up yer breeks, and gang yer gate, my chick: G—d for sakes! My man; I'm na going to fornicate the nicht wi' a man who whiustles on the Sabbath!'

John Russell,
The Amberley Papers (1937)

THE LAW

Scotland did retain two institutions of her own, and of these the greatest factor in the preservation for Edinburgh of the ethos of a Capital has been not the Church but the Law. The Presbyterian Church could have maintained its headquarters in any provincial town, for its constitution is democratic, its Moderator annually elected from any part of the country. But, although the Scottish legal system is in form less centralised than the English, the Law demanded somewhere a High Court and a background for its judges and senators. The Supreme Judicature set up by James V first met in the Edinburgh Tolbooth in 1532, and moved across to the Parliament House with the Estates. The Faculty of Advocates, from whom the Judges are nominated, is a body with a distinguished record of integrity and patriotism; it is also the last actively surviving trade guild in Scotland, retaining many of its ancient powers and privileges. No better fate could have befallen the Parliament House when it lost its place as the seat of government, than that it should have devolved into the home of Scottish Law. The legal fraternity from thenceforward became increasingly important occupying a unique position as the centre of Scotland's intellectual life and very largely the guardians of the nation's rights and continued existence. The great Edinburgh personalities from the middle of the eighteenth to about the middle of the nineteenth centuries were practically without exception associated with the Law. It was no accident that Sir Walter Scott was a lawyer: he could hardly have been otherwise. The Profession provided the only background against which he could thrive: intellectual life had become almost identical with legal life. Boswell was a not very successful advocate: his father was a Judge. Hume became librarian to the Advocates. Jeffrey, whose criticism seemed immortal to his own generation but proved as transient as most of its genre, and Cockburn, whose *Memorials* and *Circuit Journeys* remain delightful reading, were two of the radical rebels of the turn of the century, both ending on the Bench. If such writers as Henry Mackenzie, author, of *The Man of Feeling*, are never likely to be read again, they preserved interest and judgment and taste in their way. If by its nature the Law imposed certain obvious restrictions upon the literary field that it dominated, at least it was the lawyers themselves who first welcomed Burns to the Capital, and gave him the encouragement he needed.

In losing the Court, Edinburgh lost panoply, and stimulus, also some of its less-desirable hangers-on. In losing resident politicians, she no doubt lost a good deal of liveliness and enterprise. In replacing them as leaders of her Society with lawyers trained and proud in their Profession, she has gained in dignity and honour, elements whose value seems clearer to us in days when we see responsibility becoming sterilised as the prerogative of the State. If certain ludicrous elements of social rectitude have come to be associated with the City's life, the Edinburgh man himself does not take them so seriously, for he knows how much remains of the old convivial spirit of the Noctes Ambrosianae; and that the dignity of the Legal Profession would never suffer it to become teetotal. Of course the consumption is not on the old gargantuan scale (for long helped by a happy oversight whereby Scotland was enabled to purchase claret without the heavy English tariff that the Union imposed upon all her important imports). The stories of learned juridical potations related by Cockburn and others remain to us heroic legends.

George Scott-Moncrieff, *Edinburgh* (1947)

Court of Session

1532. It was modelled out of two older courts – the one entitled the 'Sessions' and the other the 'Daily Council' – from whence the Judges are named 'The Lords of Council and Session'.

Robert Stevenson,
Annals of Edinburgh (1839)

~

The Quality of Mercy

Being one day alone in the Parliament Close, I observed that the Parliament House was open. I entered it as others did. I saw one very old man on the bench; his head was shaking, and he shook the papers, which he held in his trembling hands; with a feeble, broken, quivering voice, he was prattling something in broad Scotch. Very few persons were present. It was interlocutory, they said.

I asked a man, who appeared to be an usher or door-keeper, who the judge was. 'Oh! he is an old man; a poor old creature!' In England, such an answer, spoken aloud, would have appeared undecorous; but we were a less wise – a less civilized – people. Probably the superannuated Rhadamanthus was deaf as well as feeble, for he heeded it not. I still persisted in asking his name,

'It is just the Lord Ordinary.'

'But what is his name?'

'It is just the Lord Ordinary. He will have a name . It is very like – oh! he will have a name! It is very like, indeed – but I do not rightly ken what it is. I dare say he will have a

name. It is just the Lord Ordinary – poor old creature!'
And in this the bystanders unanimously concurred.

Thomas Jefferson Hogg,
The Life of Percy Bysshe Shelley (1858)

His Lordship

A professional brother informing the facetious Advocate,
John Clerk, that he had the prospect of being raised to the
Bench, asked him to suggest what title he would adopt –
'Lord Preserve Us'.

Charles Rogers,
Familiar Illustrations of Scottish Character (1861)

The Judges' Ladies

Scots law lords at one time invariably and still frequently
take a title from landed estate. This was natural. A judge
was a person with some landed property, which was in
early times the only property considered as such, and in
Scotland, as everybody knows, the man was called after his
estate. Monkbarns of the *Antiquary* is a classic instance,
and it was only giving legal confirmation to this, to make
the title a fixed one in the case of the judges. They never
signed their names this way, and were sometimes sneered
at as paper lords. To-day, when the relative value of
things is altered, they would probably prefer their paper
title. According to tradition their wives laid claim to a
corresponding dignity, but James V, the founder of the

College of Justice, sternly repelled the presumptuous dames, with a remark out of keeping with his traditional reputation for gallantry. 'He had made the carles lords, but wha the deil made the carlines leddies?' Popular custom was kinder than the King, and they got to be called ladies, till a newer fashion deprived them of the honour. It was sometimes awkward. A judge and his wife went furth of Scotland, and the exact relations between Lord A and Mrs B gravelled the wits of many an honest landlord. The gentleman and lady were evidently on the most intimate terms, yet how to explain their different names? Of late the powers that be have intervened in the lady's favour, and she has now her title assured her by royal mandate.

Francis Watt, *Book of Edinburgh Anecdote* (1912)

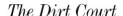

The Dirt Court

Previous to the institution of the police-court, a bailie of Edinburgh used to sit, every Monday, at that part of the Outer Parliament House where the statute of Lord Melville now stands, to hear and decide upon small causes – such as prosecutions for scandal and defamation, or cases of quarrels among the vulgar and the infamous. This jurisdiction, commonly called the *Dirt Court*, was chiefly resorted to by washerwomen from Canonmills, and the drunken ale-wives of the Canongate. A list of Dirt Court processes used always to be hung on a board every Monday morning at one of the pillars in the piazza at the outside of the Parliament Square; and that part of the piazza being the lounge of two or three low pettifoggers, who managed such pleas, was popularly called the *Scoundrels' Walk*. Early on Monday, it was usual to see one or two threadbare personages, with prodigiously clean linen, bustling about with an air of importance, and occasionally accosted by *viragoes* with long eared caps flying behind their heads. These were the agents of the Dirt Court, undergoing conference with their clients.

Robert Chambers,
Traditions of Edinburgh (1825)

Forensic Skill

In the parliament house, as the Courts of Justice are called in Scotland, he (John Clerk of Picardy House, later Lord Eldin) was a very tiger, seizing on his adversary with tooth and nail, and demolishing him without mercy, often without justice, for he was a true Advocate, heart and soul, right or wrong, in his client's cause. Standing very upright on the long leg, half a dozen pairs of spectacles shoved up over his forehead, his wickedest countenance on, beaming with energy, he poured forth in his broad Scotch a torrent of flaming rhetorick too bewildering to be often very successfully opposed. There was a story of his having mistaken a case, and so in his most vehement manner pleading on the wrong side, the Attorneys, called writers with us, in vain whispering and touching and pulling, trying in their agony every possible means of recalling his attention. At last he was made to comprehend the mischief he was doing. So he paused – for breath, readjusted his notes, probably never before looked at, held out his hand for the spectacles his old fat clerk Mr George had always a packet of ready, put them on, shoved them up over all the series sent up before, and then turning to the Judge resumed his address thus, 'Having now, my lord, to the best of my ability stated my opponent's case as strongly as it is possible for even my learned brother' – bowing to the opposite Counsel with a peculiar swing of the short leg – 'to argue it, I shall proceed point by point to refute every plea advanced, etc. etc.'; and he did, amid a convulsion of laughter.

Elizabeth Grant of Rothiemurchus,
Memoirs of a Highland Lady (1898)

An Unsuccessful Advocate

One of the most famous, and least successful, advocates was admitted to the Faculty in 1875, Robert Louis Stevenson.

It is depressing to compare the style of Stevenson's education with the rigours of a modern system. He first went to school at the age of nine and shortly afterwards spent eighteen months at Edinburgh Academy. At the age of thirteen he spent a term at a school near London and then did three more years at a day-school in Frederick Street, Edinburgh. The whole of his schooling seems to have amounted to not more than seven years. It was then decided that he should be a lighthouse engineer, like his ancestors. The training for this life consisted in winters at Edinburgh University reading for a science degree, and summers in remote parts of Scotland inspecting or building lighthouses. In fact he attended almost no classes.

It was in 1869 that Stevenson was elected a member of the Speculative Society, the literary and debating society within Edinburgh University, which at that time was largely dominated by intrants to the Faculty of Advocates . . . It appears that this new interest, which grew slowly, led

Stevenson away from engineering towards the bar . . . The course of Stevenson's legal studies was almost as desultory as his earlier education. In the winter of 1872 he attended 'some' of the necessary lectures in Civil Law and Public Law, and also attended an oral examination, set by the Faculty of Advocates, in General Scholarship. This appears to have been in French and Philosophy, and none too seriously treated. In the summers of 1872 and 1873 he spent some time in a solicitor's office, Skene and Peacock, ws. His serious study of the law began in the winter of 1874 when he attended lectures in Conveyancing, Scots Law and Constitutional Law, and he passed the last exam on 14th July. He was admitted to the Faculty on 16th July 1875. It would appear that his legal education consisted of two years at university and a few months in an office.

'Pericles',
Journal of the Law Society of Scotland, March 1972

MEDICINE

Surgeons and Physicians

Although some individuals calling themselves surgeons can be traced in the records well before the end of the fifteenth century, the vital event in the history of the Edinburgh surgeons was without doubt the ratification of their Seal of Cause by James IV in 1506.

There had been some sort of organisation of the barbers and surgeons prior to this, as witnessed by a document dated 24 April 1504, which authorised the 'kirkmaister & ouersman of the barberis to have yr divine service at St Mongos alter of St Bryde in St Giles Kirk and St Mongow to be yr patron'. This was in the tradition of such altars being maintained by the weekly contributions of the members of the various crafts of the burgh in St Giles kirk, and reflects the primarily religious and 'brotherly' nature of these early groups. The surgeons and barbers must have been of sufficient numbers to warrant formal organisation, a major and difficult objective of which would be to exclude non-members from practising in their defined area of jurisdiction.

The Seal of Cause was, at first sight, a standard document of its type – a charter of incorporation for a group of individuals following the same occupation . . . Entrant masters were obliged to swear an oath to uphold all the clauses of the Seal of Cause, but after the Reformation it was ordained that individuals must swear to keep faith with the sentiments of the charter 'excepting idolatry contained thairintill'.

Physicians, for example, were generally (but not exclusively) drawn from higher social levels, and it was consequently a little difficult for them to indulge in activities viewed as too 'practical', such as the detailed physical examination of patients. *Consultation* was the crucial factor, and it was not until the more practical philosophy advocated by men such as Boerhaave was gradually introduced that physicians began to feel a little more able to *practise* as opposed to consult and prescribe. Similarly, in the case of the surgeons, who were generally drawn from slightly lower social ranks, it may have been a problem for patients in the upper ranks of society to submit themselves to the ministrations of their social inferiors . . . however, the universal literacy and high levels of learning achieved by the surgeons of Edinburgh helped them to overcome at least some of these difficulties. The importance of education and learning were deeply embedded in the Scottish character, and the acquisition of knowledge allowed at least a few rungs of the social ladder to be climbed, to a higher level than was the case in England, where surgeons were not so highly regarded.

Helen M. Dingwall,
Physicians, Surgeons and Apothecaries (1995)

The Hospitals

Excluding the leper houses, like those at Liberton and Greenside, there was literally little in-patient provision for fever victims except during epidemics when hastily built huts in the city outskirts were used to isolate them. During these outbreaks the services of religious houses of charity like those of St Catherine of Sienna (now Sciennes) and the Chapel of St Roque (now in the Astley Ainslie Hospital) would be overstretched but there is reason to think they also provided for fever patients during the quieter, inter-epidemic periods. Bailie Pollard records that in the reign of Mary, Queen of Scots the city had at least eight houses for the relief of the infirm, all supported by charity. After the sixteenth century they had either closed, due to falling support, or else they became homes for the aged and decrepit rather than hospitals.

. . .

A Royal Charter from George II was granted in 1736 for the new Royal Infirmary of Edinburgh, under the guidance of the far-seeing Lord Provost Drummond. After a massive public subscription, the foundation stone was laid was laid in 1738.

James A. Gray,
The Edinburgh City Hospital (1999)

∾

The City Hospital

Edinburgh suffered serious outbreaks of cholera in 1832, and again in 1849, at a time when the city was ill-equipped to deal with the ravages of infectious diseases. The Town Council purchased Canongate Poorhouse in 1867 for £1,600 and converted it into a fever hospital. This work was continued at the new Royal Infirmary when it was opened at Lauriston in 1879. However there was a setback in 1885 when the Royal Infirmary informed the Town Council that it could no longer accommodate patients with infectious diseases. As a result, the wards were transferred to the site of the old Infirmary building in Infirmary Street. This unsatisfactory state of affairs came to a head in 1894 when the Old Infirmary site could not cope with the outbreak of smallpox, requiring some patients to be admitted to 'large wooden structures' in Holyrood Park . . . If nothing else, the 1894 outbreak of smallpox acted as a catalyst for a more comprehensive approach to the problem. After all the arguments had been considered, it was decided that the new hospital should be located outside the city, rather than in any piecemeal development of a city-centre site. On the question of accessibility, the committee were obviously influenced by the finding that 'ambulance waggons are now so constructed that fever patients can be carried in them over considerable distances without serious risk.'

Various sites were considered. Colinton Mains Farm was bought by the Town Council for £20,000, providing 130 acres, of which 72 acres were set aside for the new hospital.

Malcom Cant,
The District of Greenbank (1998)

Joseph Bell (1837–1911)

The great mystery, which has never as yet been cleared up, is whether Holmes ever really existed. Is Holmes merely the creation of Doyle's ingenuious brain? Or is there really an individual who is the living embodiment of Sherlock Holmes?

Conan Doyle is essentially an Edinburgh product. He was born there. His medical studies were pursued in that ancient city of medical lore . . . To a man of Doyle's alertness, memory and imagination, this training was invaluable. It was in the infirmary wards at Edinburgh, in the dispensaries and in the out-patient department that he first encountered that subtle and wonderful character who is now world-renowned, the original of the great detective, Sherlock Holmes . . . All Edinburgh medical students remember Joseph Bell – Joe Bell – as they called him

The Edinburgh Magazine

Bell was a very remarkable man in body and mind. He was thin, wiry, dark, with a high-nosed acute face, penetrating grey eyes, angular shoulders, and a jerky way of walking. His voice was high and discordant. He was a very skilful surgeon, but his strong point was diagnosis, not only of disease, but of occupation and character.

Arthur Conan Doyle,
Memories and Adventures (1924)

EDUCATION

Edinburgh University

The Scottish universities, which were the apex of the national education system, were of course exclusively masculine. All the universities, except Edinburgh had been originally clerical corporations, products of a medieval church, and John Knox and the other fathers of the Scottish Reformation were determined to maintain the grip of the Kirk on the colleges. The latter, after all, provided the vocational training for the clergy and their secular partners, the parish dominies, some of whom were always young aspirants to the ministry awaiting a charge. Edinburgh, despite being a Renaissance 'tounis college', was not really different. It was the biggest and the most prestigious of Scottish universities in the eighteenth century. Its principal was *ex officio* a member of the General Assembly of the Kirk, and in the 1760s and 1770s he was usually the dominant figure in that body.

In no sense, however, were the universities subject to clerical tyranny. Edinburgh is the classic case. Its Faculty of Divinity was the senior one in terms of status and symbolism, but it produced no major works of theology. Robertson, who became principal in 1762, was an historian, while his main Moderate clerical ally, Hugh Blair, was Professor of Rhetoric. There were no confessional tests for admission as a student to Scottish universities. English Dissenters or Polish Roman Catholics were perfectly welcome if they paid the modest class fees. In theory, professors had to sign the Westminster Confession of Faith.

In practice, only one professor in Edinburgh did so between 1758 and 1826. Moderate ecclesiastical historians, for instance Fraser Tytler of Edinburgh, were clear that tolerance towards all major faiths was a virtue. In lectures in 1798–1800 Tytler expressed admiration for aspects of the Koran and saw all churches, including the Church of Scotland, as flawed products of their time . . . There was a complete alliance in Edinburgh between city and university. They were interdependent. A distinguished professoriate confirmed Edinburgh's 'capital' status in the post-1707 world and attracted students.

R. A. Houston & W. W. J. Knox,
New Penguin History of Scotland (2001)

In 1582 the Town Council, after long hesitation, decided that the Scots capital should no longer be in a position of inferiority to St Andrews, Glasgow, and Aberdeen. Not that they can claim the merit of initiating the proposal. That was due to Robert Reid, who, in 1558, bequeathed to the town the sum of 8000 merks for the purpose of erecting a University. Queen Mary eagerly supported the proposal and in 1566 drew up a charter . . .

But her abdication soon after, rendered her scheme null and void, and the Council was left to undertake the work itself, with the 'royal approbation' of James VI, and in 1617 his gracious permission that the college might be called after himself. In 1582 the members of the Town Council busied themselves in securing suitable buildings at Kirk-of-Field, where Darnley had met his death, and next year, Robert Rollock, then a professor at St Andrews, was invited to become the first 'Regent and Master of the New College'. He had virtually to formulate an academic system and curriculum, and as at the outset he had to do all the teaching himself, he was compelled to place all the students in one class. Such a course was very discouraging for those who were more advanced . . . From its foundation until the present day, the institution has steadily advanced along the best lines of progress and development, until now albeit the youngest, it is by far the largest of the Scots universities. Its system of teaching has in most cases been admirably adapted to the needs of life, as is proved by the large number of its *alumni* who have taken leading places in all departments of human activity and in all parts of the globe.

Oliver Smeaton,
Edinburgh and its Story (1904)

The National Character

In the history of the University of Edinburgh we may clearly trace the national character of Scotland. We find there all that hardy energy, that gift of extracting much from little, and husbanding every available provision – of supplying the defects of external appliances and means from within by the augmented effort and courage of man, that power to make an uncongenial climate smile and a hungry soil teem with all the bounties of providence, which have given Scotland a place and a name among men so far beyond what was due to her geographical extent or to her natural resources.

William Ewart Gladstone,
Rectorial Address, 1853

It is within this city that I spent three happy years of my life, receiving from the University of Edinburgh part – and I will say the most valuable part – of the instruction which I have received.

Lord Palmerston (1784–1865)

Modern Athenians

Edinburgh University may call herself with grim jocoseness the 'alma mater' of her students, but if she be a mother at all she is one of a heroic and Spartan cast, who conceals her maternal affection with remarkable success. The only signs of interest which she ever deigns to evince towards her alumni are upon those not infrequent occasions when guineas are to be demanded from them. Then one is surprised to find how carefully the old hen has counted her chickens, and how promptly the demand is conveyed to each one of the thousands throughout the empire who, in spite of neglect, cherish a sneaking kindness for their old college. There is symbolism in the very look of her, square and massive, grim and grey, with never a pillar or carving to break the dull monotony of the great stone walls. She is learned, she is practical, and she is useful. There is little sentiment or romance in her composition, however, and in this she does but conform to the instincts of the nation of which she is the youngest but the most flourishing teacher.

A. Conan Doyle,
The Firm of Girdlestone (1890)

Graduation

Graduations at Edinburgh University were picturesque ceremonies. Wall space climbing up to the roof was filled with pictures of Greek or Roman figures sitting or standing on steps leading to classical buildings and engaged in intellectual discussion. The organist played *Il Penseroso*-like music on the pealing organ while the parents and friends assembled. There were parents accustomed to the occasion and at ease, approvingly seeing their children tread successfully the paths they themselves trod a generation ago. There were other parents in their Sunday best, proud of their children who had made the grade into a socially approved status . . .

The procession began, the entry of the priests. The Dean of the Faculty of Divinity said a prayer. The words were beautifully chosen and appropriate and rang true. Almost I was persuaded that this was not ritual but reality. The capping of the doctors of philosophy drew attention to the programme which listed the subjects of their research. The other graduands were capped, received a word from the acting vice-chancellor and walked across to accept from a girl in a beautiful summery hat the red cylinder containing their Latin-worded degree certificate. The acting vice-chancellor addressed the new graduates. The organ struck up, the procession re-formed and filed out. The sun shone beautifully. Cameras recorded the scene. Graduates posed against the monument in the gardens, or the hall, or the more distant Salisbury Crags, happily. Parents greeted unknown parents, sharing a success, wondering about a future. Then they drifted away to restaurants to mark the occasion, laughing with the waiter in Denzil's, ordering salmon or lamb, drinking toasts in sherry or Bordeaux or champagne.

R. F. Mackenzie, *A Search for Scotland* (1989)

Special Graduation

On a Sunday afternoon just before Graduation, two members of the Edinburgh University staff met over a cup of tea. One was the Professor of Greek, the other had some responsibility for the arrangements of that day. Had his friend realised, the Greek Professor wondered, that Eric Liddell, the Olympic champion and sporting hero of the University, would be among the graduates in Science at that time? The students, it was certain, would look for something special to mark the occasion. In the course of conversation, the idea of a crowning ceremony was mooted, with a Greek epigram and an olive wreath as its principal features, and it was decided to approach the Principal and Vice-Chancellor and put the proposition before him . . . The Keeper of the Royal Botanic Gardens was next approached, and he was asked to supply the nearest thing he could get to a crown of wild olive – the award to the victor at the Olympic Games of old. Oleaster, a garden derivative, was chosen for the purpose.

The degree for which Eric Liddell was to be presented in the McEwan Hall of Edinburgh University at the Summer Graduation on the forenoon of Thursday, 17th July, 1924, was that of Bachelor of Science in the department of Pure Science. . . . As Mr Liddell stepped forward to receive the ordinary degree of Bachelor of Science, the vast audience rose and cheered him to the echo . . . The Vice-Chancellor said: 'Mr Liddell, you have

311

shown that none can pass you but the examiner. In the ancient Olympic tests the victor was crowned with wild olive by the High Priest of Zeus, and a poem written in his honour was presented to him. A Vice-Chancellor is no High Priest, but he speaks and acts for the University; and in the name of the University, which is proud of you, and to which you have brought fresh honour, I present you with this epigram in Greek, composed by Professor Mair, and place upon your head this chaplet of wild olive.'

The scroll thus put into the hand of the Olympic victor and newly-made B.Sc. Read as follows:

> The University of Edinburgh congratulates
> Eric Henry Liddell
> Olympic Victor in the 400 Metres.

Translated into English, the Greek epigram read thus:

> Happy the man who the wreathed games essaying
> Returns with laurelled brow,
> Thrice happy victor thou, such speed displaying
> As none hath showed till now;
> We joy, and *Alma Mater*, for thy merit
> Proffers to thee this crown:
> Take it, Olympic Victor. While you wear it
> May Heaven never frown.

Immediately the ceremony was over, the students seized the Olympic champion, still wearing gown, hood and crown, and carried him shoulder high to St Giles' Cathedral.

> D. P. Thomson,
> *Eric Liddell: Athlete and Missionary* (1945)

The General Strike – 1926

Of all the numerous activities that were available during the strike, none could offer greater variety, or more romantic possibilities than service with the LNER. At once it conjures up visions of eminent lights of the University, coal black from head to foot, exploring the inner workings of engines, labouring under the delightful delusion that the engines were benefiting by their ministrations; or, better still, was the thought of those gentlemen spending a happy day shovelling cinders! Another pleasing spectacle was the sight of a large band of students shepherding passengers about complete with their luggage, with a politeness that was a joy to witness, and an edifying spectacle to boot, until one realised that it was merely the hope of an extra large tip that prompted this unwonted display of manners. Another familiar sight was two persons, one diminutive and one large, who trailed about with spanners, oil-cans, hammers, and all kinds of gadgets. Their technical name was 'greasers', their occupation to make sure that every train arrived and departed whole. The greasers lived in the station, a calm and placid life marred by one tragedy alone. One day, unbeknown to them, their 'bedroom' was shunted, and great were their wailings till it was restored to them. An evil set of ruffians, attired in wondrous garments, went by the euphemistic name of 'carriage cleaners'. Concerning these it will be suffice to state that they could only be trusted with the third class compart-ments. There was one band of workers whose work, though of the greatest responsibility, and of extreme national importance, received but little recognition. These ardent souls spent a riotous time cleansing cattle-trucks at Gorgie. Another body, but a far more select and exclusive one, which recruited its ranks from some of Edinburgh's most distinguished professional men, employed its leisure moments, disporting itself among boxes of kippers which had long passed their prime, among sacks of bacon and hams, sides of beef, boxes of fish, and whales of prodigious size from Aberdeen, and last but not least, among milk churns. Two important people have not yet received recognition, the guards and the stokers. These are classed together because they formed the fighting squad. The guard was walled up in a van with luggage, leaving him about a square ft. of breathing space, and then told that he could sort that stuff as he went along. In the intervals he might fight a successful rearguard action. The firemen, when not actively engaged in stoking, were expected to field any brickbats, bottles, boulders, &c., that might come their way. The stationmaster's clerks baffle all description. They spent their time giving fatuous answers to foolish questions, and shouting information of dubious worth down the telephone

I. B. W, The Student, June 2, 1926

Thomas Carlyle (1795–1881)

'Sartor Resartus' is only intermittently biographical, but it is not difficult now, in view of the evidence available to pick out the bits that depict Carlyle's own career, and the references to Teufelsdörckh's University as unquestionably applicable to Edinburgh. 'Had you anywhere in Crim Tartary,' he writes, 'walled in a square enclosure, furnished it with a small ill-chosen library, and then turned loose into it eleven hundred Christian striplings, to tumble about as they listed from three to seven years, certain persons, under the title of Professors, being stationed at the gates to declare aloud that it was a University, and extract considerable admission fees – you had, not indeed in mechanical structure, yet in spirit and results, some imperfect resemblance of our high seminary . . . We boasted ourselves a rational University in the highest degree, hostile to mysticism; thus was the young mind furnished with much talk about progress of the species, dark ages, prejudice, and the like, so that all were quickly enough blown out into a state of windy argumentativeness, whereby the better sort had soon to end in sick impotent scepticism; the worst sort explode in finished self-conceit, and to all spiritual intents become dead . . . The hungry young looked up to their spiritual nurses, and for food were bidden eat the east wind. What vain jargon of controversial metaphysic, etymology, and mechanical manipulation, falsely named science, was current there indeed learned better than most. Among eleven hundred Christian youths there will not be wanting some eleven eager to learn. By collision with such a certain warmth, a certain polish was communicated; by instinct and happy accident I took less to rioting than to thinking and reading, which latter also I was free to do. Nay, from the chaos of the library I succeeded in fishing up more books than had been known to keepers thereof.'

'Famous Edinburgh Students' – *The Student* 1914

Student Song

To the air: 'Bonnie Dundee'

We sing not thy praises in Latin or Greek,
But just in the common old language we speak;
When we sound thy fair fame no such hindrance
                                        we brook –
All hail to the Thistle and Castle and Book!

Chorus. Come fill up your bumpers as full as you can,
And drink to this toast every true-hearted man,
Be ye living by land, be ye sailing by sea,
'Love, life, and all honour to our Varsitee!'

Where thy old buildings stand in a regular square
Poor Darnley went rocket-like up in the air,
And as Kirk o' Field down to her foundations shook
Then sprang up the Thistle and Castle and Book!

Chorus.

Dr David Rorie,
The Tounis Colledge (1891)

[*Editor's Note*: Thistles, Castle and Book are the arms of
Edinburgh University]

An Undergraduate in the Nineteenth Century

The next day I matriculated as an Arts student in the
University, and joined the class of Professor (Alexander)
Christison in Latin, and in Greek that of Professor
Dunbar. At that time the college, as a building, was

neither the College of the past, nor yet that of the present day. It was in a state of transition. Part of the quadrangle had been built after the original design by Adam; but on the south side was a row of old houses, one storey and a half high, with storm windows, which in all probability had seen the day of Principal Rollock. At the very entrance to the quadrangle was the old library, which, besides its stately surroundings, looked like an old country house that had strayed and lost its way. A flock of starlings built their nests among the unfinished pediments, and both professors and students fed them with bits of bread.

As to my own feelings, it is usual (in books especially) for a young student, as he enters the University gates, to have lofty aspirations, high resolve, and glowing thoughts as to work and fame in the far-off future. To me these came in certain fashion after a season. . . . but the first weeks of my life in Edinburgh College chill me yet with a memory of utter loneliness. The massive stonework numbed my very soul . . .

But the weather changed and brought changes. A snow-storm set in towards the end of December. The shepherd meteorologists of the Borders recognised four types of snowflake – Harefoot, Birdwing, Poppler, and Sparevvil. If the first snowstorm of the year was Harefoot, it betokened the storms of an old-fashioned winter. Harefoot flakes had fallen on Edinburgh College all night and all morning, and, though the sun had blinked out, it was evident that more snowflakes were coming.

Alison Hay Dunlop,
Anent Old Edinburgh (1890)

Undergraduates in the Twenties

There used to be a back entrance to the Old Quad of Edinburgh University –is it still there?– through which I hurried to my classes. My feet echoed on the flagstones – I can hear them now – and there was always a faint lifting of the heart, for, beyond the passage, was escape from school and from family into a world where I was called, not by my Christian name, but *Miss* Burnett it was in those days – and very heady I found it – where I wore hairpins and hatpins, where I read Logic – '*Barbara celarent darii ferioque prioris*' I used to chant to myself on my daily walk through the Meadows – what intoxicating nonsense! – a world which contained the Sellar and Goodhart Classical Library, where up a long flight of stairs – goodness, who carried coal all that way up? – a statue of Hermes watched me devour the Agamemnon raw, in a blaze of excitement, and, behind propped-up lexicons, small love-affairs, and some corrosive ones, waxed and waned. Forty years have passed since then, but I can hear my footsteps echo still and I can see myself, sometimes with a fiddle of which I was vaguely ashamed, often with a hockey stick and always with a pile of lecture notes, for I was an earnest attender at lectures. Is the Humanity lecture room still guarded by a servitor with top hat and silver buttons? And does he still hold the door open for the Professor to Make an Entrance. How naive we seem to have been when I compare us with the under-graduates of to-day. What a passion we had for simple-minded activities, such as going for rambles on the Pentland Hills – hikes, I suppose they would be called now, but we called them, unselfconsciously, rambles. And ramble we did, for miles. Money, in fact, was not a barrier. Books were cheap and second-hand. There was no insistence on the latest edition. Many of mine bore my father's name on the flyleaf and they saw me through well enough. I liked the ticking of the clock in the Sellar and Goodhart Library. The drop of ash in the grate and the moment when I surfaced into the moonlight world of the Old Quad. That was what I liked best – the place and the people. Across the years I can hear their footsteps echoing, and, somewhere among them is a girl with a fiddle and a hockey stick who once was me.

Maida Burnett Stanier,
University of Edinburgh Journal (Autumn 1967)

I don't quite know what I expected from a university. Certainly something a little less reach-me-down than the degree-collecting process turned out to be. One or two of our professors lectured with a freshness and enthusiasm that, looking back on, I can appreciate now better than I did then. Old Professor Grierson of the English Department, for instance, had a warm, infectious intensity that few of us could resist. Apparently undismayed by the rows upon rows of us, he would abandon himself to a favourite author, declaiming from selected passages for a solid hour on end with all the ardour of a young lover for a new-found love. We were all on our best behaviour in the old man's classroom, for we liked him, and those who by temperament were unable to share his enthusiasms, at least marvelled at them. I boggled a bit over some of his Wordsworth, but otherwise was one of his most impressionable disciples. But most of our lecturers were dreary and circumspect. I suppose they had to be in order to survive. Edinburgh is not the sort of place to encourage any kind of unorthodoxy. Only one of them during the four and a half years I attended classes made any attempt to break away from the mechanical routine.

Jeannie Lee,
This Great Journey (1963)

Rectorials

It all started in Bologna in 1155. The students of that University had many grievances to lay before Frederick the German Prince, but their chief complaint was that landlords charged them extortionate rates for lodgings. Frederick had his eye on the crown of the Cæsars, and realising that many of the students were his own country-men, decided that he had better gain the support of the University to further him in his imperial ambition. Therefore he granted to the students such powers of self-government as virtually placed the control of all University affairs in their hands. The 'Student Universities' of Italy, for so they are called in contrast to the 'Master Universities' of Paris, Oxford and Cambridge, were essentially democratic institutions. The Rector (his actual title was Dominus Rector) was the actual ruler, the Chancellor merely being a figure of ceremony. The Professors were within his jurisdiction, and he frequently fined or deposed them. When the older Universities of Scotland were founded in the fifteenth century – St Andrews, 1411; Glasgow, 1450; and Aberdeen, 1494 – they were modelled on those of Italy. Indeed in the Bull of Pope Nicholas V giving the right to found a *Studium Generale* in Glasgow, it is specifically stated that the University is to enjoy similar privileges to those of the

University of Bologna. In this way, then, was the Rector-ship introduced into Scotland. On the founding of the 'Tounis College' in 1582 the office of Rector was combined with that of Principal. In 1640 they were dissociated. In 1665 a change took place, and it was decided that the Lord Provost of Edinburgh should also be the Rector of the University. In 1859 the present system of choosing a Rector triennially, by the vote of the student electorate, was introduced. The Lord Provost has not been forgotten, however. In the four Scottish Universities he has a seat *ex officio* on the University Court. That is a brief account of the history of the Rectorship. It at least shows that the Scottish Universities are far more the direct heirs of the Renaissance tradition than are the English Universities.

> J. H. Burns and D. Sutherland-Graeme,
> *Scottish University* (1944)

Speculative Society

A hall, turkey-carpeted, hung with pictures, looking when lighted at night with fire and candle, like some goodly dining-room; a passage-like library, walled with books in their wire cages and a corridor with a fireplace, benches, a table, many prints of famous members, and a mural tablet to the virtues of a former secretary. Here a member can warm himself and loaf and read: here, in defiance of Senatus-consults, he can smoke.

> Robert Louis Stevenson,
> *A College Magazine* (1887)

SCHOOLS

An Edinburgh High School

There is in this place, which everybody talks about – the High School, I think they call it. 'Tis said to be the best school in the whole island; but the idea of one's children speaking Scotch – broad Scotch!. . . Let me call thee up before my mind's eye, High School, to which, every morning, the two English brothers took their way from the proud old Castle through the lofty streets of the Old Town. High School! – called so, I scarcely know why; neither lofty in thyself nor by position, being situated in a flat bottom; oblong structure of tawny stone, with many windows fenced with iron netting – with thy long hall below, and thy five chambers above, for the reception of the five classes, into which the eight hundred urchins who styled thee instructress, were divided. Thy learned rector and his four subordinate dominies; thy strange old porter of the tall form and grizzled hair, hight Boee, and doubtless of Norse ancestry, as his name declares . . . Yes, I remember all about thee, and how at eight of every morn we were gathered together with one accord in the long hall, from which, after the litanies had been read (for so I will call them, being an Episcopalian), the five classes from the five sets of benches trotted off in long files, one boy after the other, up the five spiral staircases of stone, each class to its destination; and well do I remember how we of the third sat hushed and still, watched by the eye of the dux, until the door opened, and in walked that model of a good Scotchman, the shrewd, intelligent, but warm-heart and kind dominie, the respectable Carson.

And in this school I began to construe the Latin language, which I had never done before, notwithstanding my long and diligent study of Lilly, which illustrious grammar was not used at Edinburgh, nor indeed known. Greek was only taught in the fifth or highest class, in which my brother was; as for myself, I never got beyond the third during the two years that I remained at this seminary. I certainly acquired here a considerable insight in the Latin tongue; and, to the scandal of my father and horror of my mother, a thorough proficiency in the Scotch, which, in less than two months, usurped the place of the English, and so obstinately maintained its ground, that I still can occasionally detect its lingering remains. I did not spend my time unpleasantly at this school.

George Borrow, *Lavengro* (1851)

Boys will be Boys

1595 – High School Riots

The boys of the High School, having become exceedingly riotous; one of the magistrates is shot by a boy named Sinclair, while endeavouring to quell the tumult.

Robert Stevenson, *Annals of Edinburgh* (1839)

Another Institution

In Edinburgh there are many unique things and the city has claims to distinction in many spheres, but among the first of these claims is the Company of Merchants of the City of Edinburgh. The Company of Merchants of the City of Edinburgh, incorporated in 1681, has for its aim 'the improving of their trade and preventing abuses therein, and especially for enabling them to prosecute the design and manufactories, and carrying on and so good and great a work.' Its proudest activities are, however, its schools, and although these are being limited, cribbed, cabined and confined by increasing interference by the State in the right of individuals to provide schools of their own pattern for their children, they still have a unique place in the lives of the citizens of Edinburgh. The Company, in the 'nineties, had five schools – George Watson's and Daniel Stewart's for boys, James Gillespie's for boys and girls, and Edinburgh Ladies' College and George Watson's Ladies' College for girls. Of these five, James Gillespie's was the only mixed school the Company had. It has now passed from the management of the Merchant Company and is under the local authority. Its name remains, but to those who were at Gillespie's its glory, if not departed, has been transmuted.

Sir William Y. Darling,
So it Looks to Me (1952)

George Watson's

I was very lucky indeed that I received my schooling at Watson's. It was, and is, a very fine rugby school and, in a sense, because we got first-rate tuition from primary six onwards, we had a head start on other schools which didn't begin to take the game seriously until secondary level.

. . .

Rugby, then, ran in the blood and for me it started in 1974 as a nine-year-old with the JB1s at George Watson's College. That was the primary six first team. I was fly-half and captain. Probably here the Hastings name worked in my favour. Graeme and Gavin had both been trailblazers for me at Watson's and they had both proved that they could play a bit. The masters probably thought, here's another Hastings boy, we'll make him captain. Because of all the bounce games that I had already played on those Saturday afternoons at Myreside I wasn't a total novice but my first real, official game of rugby was for the JB1s against old Edinburgh rivals Daniel Stewart's and Melville College, away at Ferryfield.

. . .

There was great tradition and rivalry associated with those games against other Edinburgh schools and, in fact, the rivals that you would come up against as a nine-year-old – people like Jeremy Richardson, for instance, who played for Edinburgh Academy – you would still be playing against over 20 years later, Jeremy for Edinburgh Accies and me for Watsonians.

Scott Hastings, *Great Scot* (1996)

A Final Tribute

~

New Zealand

To-day, were any of you to go to the city of Dunedin, you would find that the Scotsmen who lived there at the time referred to by the Lord Provost had not forgotten the land from which they sprang. There you will find Princes Street, High Street and the Water of Leith . . . The new Edinburgh of New Zealand.

Sir Joseph Ward – Prime Minister of New Zealand,
Freedom of the City – 1907

Canada

It is not for me to try and praise Edinburgh. Great writers of poetry and prose have tried to do it, but none of them has said the last word, for Edinburgh is more than the capital of Scotland. It is Scotland itself in miniature, a microcosm of our land, and its history is a summary of the story of Scotland.

John Buchan, on his appointment to be
Governor-General of Canada – 1935

United States of America

There is a quality in your city which charms an American who comes from the vast distances and endless millions of his own continent. Though your suburbs spread for miles about you, your own area is not large. The Pentlands are not mountains; they are hills. Your population is not millions, but measurable, companionable thousands. Your houses are many-storied, but they do not assault high heaven and blot out the sky. You have escaped the worst atrocities of the machine age, and somehow preserve a metropolitan character with a reasonable size. Then, too, if the style be the man, as the Frenchman said, certainly the employment is the town. You seem to have chosen even your industries with the genius of fitness. Litigation and education, the manufacture of biscuits, books and – I hesitate to use the word – beer, the banking of people's money safely, checking their accounts carefully, and insuring their bodies in this world and their souls in the next on a sound actuarian basis – these are occupations which have combined in such graceful proportions as to justify the envy and admiration which you undoubtedly excite.

Ambassador Alanson Houghton, at the time of the
hand-over of the Scottish-American
War Memorial in Princes Street Gardens – 1927

In Edinburgh every newcomer must feel, as I have felt, the impact of history. It is part of the city's backbone. Edinburgh has stood firm through many ups and downs; but that is to be expected of a city built so deftly upon hills and valleys.

Ambassador Joseph Patrick Kennedy,
Freedom of the City – 1939

Edinburgh is neither the oldest nor the largest of the world's cities, but it typifies, better than most, man's age-long search for peace and betterment of his lot and his tortuous progress on the path towards it.

Cities like Edinburgh, far from being mere structures of brick and stone, are living symbols of mankind's fundamental need of and faith in co-operative action.

General Dwight D. Eisenhower,
Freedom of the City – 1946

To all true Scotsmen, wherever their wanderings may have led them, *Edinburgh will still be the centre of the Universe*; with the axletree sticking up visibly into space, somewhere between the Castle and St Giles Cathedral.

John A. Ross, *The Early Home of Robert L. Stevenson*, (1895)

I was born likewise within the bounds of an earthly city illustrious for her beauty, her tragic and picturesque association, and for the credit of some of her brave sons. Writing as I do in a strange quarter of the world, and a late day of my age, I can still behold the profile of her towers and chimneys, and the long trail of her smoke against the sunset; I can still hear those strains of martial music that she goes to bed with, ending each day like an act of an opera to the notes of bugles; still recall with a grateful effort of memory, any one of a thousand beautiful and spacious circumstances that pleased me and that must have pleased anyone in my half-remembered past. It is the beautiful that I thus actually recall, the august airs of the castle on its rock, nocturnal passages of lights and trees, the sudden song of the blackbird in a suburban lane, rosy and dusky winter sunsets, the uninhabited splendours of the early dawn, the building up of the city on a misty day, house upon house, spire above spire, until it was received into a sky of softly glowing clouds, and seemed to pass on and upwards by fresh grades and rises, city upon city, a New Jerusalem bodily scaling heaven.

Robert Louis Stevenson

Acknowledgements

The editor and publisher gratefully acknowledge permission
to reprint copyright material in this book as follows:

Birlinn Ltd for passages by James Thomson (*Edinburgh
  Curiosities*, 1996), Joyce Wallace (*Traditions of
  Trinity and Leith*, 1984 and *Historic Houses of
  Edinburgh*, 1987) and Helen Dingwall (*Physicians,
  Surgeons and Apothecaries*, 1994)
Des Brogan for the extract from *Hidden and Haunted
  Underground Edinburgh* (Mercat Tours Publications,
  1999)
Donald Campbell for his poem 'Tynecastle'
Stewart Conn for 'Lothian burn' and 'Westlandman'
  from *Stolen Light*, (Bloodaxe, 1999) 'Choral
  Symphony' from *In the Kibble Palace* (Bloodaxe Books,
  1987) and 'Charlotte Square' which is un-collected.
Professor David Daiches for the extracts from *Two
  Worlds* (Macmillan, 1957)
Sheil Land Associates Ltd on behalf of Elspeth Davie for
  the extract from *Coming to Light* (Hamish Hamilton,
  1989). Copyright © 1989 Elspeth Davie
Richard Demarco for the extract from *A Life in Pictures*
  (Northern Books, 1995)
James Allan Ford for the passage from *A Statue for a
  Public Place* (Hodder & Stoughton, 1965)
Duncan Glen and Akros Publications for the inclusion of
  his poems
Steve Savage Publishers for the extract from *The Place
  Names of Edinburgh* by Stuart Harris (Gordon Wright
  Publishing, 1996 and Steve Savage Publishers , 2002)

Edinburgh University Press for 'Edinburgh Weather' from *Collected Poems and Songs of George Campbell Hay* edited by Michael Byrne (Edinburgh University Press, 2000)

The editor of *History Scotland* for the article from the Winter 2001 issue

Andrew Jeffrey for the extract from *This Present Emergency* (Mainstream, 1992)

Paul Johnston for an extract from *Water of Death* (Hodder & Stoughton, 1999), copyright 1999 Paul Johnston

The Society of Authors as the Literary Representative of the Estate of Robert Kemp for the extract from *The Maestro* (Duckworth, 1956)

Sir Ludovic Kennedy for the extract from *On My Way to the Club* (Collins, 1989)

The Estate of Eric Linklater for the extracts from *Magnus Merriman* (Cape, 1934), *Edinburgh* (Newnes, 1960), *The Survival of Scotland* (Heinemann, 1968)

Carcanet Press Limited for the extract from Hugh MacDiarmid's *Complete Poems* edited by Michael Grieve and W. R. Aitken (Carcanet, 2000)

Charles McKean for extracts from *Edinburgh: Portrait of a City* (Century, 1991)

John Mackie for the passage by Albert Mackie in *Scottish Pageantry* (Hutchinson, 1967)

Magnus Magnusson for the extract from *Scotland: the Story of a Nation* (Harper Collins, 2000)

Mainstream Publishing for extracts from Sandy Mullay (*The Edinburgh Encyclopedia*, 1996), Jan-Andrew Henderson (*The Town Below the Ground*, 1999), Scott Hastings (*Great Scot*, 1996)

Acknowledgements

Tessa Ransford for 'Holyrood Park at Night' from
  Shadows from the Greater Hill (Ramsay Head Press,
  1987) reprinted in Scottish Selection (Akros, 1998)
Juliet Rees for the extract from *Once Upon a Haugh*
  (Scotland Yard Adventure Centre, 1991)
Trevor Royle for the passage from *Precipitous City*
  (Mainstream, 1980)
Edinburgh University Press for the extracts from A. J.
  Youngson's *The Making of Classical Edinburgh*
  (Edinburgh University Press, 1966)

Every effort has been made to contact copyright holders
and any errors or omissions are entirely unintentional.
If contacted the publisher will be pleased to make
corrections at the earliest opportunity.

Some extracts have had to be dropped because the
copyright holder did not give permission for the piece to be
used. The editor would welcome suggestions for extracts
he may have missed.